Current Issues in Australian Constitutional Law

Edited by A. Keith Thompson

SHEPHERD
STREET PRESS

Shepherd Street Press is an imprint of Connor Court Publishing and The School of Law, The University of Notre Dame Australia, Broadway.

Shepherd Street Press Editorial Executive: Michael Quinlan, A. Keith Thompson and Iain T. Benson

Published in 2022 by Connor Court Publishing Pty Ltd under the imprint Shepherd Street Press.

Shepherd Street Press is an imprint of Connor Court Publishing and The School of Law, The University of Notre Dame Australia, Broadway.

Shepherd Street Press Editorial Executive:

Michael Quinlan
A. Keith Thompson
Iain T. Benson

Connor Court Publishing Pty Ltd
PO Box 7257
Redland Bay QLD 4165
sales@connorcourt.com
www.connorcourtpublishing.com.au
Phone 0497-900-685

Printed in Australia

ISBN: 9781922815125

Front Cover Image: annotated copy of the 1891 draft of the Constitution, Wikipedia Commons.

Peer Review Policy

This book has been prepared in compliance with the Peer Review Policy of the Shepherd Street Press which provides for double blind peer review by at least two expert reviewers.

Table of Contents

Foreword – Gabriël A. Moens   7

Introduction – A. Keith Thompson   15

About our Contributors   23

I - The powers of the states and the Commonwealth

1 - What is the Melbourne Corporation Principle? – Michael Dimarco   27

2 - The Separation of Powers and the Mineralogy/Palmer Litigation – Anthony Gray 63

3 - National Emergency Powers in Australia – the current constitutional limits – Lorraine Finlay   93

II - The implied freedom of political communication and structured proportionality

4 - No More Than Legal Fiction? A Critical Evaluation of the Implied Freedom of Political Communication in Australia - Augusto Zimmermann   129

5 - The importance of Gageler and Gordon JJ's continuing dissent against structured proportionality – Thomas Boyle   163

III - Aboriginal reconciliation

6 - The Australian Constitution and our First Peoples – a statutory solution seeded by Mabo (No.2)? – A. Keith Thompson   211

Index   259

Foreword

I was delighted when Professor Keith Thompson invited me to write the Foreword to his latest book on Australian constitutional law. My delight stems from the fact that I have the highest admiration for his scholarly achievements, especially in the areas of constitutional law, history of law, and law and religion. Two contributions to this volume have been authored by Honours students at the University of Notre Dame Australia, Sydney, whose Honours theses were supervised by Professor Thompson.

In any event, it is always a pleasure to contribute to a book that is clearly written, superbly researched, rich in content and accessible to practising lawyers, law students, and scholars. This book illustrates that constitutional law is a rich tapestry which is indispensable in the education of lawyers.

The book contains six chapters, distributed over three parts. The first part deals with the relationship between the states and the Commonwealth – a relevant topic during the COVID-19 pandemic; the second part addresses the implied freedom of political communication, and the concept of 'structured proportionality'; and the third part, containing a solitary chapter, concerns Aboriginal reconciliation.

Michael Dimarco has contributed a chapter to the first part of the book on the important *Melbourne Corporation* principle. The High Court developed the principle in *Melbourne Corporation v Commonwealth*,[1] also known as the *State Banking Case*. The case dealt with legislative attempts by the Commonwealth to deprive the states of the freedom to choose their preferred banking institution for banking purposes. However, the High Court held the relevant legislation invalid because it interfered with the constitutional powers of the states. Chief Justice Latham considered that the impugned legislation was a law with respect to state governmental power and, hence, did not come within one of the heads of power in s 51 of the *Constitution*. And Justice Dixon postulated that legislative powers should not be understood 'as authorizing the Commonwealth to make a law aimed at the restriction or control of a State in the exercise of its executive authority.'[2]

Professor Anthony Gray wrote an informative chapter on the Mineralogy/Clive Palmer litigation against Western Australia, that had enacted legislation to invalidate arbitral awards rendered in relation to these two parties. But, in adopting this contentious legislation, the State denied its liability in relation to these arbitral matters and revoked Palmer's ability to commence legal action. Palmer argued that the State, in abrogating his right to litigate, violated the separation of powers doctrine. The High Court, however, condoned the legislation and refused to find a violation of the doctrine.[3]

Palmer, controversially branded 'an enemy of the state'[4] by Premier Mark McGowan, was also involved in another case against Western Australia – not the subject of Gray's article

---

1 (1947) 74 CLR 31. For a discussion of this case, see Gabriël A Moens & John Trone, *The Constitution of the Commonwealth of Australia Annotated*, (LexisNexis Butterworths, 9th ed, 2016), 123-126.

2 (1947) 74 CLR 31 [83].

3 *Mineralogy Pty Ltd v Western Australia* [2021] HCA 30; *Palmer v Western Australia* [2021] HCA 31.

4 Mas Mason, 'McGowan labelling Palmer 'enemy of the state' needs context: judge', *Financial Review*, 14 February 2022, <https://www.afr.com/politics/mcgowan-labelling-palmer-enemy-of-the-state-needs-context-judge-20220214-p59w72>.

but nevertheless uppermost in the minds of constitutional scholars – relating to the closure of the Western Australian border during the COVID-19 pandemic. Palmer sought to argue that the *Quarantine (Closing the Border) Directions* (WA) and the authorising *Emergency Management Act 2005* (WA) were constitutionally invalid because they violated s 92 of the *Constitution*, according to which 'trade, commerce, and intercourse among the States…shall be absolutely free.'

However, the High Court held that the burden on interstate intercourse was justified by the non-discriminatory purpose of preventing transmission of the coronavirus. The Court also held that the State measures were proportionate to the objective the State sought to achieve, namely the prevention of the spread of the coronavirus.

One could take issue with the High Court's claim that there was 'no effective alternative'[5] to the closure of the State's border. Professor Augusto Zimmermann, also a contributor to this volume, argued in another paper that the Court misinterpreted s 92 because it overlooked the meaning of the word 'absolutely'. He opined that the closure of the border 'unconstitutionally prohibited cross-border movement to Western Australia' and not only 'imposed a direct burden on the freedom of intercourse, but also a discriminatory burden with a naturally protectionist effect', thereby contravening 'the freedom of trade and commerce also protected under the relevant constitutional provisions.'[6] I am confident that Professor Gray would agree with Professor Zimmermann's interpretation of s 92. Indeed, in an article published in an influential study on the violation

---

5 *Palmer v Western Australia* (2021) 388 ALR 180 [80] (Kiefel CJ and Keane J). For a discussion of this case, see John Trone, *The Constitution of the Commonwealth of Australia Annotated*, (LexisNexis, 10th ed, 2021), 459-461.

6 Augusto Zimmermann, 'How the High Court Redefine 'Absolutely', *Quadrant*, 4 March 2020, <https://quadrant.org.au/opinion/qed/2021/03/how-the-high-court-redefined-absolutely/>.

of rights in the age of COVID-19, he wrote that it 'is clearly evident' that s 92 represents '[t]he vision of a unified, connected nation' and that '[t]he measures are arguably disproportionate to achievement of their legitimate objective.'[7]

The book's foray into the COVID-19 tribulations continues with a paper authored by Lorraine Finlay, now the Human Rights Commissioner. She discusses the limits of the states' emergency powers. Specifically, she analyses the *National Emergency Declaration Act 2020* (Cth) which purports to provide a national framework for the calling of an emergency.

Professor Augusto Zimmermann, in a thought-provoking piece, recalls the decisions of the High Court that created a right to political communication. He argues that this right is not readily available to non-parliamentarians. If so, his arguments are a brutal reminder that freedom of speech is merely a chimera of what freedom should be like.

The veracity of Zimmermann's claim was recently on display in the Australian Parliament. From time to time, parliamentarians, especially those making their valedictory farewell speeches, display a remarkable tendency to speak without fear. Their willingness to use their parliamentary right to criticise their enemies does not rely on courage and a concern for the truth, but on the fact that their statements read in parliament are protected by parliamentary privilege.

This privilege, the scope of which is essentially the same as the individual privileges existing in the House of Commons in 1901, 'is based upon the idea that only if members are immune from the possibility of suit for defamation for their statements in Parliament will they be able to speak their minds freely

---

7 Anthony Gray, 'Covid-19 Border Restrictions and Section 92 of the Australian Constitution', in Augusto Zimmermann and Joshua Forrester (eds. *Fundamental Rights in the Age of COVID-19*, 2020, (Connor Court Publishing, 2021) 99, 135.

regarding public affairs.'[8]

A good example was on display on 30 March 2020, when Liberal Senator Concetta Fierravanti-Wells savagely attacked the character of the Prime Minister, Scott Morrison, and his fitness to be prime minister. Protected by parliamentary privilege, she described the Prime Minister as an autocratic leader and a bully who lacks a 'moral compass.'[9]

Of course, the Prime Minister's office suggested that the senator was merely miffed because she had been relegated to an unwinnable position on the Liberal Senate ticket in New South Wales – a case of very sour grapes. Regardless, the uses or abuses of parliamentary privilege remind us that non-parliamentarians would be subjected to defamation claims if these statements were made outside the parliament.

In his contribution to this volume, Thomas Boyle deals with 'structured proportionality', a tool used in freedom of communication cases but now also extended to s 92 analysis, as mentioned above. 'Proportionality' requires that there is a cogent relationship between the measures embraced by the legislature and the achievement of its objectives. Specifically, Boyle discusses the deconstruction of this concept by Justices Gageler and Gordon of the High Court.

Finally, Professor Keith Thompson authored the third part, which is the sixth chapter of the book. It concerns Aboriginal reconciliation, based on the New Zealand model. Thompson's chapter represents a veritable *tour de force* because it purports to offer a solution to the continuing fractious relationship between the First Nations people, and other Australians.

---

8 Gabriel A Moens & John Trone, *The Constitution of the Commonwealth of Australia Annotated*, (LexisNexis Butterworths, 9th ed, 2016), 115.

9 See Gabriël Moens, 'Australia: The Unlucky Country?, *The Epoch Times*, 7-13 April 2022, A10.

This book is published by the Shepherd Street Press, which is fast becoming the premier Australian publisher of quality constitutional law, and law and religion scholarship.

Although this book is not written for a general audience, I am confident that those who have been trained in the rigorous discussion of social and moral issues or exhibit a curiosity for the way in which Australia is governed, will be able to benefit from reading this book. In publishing this book, the publisher, editor and contributors have made the study of constitutional law rewarding, even exciting, and certainly intellectually stimulating. As such, the book will enlighten those who are interested in the governance of Australia and the protection of the rights of its citizens, especially those who are attentive to how the *Constitution* responds to current social issues.

I predict that this book will easily figure on the compulsory reading list of students of constitutional law in Australian law schools. This is because the contributors' articles enlighten the study of constitutional law, and even clarify historical constitutional law developments. The book's chapters, and their erudite arguments, are intricately connected with the aspirations, expressed by all contributors to this book, to promote good governance of Australia. As such, the book, over time, will become a classic text on the areas covered in it.

In predicting that this book will become a widely consulted text in these areas, I am not merely making a platitudinous statement, sometimes expected of writers of Forewords. Indeed, in this case, it is a truthful expression of a sentiment about a wonderful book that richly deserves praise because of the quality of the writing, research, and historical interest.

Although the book will undoubtedly stimulate some scholars into disagreeing with the arguments and conclusions of the contributors, they will not be able to complain about the quality of the scholarship on offer.

Professor Thompson, as editor, has been responsible for guaranteeing the quality of this publication and mentoring the student contributors to the volume. In his preface, he expresses the wish 'to live forever' to be able to cajole students into writing articles which enable 'wider accessibility'. But for the time being, he can justifiably be proud of this fine achievement.

Gabriël A. Moens AM
Emeritus Professor of Law, The University of Queensland
Friday, 22 April 2022

Introduction

The question that unites this short and eclectic collection of essays about the *Australian Constitution* is "what changes would we like to make"? During my last ten years of teaching law students Australian constitutional law, the changes my students wish would happen have been diverse but several major themes have distilled. "Do we really need three levels of government in Australia", and if not, "should we do away with the state governments?" "Why don't we have a constitutional bill of rights" and "how could we get one"? And "what physical changes would we be required to make Australia a republic" or "to make the existing *Australian Constitution* just towards our First Peoples?"

Some of those questions are implicated here but not completely answered. This particular book began its life as one of a series intended to feature the research work of some of our best students at the Sydney campus of The University of Notre Dame Australia – particularly those who had been invited to write honours theses at the conclusion of their candidature as students in the Bachelor of Laws program. This is the third book in that series. The first addressed *Current Issues in Law and Religion* and the second, *Current Issues in the Law of Evidence*. While the themes addressed in this book were subliminally identified at the outset, the collection finally available in these books is a consequence of the practical realities that descend upon law students when they graduate after completing their honours theses. They have to make a living. Most of them are immediately engaged in demanding legal roles as judicial staffers and as junior associates in major law firms, and that leaves little time to make the changes involved in turning an insightful research thesis into a double blind peer reviewed article worthy of publication. Thus, several of the theses early identified for publication here have not become chapters in this book. More is the pity. If they had proceeded, there would be more about Indigenous reconciliation and the ironies of the implied freedom of political communication, and there would also have been suggestions as to how we might engage Australia's many dual citizens in the government in the future. But at least we have made a start. We are also grateful that some adjuncts and other friends of the Law School have responded to the opportunity here to say something current in Australia's constitutional space.

I have divided the book into three parts. The first is the largest and responds to the most obvious constitutional questions that have engaged all Australians in the last two years during the Covid pandemic. Where do the boundaries lie between the power of our state and federal governments and how far can any of those laws go in abrogating personal freedoms since our freedoms are not protected by a written bill of rights?

Michael Dimarco started writing about the *Melbourne Corporation* principle before the pandemic broke out and did not anticipate the level of cooperation between state and Commonwealth governments that has come out of Scott Morrison's new National Cabinet. But when the Covid urgency retreats and the Commonwealth no longer needs to rely on the states to pass laws which (for example), prevent people attending church, the old questions will return and we will again want to know when and how much the Commonwealth can interfere with state autonomy. Michael's chapter discusses constitutional cases where the High Court has considered the Commonwealth-states relationship with the *Melbourne Corporation Case*

(1948) as the focus. In that case, Commonwealth legislation that sought to control state banking was found invalid because it infringed an implication in the *Constitution*. But exactly what that implication is and how it works remains unclear. Michael suggests that confusion surrounding the *Melbourne Corporation* principle falls away if one thinks about it as an intergovernmental immunity rather than as a prohibition or limitation on Commonwealth power - despite the High Court's dismissal of the idea of state immunity from Commonwealth action in the *Engineers' Case*. His immunity analysis also factors in the principles outlined in the *Cigamatic* (1962) and *Spence v Queensland* (2019) *Cases.*

Anthony Gray asks whether an Australian government should be able pass laws overruling valid arbitral awards and protect itself from law suits to which everyone else should be subject. Doesn't that offend the rule of law idea which is at least as old as *Magna Carta*? It certainly resonates with our recoil at George Orwell's idea that some animals are more equal than others. Anthony's particular focus is the High Court's decisions in the *Mineralogy* and *Palmer Cases* in 2021 after the Western Australian government used legislation to reverse arbitral awards which it did not like following a good faith agreement made with Palmer and his companies in 2002. Anthony was disappointed that the High Court relied on technicalities to rule in Western Australia's favour rather than take the opportunity to restate the invalidity of any Australian legislation that tells any Australian court how to exercise its exclusive judicial power.

Lorraine Finlay's chapter directly addresses the constitutional issues raised by both the 2019 bushfire and 2020-2022 Covid crises. She draws attention to the fact that there is no provision in the *Commonwealth Constitution* that directly allows the Commonwealth to declare a national or localised state of emergency with regulations and other responsive measures.

While she identifies Prime Minister Scott Morrison's initiative in creating the National Cabinet as an attempt to facilitate a coordinated response to the Covid pandemic, the lack of an emergency power in the *Commonwealth Constitution* is a lacuna that needs to be filled. While she infers that the High Court would be sympathetic to the validity of *National Emergency Declaration Act 2020* under the defence, external affairs, executive and nationhood powers, the law would be much clearer if the states referred further powers to the Commonwealth to deal with national emergencies under s 51(xxxvii) or if a referendum were passed to formally create a new power under s 128 of the *Constitution*.

Augusto Zimmermann reminds us that the implied freedom of political communication which the High Court began to recognise as a limitation on Australian Commonwealth law-making capacity in 1992 is not free speech. In fact, it is nothing like it. Though our constitutional framers hoped that our legislatures would protect our common law rights including freedom of speech by voting against laws that interfered with them at all, party discipline creates an elitism that prevents most elected politicians from disagreeing with policy despite the interests of many electors. Augusto is particularly unimpressed by affirmative action which he identifies in some federal and state anti-discrimination laws. While there is virtue in passing laws that prevent the harassment and vilification of minorities, laws that penalise speaking against the views and orientations of those minorities are anti-democratic – and ironic, since our constitutional implied freedom of political communication allows us to use invective to insult and offend any public figure without any regard to the consequence.

Thomas Boyle draws attention to another irony in our High Court jurisprudence. As Leslie Zines has said, precedent has less impact in constitutional matters because the text of the *Constitution* remains the most important thing. Perhaps that lesser significance of precedent in the High Court is one of the reasons why some High Court judges maintain their disagreement with majority decisions of their own court. Some of those maintained disagreements finally result in doctrinal changes and new precedents that ironically bind lower courts. But not always. In Thomas' chapter he asks why Justices Gageler and Gordon have maintained their opposition to the doctrine of structured proportionality and what that means? While he does not labour the question of how the doctrine of proportionality may be reconciled with Dicey's concept of parliamentary sovereignty in an Australian context, he does ask whether these dissenting views are more consistent with Australia's common law heritage since proportionality is an unashamed European import.

In my chapter I suggest that there is no need for constitutional change in Australia to effect a reconciliation with our First Peoples. But the primary reason for that observation is not that constitutional change in Australia is notoriously difficult. Rather, the point is that New Zealand has achieved a genuine reconciliation with its First Peoples in the period since our High Court handed down the *Mabo* (*No. 2*) decision...while we have been sitting on our hands and wringing them from time to time. Constitutional change is not required in Australia because it was not required in New Zealand. In part that is because New Zealand does not even have a written constitution. We simply need to follow New Zealand's example and empower a Tribunal or Commission to investigate and recommend reparations to the Commonwealth. I suggest that is what Justice Deane, Toohey and Gaudron had in mind when they wrote their judgments in *Mabo* (*No. 2*) even though Chief Justice Mason and Justices Brennan and McHugh thought that was too hard in 1992. I observe the High Court's revived empathy for the plight of our

First Peoples in *Love* in 2020 suggests that the time is right for the Commonwealth to pass more generous legislation in favour of our First Peoples than the *Native Title Act* which the Keating government passed in 1993.

So what changes would these authors like to make in Australian constitutional law and society? I think Michael Dimarco would like to see more clarity regarding the distribution of power within the federation, but Anthony Gray would like the High Court to develop some active jurisprudence around Sir Owen Dixon's idea that our *Constitution* is founded on the rule of law. Perhaps ironically, that would close down the autonomy that the High Court allowed Western Australia in the *Mineralogy* and *Palmer* cases. Lorraine Finlay wants more defined powers for the Commonwealth government to deal with emergencies, and since we have failed many times to implement a constitutional Bill of Rights, Augusto Zimmermann wants the High Court to find a more expansive version of free speech implied in the *Constitution* so that bona fide opinion short of vilification cannot be punished by PC tribunals enforcing affirmative anti-vilification laws. Thomas Boyle does not recommend any changes. Rather he implicitly observes that the High Court majority's infatuation with structured proportionality is not consistent with our common law history and mythical deference to the doctrine of parliamentary sovereignty. And I want us to get serious about Aboriginal reconciliation and I say we have been making excuses for too long.

I think there will be more constitutional offerings from Honours students at The University of Notre Dame Australia. I would like to live forever so that I can cajole and marshal them into a form which enables their wider accessibility. But I suspect the ravages of age may require me to leave that to others, though I have wanted to exhort that it be done!

The intent here is unashamedly provocative. We want to provoke you to thought, perhaps to rebuttal, but certainly to engagement. All of us believe in the virtues of the marketplace of ideas. Though truth may not immediately distil from robust adversarial disagreement, the process is virtuous to the extent that it explores progress without violence.

A. Keith Thompson
April 2022
Sydney

About our contributors

Thomas Boyle graduated from the University of Notre Dame (Fremantle) with honours in 2021 and also holds a Bachelor of Arts from the University of Western Australia.

He is currently employed as an Associate at the Supreme Court of Western Australia and will be admitted to practice in November 2022. He previously worked for a large national law firm where he will return as a lawyer in 2023. His research interest is primarily in constitutional and administrative law as well as public international law.

Michael Dimarco was admitted as a legal practitioner in New South Wales in March 2021. Having spent time practicing law in a commercial firm in Sydney, Michael then commenced as Tipstaff to the Honourable Justice Ball of the Equity Division of the Supreme Court of New South Wales in October 2021. He holds a Bachelor of Laws (Hons I) from the University of Notre Dame Australia and a Master of Laws from the University of Sydney. His Honours thesis, entitled "What is the Melbourne Corporation Principle?", formed the basis of his chapter in this book. He was the Secretary of the United Nations Association of Australia (NSW Division) between October 2019 and October 2021.

Lorraine Finlay (ORCID: 0000-0002-4801-4028) is Australia's Human Rights Commissioner, commencing in this role in November 2021. Prior to joining the Australian Human Rights Commission Lorraine has worked as a lawyer and academic specialising in human rights and public law. This includes recent roles as a law lecturer at Murdoch University and as senior human trafficking specialist with the Australian Mission to ASEAN. Lorraine has a dual Masters in Law from New York University and the National University of Singapore, where she studied as a Singapura Scholar.

Anthony Gray (ORCID: 0000-0001-9565-475X) is Professor and Associate Head – Research within the School of Law and Justice, University of Southern Queensland. He has published approximately 140 sole-authored journal articles in refereed outlets, including the most prestigious Australian journals, international journals, and published numerous monographs. One of these is *Criminal Due Process and Chapter III of the Australian Constitution* (Federation Press, 2016) in which he explores the separation of powers principle in more detail.

Gabriël A. Moens AM is Emeritus Professor of Law, The University of Queensland. He served as Pro Vice Chancellor, Dean and Professor of Law at Murdoch University, and Garrick Professor of Law, at The University of Queensland. In 1999, Professor Moens received the Australian Award for University Teaching in Law and Legal Studies. In 2003, the Prime Minister of Australia awarded him the Australian Centenary Medal for services to education. He was named the 'International Alumnus of the Year' by the Pritzker Law School of Northwestern University in 2019.

He is the author/co-author/editor/co-editor of *Emergency Powers, COVID-19 Restrictions & Mandatory Vaccination: A 'Rule of Law' Perspective* (Connor Court Publishing, 2022); *Enduring Ideas*, (Connor Court Publishing, 2020); *Law of International Business in Australasia*, (The Federation Press, 2nd ed, 2019); *The Constitution of the Commonwealth of Australia Annotated*, (LexisNexis Butterworths, 9th ed, 2016); *Jurisprudence of Liberty*, (LexisNexis, 2nd ed, 2011); and *Commercial Law of the European Union*, (Springer, 2010).

A. Keith Thompson (ORCID: 0000-0001-9443-9644) is a Professor of Law at the University of Notre Dame Australia (UNDA). His books include *Religious Confession Privilege and the Common Law* (Leiden: Brill, 2011) and *Trinity and Monotheism: A historical and theological review of the origins and substance of the doctrine* (Queensland: Connor Court, 2019). He formerly practised as a partner in a commercial firm in Auckland and as International Legal Counsel for The Church of Jesus Christ of Latter-day Saints in the Pacific and through the African continent.

Augusto Zimmermann (ORCID: 0000-0002-6577-2090) is Professor and Head of Law at Sheridan Institute of Higher Education in Perth, WA. He is also Adjunct Professor of Law at the University of Notre Dame Australia, Sydney campus. From 2004 to 2006 he served as a board member of the Church and Nation Committee of Presbyterian Church of Victoria, which is charged with the responsibility of investigating moral and ethical questions on the denomination's behalf. From 2012 to 2017, he served as Law Reform Commissioner in Western Australia. He is the author/co-author/editor/co-editor of numerous academic articles and books, including *Christian Foundations of the*

Common Law (3 Volumes, Connor Court, 2018), and *Emergency Powers, COVID-19 Restrictions & Mandatory Vaccination – A Rule-of-Law Perspective* (Connor Court, 2022).

1

What is the Melbourne Corporation Principle?

Michael Dimarco

Abstract

In 1947 the High Court recognised and expounded upon an important implication of constitutional federalism in *Melbourne Corporation v Commonwealth* ('*Melbourne Corporation*'). But despite more than seven decades of judicial and academic treatment the nature and operation of the '*Melbourne Corporation* principle' remain ambiguous. This chapter argues that the prevailing approach for applying the principle, established by the High Court in *Austin v Commonwealth* and affirmed most recently by a High Court majority in *Spence v Queensland*, is inappropriate. It examines the principle to explain what it is and how it should be applied. The core contention is that the principle should be conceptualised as an inter-governmental immunity the application of which requires consideration of whether an exercise of power encroaches upon the autonomy of an independent body politic operating in a federal system.

Keywords

Federalism, *Melbourne Corporation v Commonwealth*, constitutional implications, inter-governmental immunities, implications of federalism, *Melbourne Corporation* principle

I.   Introduction

In *Melbourne Corporation v Commonwealth*[1] the High Court recognised a doctrine that concerns the Commonwealth's and the states' ability to affect one another. Through the relevant cases the doctrine was developed into a recognisable principle that has important consequences on the balance of power in the Australian federation. But despite its importance and the 'longevity'[2] of its broader aspects what the *Melbourne Corporation* principle is and how it ought to be applied remain unclear. That may be because, as some High Court judges have observed, a formula for applying the doctrine would be inappropriate[3] and 'it is difficult, if not impossible, to articulate it except in negative terms which are cast at a high level of abstraction.'[4] Nevertheless, it will be argued, the jurisprudence has obfuscated the doctrine with the consequence that clarification regarding what it is and how it should operate is required.

Following the High Court's recognition of the doctrine in *Melbourne Corporation*, its gradual application in the subsequent cases resulted in a principle comprised of two branches. One branch would render invalid action by one polity that discriminated against another, that is action by one polity that isolated another from the general law. The other branch would render invalid

1 *Melbourne Corporation v Commonwealth* (1947) 74 CLR 31 ('*Melbourne Corporation*').
2 *Spence v Queensland* (2019) 93 ALJR 643, 716 [313] (Edelman J) ('*Spence*').
3 See *Austin v Commonwealth* (2003) 215 CLR 185, 257–8 [143] (Gaudron, Gummow and Hayne JJ) ('*Austin*'); *Clarke v Federal Commissioner of Taxation* (2009) 240 CLR 272, 306 [65] (Gummow, Heydon, Keifel and Bell JJ) ('*Clarke*').
4 *Austin* (n 3) 246 [115] (Gaudron, Gummow and Hayne JJ).

laws of general application by one polity that curtailed another polity's capacity to function.[5] In *Commonwealth v Tasmania*[6] Mason J summarised this conception of the doctrine when he observed that the Commonwealth cannot 'enact a law which discriminates against or "singles out" a State or imposes some special burden or disability upon a State or inhibits or impairs the continued existence of a State or its capacity to function'.[7] At least until recently all of the cases in which the doctrine has been applied concerned Commonwealth action that affected one or all the states. But as a majority of the High Court (as well as Edelman J in dissent) confirmed in *Spence*, it is an error to regard the principle solely as a constraint on Commonwealth power; it can apply to invalidate Commonwealth or state action.[8]

A significant turning point in understanding the doctrine came in *Austin* in which the plurality rejected the discrimination branch of the principle and held that the doctrine really consists of a single limitation.[9] That change in understanding led some commentators to criticise *Austin*, arguing that the plurality's decision in that case has obfuscated on the doctrine.[10] Nevertheless the plurality's decision in *Austin* was followed in *Clarke*,[11] *Fortescue Metals Group Ltd v Commonwealth*[12] and by extension in *Spence*.[13] The prevailing conception of the doctrine is that of a principle that 'requires consideration

---

5 *Queensland Electricity Commission v Commonwealth* (1985) 159 CLR 192, 217 (Mason J) (*'Queensland Electricity Commission'*).

6 *Commonwealth v Tasmania* (1983) 158 CLR 1 (*'Tasmanian Dam Case'*).

7 Ibid 128 (Mason J).

8 *Spence* (n 2) 673 [107] (Kiefel CJ, Bell, Gageler and Keane JJ), 714–15 [308]–[310] (Edelman J).

9 *Austin* (n 3) 249 [124] (Gaudron, Gummow and Hayne JJ).

10 See, eg, James Stellios, *Zines's The High Court and the Constitution* (The Federation Press, 6th ed, 2015) 501 ('Stellios'); Anne Twomey, 'Federal Limitations on the Legislative Power of the States and the Commonwealth to Bind One Another' (2003) 31(3) *Federal Law Review* 507, 511 ('Twomey').

11 *Clarke* (n 3) 306 [65] (Gummow, Heydon, Kiefel and Bell JJ).

12 *Fortescue Metals Group Ltd v Commonwealth* (2013) 250 CLR 548, 609 [130] (Hayne, Bell and Keane JJ) (*'Fortescue'*).

13 *Spence* (n 2) 673 [108] (Kiefel CJ, Bell, Gageler and Keane JJ).

of whether impugned legislation is directed at States, imposing some special disability or burden on the exercise of powers and fulfilment of functions of the States which curtails their capacity to function as governments'.[14]

This chapter contends with that way of understanding and applying the *Melbourne Corporation* principle. It discusses the origin (Part I), nature (Part II) and application (Part III) of the *Melbourne Corporation* principle. The aim is to clarify what the doctrine is to facilitate its proper application. It is argued that the *Melbourne Corporation* principle is best understood as an inter-governmental immunity that requires consideration of whether an exercise of power encroaches upon the autonomy of an independent body politic operating in a federal system. In developing that contention, the chapter also addresses the inter-relation of the *Melbourne Corporation* principle with other constitutional implications of federalism in Australia.[15]

II.   Origin of the *Melbourne Corporation* principle

The *Melbourne Corporation* principle is an implication of the *Constitution*, specifically, an implication of the fact that the *Constitution* was framed upon the concept of a federal system for governing the country. Accordingly, although the principle was first recognised by the High Court in the *Melbourne Corporation Case*, it is incorrect to assume that it emanates from the Court's decision in that case; the High Court's role involves uncovering, not making, constitutional implications.[16]

---

14 Ibid [107] (Kiefel CJ, Bell, Gageler and Keane JJ), quoting *Fortescue* (n 12) 609 [130] (Hayne, Bell and Keane JJ).

15 Such as the principles established in *Amalgamated Society of Engineers v Adelaide Steamship Co Ltd* (1920) 28 CLR 129 ('*Engineers' Case*'); *Commonwealth v Cigamatic Pty Ltd (In Liquidation)* (1962) 108 CLR 372 ('*Cigamatic*').

16 *Victoria v Commonwealth* (1971) 122 CLR 353, 402 (Windeyer J) ('*Payroll Tax Case*'). His Honour stated: 'I would prefer not to say "making implications", because our avowed task is simply the revealing or uncovering of implications that are already there'.

A. Federalism and the *Constitution*

The preamble to the *Commonwealth of Australia Constitution Act 1900* (Imp) relevantly states:

> WHEREAS the people of New South Wales, Victoria, South Australia, Queensland, and Tasmania, humbly relying on the blessing of Almighty God, have agreed to unite in one indissoluble Federal Commonwealth.[17]

The word indissoluble in the preamble is noteworthy because it suggests that a purpose of the *Constitution* was to establish a federal system that would endure.

The *Constitution* has been described as 'a hybrid of ideas and models'.[18] Australia has a Westminster system of government and is a constitutional monarchy, but the framers of the *Constitution* were also guided by the United States' model of federalism.[19] Like the United States' model, the Australian *Constitution* establishes a federal system for running the country that comprises a central government and independent state governments. The powers of the central government are enumerated;[20] the states' power is residual.[21] A state law that is inconsistent with a Commonwealth law will be inoperative to the extent and duration of the inconsistency.[22]

The first High Court justices, Griffith CJ and Barton and O'Connor JJ, were among the framers of the *Constitution*. They were also familiar with American constitutional law and were influenced by Chief Justice John Marshall of the Supreme

---

17 Preamble to the *Commonwealth of Australia Constitution Act 1900* (Imp).

18 George Williams, Sean Brennan and Andrew Lynch, *Blackshield & Williams Australian Constitutional Law and Theory* (The Federation Press, 6th ed, 2014) 2 [1.1] ('Williams, Brennan and Lynch').

19 See Constitutional Commission, *Final Report of the Constitution Commission* (Australian Government Publishing Service, volume 1, 1988) 53 [2.15].

20 *Constitution* s 51.

21 Ibid ss 107–108. See *United States Constitution,* Tenth Amendment.

22 *Constitution* s 109.

Court of the United States.[23] They were therefore concerned with how the Commonwealth and the states would interact.[24] Consequently, two constitutional interpretive doctrines were developed that effectively preserved the states' power, namely, the doctrines of implied immunities and reserved powers.[25] The implied immunities doctrine provided that the Commonwealth and states, and their organs or instruments, were immune from each other's laws.[26] The reserved powers doctrine provided that s 107 of the *Constitution* reserved powers to the states and thereby constrained Commonwealth power.[27]

By 1920 the composition of the High Court had changed. Sir Adrian Knox was the Chief Justice, but Isaacs J, who favoured the centralisation of power and was a longstanding critic of the immunities and reserved powers doctrines, dominated the High Court.[28] The First World War also had a profound impact on developing a sense of national identity among Australians, who had formerly identified more closely with their state of origin.[29] Those factors, in addition to legal problems, underly the High Court's seminal decision in the *Engineers' Case* about which several things must be said.[30]

The *Engineers' Case* concerned whether through its conciliation and arbitration power in s 51(xxxv) of the *Constitution* the

---

23 Owen Dixon, *Jesting Pilate and Other Papers and Addresses* (Collected by His Honour Judge Woinarski, The Law Book Company Limited 1965) 114 ('Dixon').
24 Ibid 114–15.
25 For a discussion about the how the framers' intent influenced the manifestation of those doctrines, see generally Michelle Evans, 'Engineers: The Case that Changed Australian Constitutional History' (2012) 24 *Giornale di Storia Constituzionale* 65, 66; Williams, Brennan and Lynch (n 18) 242 [6.14].
26 See, eg, *D'Emden v Pedder* (1904) 1 CLR 91; *Deakin v Webb* (1904) 1 CLR 585.
27 See, eg, *R v Barger* (1908) 6 CLR 41.
28 See Dixon (n 23) 114; Anthony Mason, 'The High Court of Australia: A Personal Impression of its First 100 Years' (2003) 27(3) *Melbourne University Law Review* 864, 872.
29 See generally *Payroll Tax Case* (n 16) 395–7 (Windeyer J).
30 For a discussion about the political factors that influenced the Court's judgment in the *Engineers' Case* (n 15) see R.T.E. Latham, 'The Law and the Commonwealth' in WK Hancock, *Survey of British Commonwealth Affairs: Problems of Nationality 1918-1936* (Oxford University Press, 1937) 1, 510.

Commonwealth could render an award binding upon the states as employers in an employment dispute. By 5:1 majority, the High Court held that the Commonwealth laws could bind the states.[31] The *Engineers' Case* has in turn been described as having 'exploded and unambiguously rejected'[32] the reserved powers doctrine (although it has been argued that the High Court adopted some 'reserved powers reasoning' again in *Spence*).[33] Nevertheless the decision continues to influence constitutional interpretation.[34] In *Spence* a majority of the High Court observed that the principles for determining whether a Commonwealth law is within the scope of legislative power 'have become "well settled" since the *Engineers' Case* and have even been described as "established, if not trite, constitutional law"'.[35] But the impact of the *Engineers' Case* on the extent to which inter-governmental immunities operate in the federation remains opaque. The inter-governmental immunity that operated between federation and 1920 did not survive the *Engineers' Case* and has not been revived.[36] But even during the period between the *Engineers' Case* and *Melbourne Corporation*, the High Court acknowledged limits on the Commonwealth's and the states' capacity to affect each other.[37]

---

31 *Engineers' Case* (n 15) 154 (Knox CJ, Isaacs, Rich and Starke JJ).

32 *Strickland v Rocla Concrete Pipes Ltd* (1971) 124 CLR 468, 485 (Barwick CJ).

33 See, eg, Nicholas Aroney, 'Spence v Queensland and the Federal Balance: How Many Swallows Make a Summer?' (2020) 31 *Public Law Review* 33 ('Aroney').

34 See David Hume, Andrew Lynch and George Williams, 'Heresy in the High Court? Federalism as a Constraint on Commonwealth Power' (2013) 41(1) *Federal Law Review* 71, 73–4. Cf Aroney (n 33).

35 *Spence* (n 2) 663–4 [57] (Kiefel CJ, Bell, Gageler, Keane JJ) (citations omitted).

36 See ibid 673 [107] (Kiefel CJ, Bell, Gageler, Keane JJ). See also Stephen Donaghue and Christine Ernst, 'The Engineers' Case and Intergovernmental Immunities: A Century On' (2020) 31 *Public Law Review* 46, 56–7 ('Donaghue and Ernst').

37 See, eg, *Pirrie v McFarlane* (1925) 36 CLR 170, 191 (Isaacs J); *Australian Railways Union v Victorian Railways Commissioners* (1930) 44 CLR 319, 390 (Dixon J); *West v Commissioner of Taxation (NSW)* (1937) 56 CLR 657, 681–3 (Dixon J).

B.   *Melbourne Corporation*

Melbourne Corporation concerned the constitutionality of s 48 of the *Banking Act 1945* (Cth) (*'Banking Act'*). During the Second World War, the Commonwealth's power expanded such that the Commonwealth Bank could control the supply of money. Section 48 was an attempt to make those arrangements permanent[38] by prohibiting any private bank from conducting banking with the states or a local governing authority without the written consent of the Federal Treasurer.[39]   Had it been upheld, s 48 would have enabled the Commonwealth to control the states' banking arrangements.[40]

Two features of s 48 should be pointed out. The first is that it discriminated against the states. That is, it isolated the states from the general law and imposed a special disability upon them.[41] The second is that, insofar as it would have controlled the states' capacity to bank, s 48 would have curtailed their capacity to govern since the ability to conduct banking is essential to the functioning of a government.[42]

In holding s 48 invalid the High Court's reasoning was not uniform. However, underlying all the judges' reasons except for McTiernan J's, which comprised a dissent, was some notion that either or both those two features of s 48 made it unconstitutional. Justices Rich, Starke and Dixon each held that s 48 was invalid because it infringed an implication of the *Constitution*, although their Honours differed in their expression of the implication and the nature of the inquiry for determining whether it has been breached.[43]   Chief Justice Latham held that s 48 was unconstitutional on the basis that it was in substance a law that

---

38 See Williams, Brennan and Lynch (n 18) 1084 [25.10].
39 *Melbourne Corporation* (n 1) 43 (Latham CJ).
40 See generally ibid 67 (Rich J).
41 *Melbourne Corporation* (n 1) 84 (Dixon J).
42 See generally ibid 52–3 (Latham CJ), 67 (Rich J).
43 See generally *Payroll Tax Case* (n 16) 421 (Gibbs J).

sought to control the states and so could not be characterised as a law relating to an enumerated Commonwealth power,[44] an argument advanced by Garfield Barwick KC on behalf of the plaintiff[45] and which it appears Williams J also accepted.[46]

Decisions in subsequent High Court cases have settled the debate surrounding the question whether s 48 of the *Banking Act* was invalid for being inconsistent with an implication of the *Constitution* or for a characterisation defect, in favour of the former view.[47] But there remain multiple ways in which one could describe the constitutional implication infringed by s 48.

Justice Rich described it when he observed that the '*Constitution expressly provides for* the continued existence of the States'.[48] Justice Starke described it when he said '[t]he *maintenance* of the States and their powers is as much the object of the *Constitution* as the *maintenance* of the Commonwealth and its powers.'[49] Dixon J described the implication when he stated: 'The foundation of the *Constitution* is the conception of a central government and a number of State governments separately organized. The *Constitution* predicates their continued existence as independent entities.'[50]

Although they employ different wording, each of those descriptions of the constitutional implication can be reduced to the proposition that the *Constitution* protects the Commonwealth and the states' existence as independent political entities. But of each of the descriptions, Dixon J's is the most appropriate

---

44 *Melbourne Corporation* (n 1) 62 (Latham CJ).

45 Ibid 34–8.

46 Ibid 99–100 (Williams J). See also Jeremy Kirk, 'Constitutional Implications (I): Nature, Legitimacy, Classification, Examples' (2000) 24(3) *Melbourne University Law Review* 645, 672, citing *Melbourne Corporation* (n 1) 97–100 ('Kirk').

47 See, eg, *R v Coldham; Ex parte Australian Social Welfare Union* (1983) 153 CLR 297, 313; *Re Australian Education Union; Ex parte Victoria* (1995) 184 CLR 188, 227 (Mason CJ, Brennan, Deane, Toohey, Gaudron and McHugh JJ).

48 *Melbourne Corporation* (n 1) 66 (Rich J) (emphasis added).

49 Ibid 70 (Starke J) (emphasis added).

50 Ibid 82 (Dixon J).

and important.[51] Accordingly, it should be analysed in detail.

In the first sentence Dixon J states that the *Constitution* was framed upon the concept of a federal system of government comprised of a central government and separate state governments. The first sentence is therefore a statement of *fact* about the essence of the *Constitution* and the circumstances in which it was made. In the second sentence Dixon J concludes that the *Constitution* predicates — that is, founds, bases, or affirms[52] — the continued existence of the Commonwealth and the states as independent entities. His Honour used the word "predicates" as a verb to describe an implication of the *Constitution*, namely the provision of the continued existence of the Commonwealth and the states as independent political entities. The second sentence is therefore a statement that describes an *implication* of the *fact* that the *Constitution* was framed upon the concept of a federal system.

That implication follows from the fact that the *Constitution* was framed upon the concept of a federal system comprised of the Commonwealth and the states because a fundamental feature of any federal system is the independent co-existence of its constituent bodies politic.[53] Section 48 of the *Banking Act* was unconstitutional because it affected the states in a manner antithetical to that precept of federalism. Accordingly, whether s 48 could be traced to some Commonwealth power enumerated in s 51 of the *Constitution* was irrelevant[54] because

---

51 Aside from its erudition, Dixon J's description of the constitutional implication has been quoted or cited on numerous occasions by other High Court judges when discussing the implication: See, eg, *Kruger v Commonwealth* (1997) 190 CLR 1, 64 (Dawson J); *Fortescue* (n 12) 609 [130] (Hayne, Bell, Keane JJ); *Spence* (n 2) 671 [99] (Kiefel CJ, Bell, Gageler and Keane JJ), 715 [309] (Edelman J).

52 The word "predicate" can have multiple meanings, including, relevantly, to proclaim, declare, affirm or assert; or to found or base (something): see *Macquarie Dictionary* (7th ed, 2017) 'predicate' (defs 1, 4). Thus, if A predicates B; B is predicated upon A.

53 See, eg, *Pirrie v McFarlane* (1925) 36 CLR 170, 191 (Issacs J); *Williams v Commonwealth* (2012) 248 CLR 156, 178 [1] (French CJ), quoting Andrew Inglis Clark, *Studies in Australian Constitutional Law* (1901) 12–13.

54 See *Melbourne Corporation* (n 1) 79, 85 (Dixon J).

every exercise of Commonwealth and state power is subject to the express and implied terms of the *Constitution*.[55]

Despite Dixon J's remarks in *Melbourne Corporation*, in *Re Residential Tenancies Tribunal (NSW); Ex parte Defence Housing Authority*[56] the plurality described the *Melbourne Corporation* principle as '[t]he fundamental principle ... that the *Constitution* is *predicated upon* the continued separate existence of the Commonwealth and the States.'[57] Along similar lines, Davis JA stated in *Local Government Association of Queensland (Incorporated) v State of Queensland*[58] that '[t]he principle underlying [*Melbourne Corporation*], and also *Cigamatic*, is that the *Constitution* is predicated upon the continued separate existence of the Commonwealth and the States as bodies politic.'[59] Professor Anne Twomey has described the *Melbourne Corporation* principle as the 'principle that the *Constitution* is predicated upon the continuing separate existence of the Commonwealth and the States'.[60] Stephen Donaghue and Christine Ernst have stated that in *Melbourne Corporation*, Dixon J said that '[t]he *Constitution* was predicated ... on "their continued existence as independent entities"'.[61]

With respect, the *Constitution* cannot both predicate the continued existence of the Commonwealth and the states as independent entities and be predicated upon their continued existence as independent entities. It may do one or the other or neither, but it cannot do both.[62] The distinction is substantive. First, it is

---

55 See, eg, *Constitution* s 51 which commences with the terms 'subject to this Constitution'. See also *West v Commissioner of Taxation (NSW)* (1937) 56 CLR 657, 681–3 (Dixon J).

56 *Re Residential Tenancies Tribunal (NSW); Ex parte Defence Housing Authority* (1997) 190 CLR 410 ('*Re Residential Tenancies Tribunal*').

57 Ibid 440 (Dawson, Toohey and Gaudron JJ) (emphasis added).

58 *Local Government Association of Queensland (Incorporated) v Queensland* (2001) 118 LGERA 195 ('*LGAQ v Queensland*').

59 Ibid 206 [47] (Davies JA).

60 Twomey (n 10) 534.

61 Donaghue and Ernst (n 36) 51, quoting *Melbourne Corporation* (n 1) 82 (Dixon J).

62 If A *predicates* B, B is *predicated upon* A: see above (n 52) and accompanying text for a discussion about the meaning of the word "predicates".

precisely because the *Constitution* predicates the continued existence of the Commonwealth and the states as independent entities that legislation that threatens the continued existence of the states as independent political entities, legislation like s 48 of the *Banking Act*, must be unconstitutional. Accordingly, when Dixon J stated that the *Constitution* predicates the Commonwealth and the states' continued existence as independent entities, his Honour was essentially articulating the "*Melbourne Corporation* principle". But moreover, the very notion of the *Constitution* being predicated upon the continued existence of the Commonwealth and the states as independent entities is incoherent. The *Constitution* established the Commonwealth and the states (the latter being colonies prior to federation). How, therefore, could it be predicated upon their continued existence as independent entities? To put it in the converse: how could the Commonwealth and the states' continued existence as independent entities predicate the *Constitution*? Respectfully, it cannot; the true position is the reverse.

III.   Nature of the *Melbourne Corporation* Principle

What is the proper way to conceptualise an implication of the *Constitution* that predicates the continued existence of the Commonwealth and the states as independent entities? The *Melbourne Corporation* principle has been called an implied limitation,[63] an implied prohibition,[64] and an immunity.[65] In the *Tasmanian Dam Case* and *Queensland Electricity Commission* Mason J referred to it as an implied prohibition.[66] But in a joint judgment with Brennan and Deane JJ in *Re Lee; Ex parte*

---

63 See, eg, *Austin* (n 3) 223 [40] (Gaudron, Gummow and Hayne JJ); *Clarke* (n 3) 298 [33] (French CJ); *Fortescue* (n 12) 591 [69] (Hayne, Bell and Keane JJ).
64 See, eg, *Austin* (n 3) 220 [30] (Gleeson CJ).
65 *Spence* (n 2) 673 [108] (Kiefel CJ, Bell, Gageler and Keane JJ).
66 *Tasmanian Dam Case* (n 6) 128 (Mason J); *Queensland Electricity Commission* (n 5) 217 (Mason J).

Harper,[67] his Honour referred to it as an implied limitation.[68] In *Austin* Kirby J referred to it both as an implied limitation and a constitutional prohibition.[69] In *Fortescue* the plurality referred to the principle as an implied limitation.[70]

One might therefore assume that the taxonomy of the *Melbourne Corporation* principle is irrelevant; that nothing is to be gained by attempting to classify the *Melbourne Corporation* principle. But such an assumption is misconceived because the way that one conceptualises the *Melbourne Corporation* principle will influence one's application of it. A sound conception of the *Melbourne Corporation* principle militates against the risk that the principle will be incorrectly or inconsistently applied. This is because, it will be argued, there are technical differences between that which prohibits power, that which prohibits a particular exercise of power, and that which provides immunity from certain effects of power. This Part concludes that the *Melbourne Corporation* principle should be conceptualised as an inter-governmental immunity.

A.   Characterisation Problem or Structural Implication?

Although the view that s 48 of the *Banking Act* was invalid because it lacked the character to relate to a Commonwealth power ("the characterisation argument") has been rejected by the High Court, an inquiry into the nature of the *Melbourne Corporation* principle would be incomplete without some consideration of it.

Section 48 of the *Banking Act* provided that '[e]xcept with the consent in writing of the Treasurer, a bank shall not conduct

---

67 *Re Lee; Ex parte Harper* (1986) 160 CLR 430.
68 Ibid 453 (Mason, Brennan and Deane JJ).
69 See *Austin* (n 3) 300 [279], 302 [285] (Kirby J).
70 *Fortescue* (n 12) 591 [69] (Hayne, Bell and Keane JJ).

any banking business for a State or for any authority of a State, including a local governing authority.'[71] It was enacted in reliance on s 51(xiii) of the *Constitution*, which provides that, subject to the *Constitution*, the Commonwealth can pass laws with respect to 'banking, other than State banking.'[72] It should be noted for completeness, that a majority of the judges in *Melbourne Corporation* held that the words "State banking" in s 51(xiii) meant the states as bankers, not banking customers.[73] Accordingly, the exception in s 51(xiii) concerning state banking was inapplicable to the case.[74]

Despite the Commonwealth's power to pass laws with respect to banking, however, Latham CJ (and, years later in the *Payroll Tax Case*, Barwick CJ) opined that s 48 of the *Banking Act* lacked the character to relate to an enumerated Commonwealth power.[75] With respect, the characterisation argument is problematic for several reasons.

First, it does not take proper account of the fact that a law may deal with multiple subjects and bear dual character.[76] More specifically the characterisation argument evades the question whether a Commonwealth law that takes multiple subjects is valid where one of those subjects is beyond Commonwealth power. According to Barwick CJ in such cases 'a decision must be made as to that which is in truth the subject matter of the law'.[77] But then his Honour proceeded to say that to decide that a law has the states, state power or a state governmental function as its subject matter 'is to decide that it cannot be a law "justified

71 *Banking Act 1945* (Cth) s 48(1).
72 *Constitution* s 51(xiii).
73 See generally Stellios (n 10) 477.
74 *Melbourne Corporation* (n 1) 78 (Dixon J).
75 Ibid 62 (Latham CJ); *Payroll Tax Case* (n 16) 372 (Barwick CJ).
76 See *Melbourne Corporation v Commonwealth* (n 1) 79 (Dixon J); *Fairfax v Federal Commissioner of Taxation* (1965) 114 CLR 1, 13 (Kitto J); *Payroll Tax Case* (n 16) 400 (Windeyer J). See also Twomey (n 10) 527–8; Williams, Brennan and Lynch (n 18) 764–5 [17.14].
77 *Payroll Tax Case* (n 16) 373 (Barwick CJ).

by the power to make laws with respect to" one of the topics enumerated in s. 51'.[78]   However, that contention avoids the question at hand, namely whether an impugned Commonwealth law that relates to two subjects, one within Commonwealth power and another beyond it, is valid.   To contend that such a law cannot relate to an enumerated Commonwealth power is to therefore reject the premise of the question.   Secondly, the characterisation argument distorts the inquiry for determining whether a Commonwealth law is within power under s 51 of the *Constitution*.   As Windeyer J observed when discussing *Melbourne Corporation* and the characterisation argument, '[t]he question under s. 51 is always whether a particular enactment is within Commonwealth power. It is not whether it invades a State's domain.'[79]

Section 48 of the *Banking Act* provided that no private bank could conduct banking with any state or local governing authority without the written consent of the Federal Treasurer. The provision clearly related to the subject of banking. Professors Leslie Zines and James Stellios have therefore observed that the characterisation test 'camouflag[es] the real ground for decision',[80] and Jeremy Kirk has aptly described the characterisation argument as a 'characterisation detour'[81] from making constitutional implications.

B.   Prohibition on Power or Restriction on Power?

In *Cigamatic*[82] the High Court recognised an implication of the *Constitution* that has occasionally been (mis)characterised as a 'reverse' *Melbourne Corporation* principle.   There are

---

78 Ibid.
79 Ibid 400 (Windeyer J).
80 Stellios (n 10) 481.
81 Kirk (n 46) 672.
82 *Cigamatic* (n 15)

similarities between the *Cigamatic* principle and the *Melbourne Corporation* principle. Both are implications of the federal structure of the *Constitution*. Both supervise the inter-governmental relationship between the Commonwealth and states. However, the principles really are distinct.

In short, the *Cigamatic* principle is a prohibition on power; the *Melbourne Corporation* principle resembles[83] a restriction or limitation on power. By a 'prohibition on power', what I mean is a principle that holds some powers to be unconstitutional. When enlivened, such a principle operates on the *power* that has been impugned and *prohibits* it. By a 'restriction on power' (or 'limitation on power'), what is being referred to is a principle that holds certain exercises of power to be unconstitutional. Thus, a prohibition on power is concerned with the use of illegitimate power whereas a restriction on power is concerned with the illegitimate use of legitimate power. Going forward, the prohibition on power is referred to as an 'implied prohibition'. The restriction/limitation on the capacity to use power is referred to as an 'implied restriction'.

The distinction between an implied prohibition and an implied restriction (as defined above) is borne out by analysis of the difference between, on the one hand, the Commonwealth and states as bodies politic and, on the other, the difference between the Commonwealth and the states' powers. As has already been explained, the *Constitution* established the Commonwealth and the states. The *Constitution* distributes powers to the Commonwealth, and the states inherited the residual colonial power.[84] However, the Commonwealth's and the states' powers do not form part of the Commonwealth and the states *themselves*

---

83 I say "resembles" because although in operation the *Melbourne Corporation* principle limits/restricts the Commonwealth and the states' capacity to affect each other, it is more correct to classify it as an inter-governmental immunity: see below Part III(C).

84 See *Uther v Federal Commissioner of Taxation* (1947) 74 CLR 508, 530 (Dixon J) ('*Uther's Case*').

as bodies politic.[85]   Justice Dixon explained this distinction between the states as political entities and the states' powers when in *Melbourne Corporation* he said:

> The framers of the *Constitution* do not appear to have considered that power itself forms part of the conception of a government. They appear rather to have conceived the States as bodies politic whose existence and nature are independent of the powers allocated to them.[86]

Because the Commonwealth and the states exist separately from their powers, Commonwealth and state power must be separate from and exist independently of the Commonwealth and the states. Accordingly, Commonwealth or state action may be invalid as a misuse of power or for requiring the support of power that is unconstitutional.

It should be mentioned that the process of finding some power to be unconstitutional in practice is obfuscated by the fact the High Court can only address 'matters' and cannot give advisory opinions or address hypothetical questions.[87] Accordingly, before some Commonwealth or state action can be impugned as based upon prohibited power, the power alleged to be prohibited must first be exercised. This in turn gives rise to an apparent paradox because power that is prohibited does not really exist and so cannot be exercised. None of this, however, contradicts the notion that Commonwealth or state action may be invalid as based upon power that is prohibited. Any so-called 'paradox' is merely a side-effect of the way the High Court must operate pursuant to ch III of the *Constitution*.

---

85 For example, the Commonwealth's power to legislate with respect to Australia's external affairs, granted to it by s 51(xxix) of the *Constitution*, is distinct from the Commonwealth as a political entity.

86 *Melbourne Corporation* (n 1) 82 (Dixon J).

87 *In re Judiciary and Navigation Acts* (1921) 29 CLR 257; *Mellifont v Attorney-General (Queensland)* (1991) 173 CLR 289. See also Williams, Brennan and Lynch (n 18) 441–2 [11.40]–[11.42].

1. Analysing an Implied Prohibition: The *Cigamatic* principle

In *Cigamatic* the High Court overruled its earlier decision in *Uther's Case*.[88] Both cases concerned the question whether a state law could displace the Commonwealth prerogative to priority over other unsecured creditors in bankruptcy cases and thus affect the inter-relation of the rights of the Commonwealth executive and rights of Commonwealth subjects.[89] The issue, at least according to Sir Owen Dixon, went to the nature of state power under the *Constitution*.[90]

In *Uther's Case* a majority of the High Court (Dixon J dissenting) upheld such state legislation.[91] In *Cigamatic* the High Court overruled *Uther's Case* and held invalid state legislation that sought to displace the Commonwealth prerogative to priority over unsecured creditors in bankruptcy cases. *Cigamatic* has since been affirmed by the High Court, albeit with modification.[92]

Central to Dixon J's reasoning in *Uther's Case* and later in *Cigamatic* when his Honour was the Chief Justice is the notion that the power required to support the state legislation impugned in those cases is unconstitutional. His Honour stated in *Uther's Case*:

> Like the goddess of wisdom the Commonwealth *uno ictu* sprang from the brain of its begetters armed and of full stature. At the same instant the Colonies became States; *but whence did the States obtain the power to regulate the legal relations of this new polity with its subjects?* It formed no part of the old colonial power. The Federal constitution does not give it.[93]

---

88 *Uther's Case* (n 84).
89 See ibid 528 (Dixon J); *Cigamatic* (n 15) 377 (Dixon CJ).
90 See *Uther's Case* (n 84) 530 (Dixon J); *Cigamatic* (n 15) 377 (Dixon CJ).
91 *Uther's Case* (n 84).
92 See generally Stellios (n 10) 531.
93 *Uther's Case* (n 84) 530 (Dixon J) (emphasis added).

According to Dixon J, ss 282 and 297 of the *Companies Act 1936* (NSW) ("the *Companies Act*") were not an exercise of state residual power. They were ultra vires laws; the states lack the power necessary to affect the inter-relation of the Commonwealth's rights and Commonwealth subjects' rights.[94] To put it another way, no state power exists to affect the inter-relation of the rights of the Commonwealth executive and the rights of Commonwealth subjects. *Cigamatic* therefore stands for the proposition that it is beyond the residual power to make laws for the peace, welfare and good government of a state to affect the inter-relation of the Crown in right of the Commonwealth and its subjects.[95]

2. Comparing *Cigamatic* and *Melbourne Corporation*

The *Cigamatic* principle has engendered prominent criticism.[96] Some contend that *Cigamatic* should be overruled and that any implication of the *Constitution* that protects the Commonwealth from state interference should be based upon a 'reverse' *Melbourne Corporation* principle.[97] But such a view overlooks important features of the two doctrines.

First, the notion of a 'reverse' *Melbourne Corporation* principle is apt to mislead. In *Spence* the majority and Edelman J (in dissent) explained that the *Melbourne Corporation* principle operates to protect both the states and the Commonwealth.[98] Their Honours did not enunciate a novel, reverse, *Melbourne*

---

94 See generally Twomey (n 10) 537.
95 See *Re Residential Tenancies Tribunal* (n 56) 424–5 (Brennan CJ).
96 R.P. Meagher and W.M.C. Gummow, 'Sir Owen Dixon's Heresy' (1980) 54 *Australian Law Journal* 25; Twomey (n 10) 534; Nicholas Aroney, 'Federalism and Subsidiarity: Principles and Processes in the Reform of the Australian Federation' 44(1) *Federal Law Review* (2016) 1, 7.
97 See *Re Residential Tenancies Tribunal* (n 56) 508–9 (Kirby J). See Twomey (n 10) 537–8.
98 *Spence* (n 2) 673 [107] (Kiefel CJ, Bell, Gageler and Keane JJ). Their Honours stated: 'The reciprocal application of that structural implication has been, and should remain, constitutional doctrine.'

Corporation principle,[99] the very notion of which tends to bifurcate a single doctrine that protects the Commonwealth and the states' continued existence as independent entities.

Secondly, and perhaps more fundamentally, unlike the legislation impugned in *Cigamatic*, the legislation impugned in *Melbourne Corporation* was not invalid because the government that enacted it lacked the power necessary to support it. Section 48 of the *Banking Act* was an invalid *exercise* of the power distributed to the Commonwealth by s 51(xiii) of the *Constitution* to make laws with respect to banking. Sections 282 and 297 of the *Companies Act* were invalid because state residual power cannot support a law that affects the inter-relation of the Commonwealth's rights and the rights of Commonwealth subjects. Accordingly, Dixon CJ was correct when he observed that the validity of the state legislation that was impugned in *Cigamatic*, '[could not] be regarded as simply governed by the applicability of the principles upon which [*Melbourne Corporation*] depended'.[100]

C.   Implied Restriction or Inter-governmental Immunity?

One might contend there is no benefit to conceptualising the *Melbourne Corporation* principle as either an implied restriction or an inter-governmental immunity. The basis of such a contention may be that any state and Commonwealth immunity would simply be consequential to a restriction on the Commonwealth and the states' capacity to use their power (or vice versa), such that the *Melbourne Corporation* principle may be considered a restriction on power that correlates with

---

99 *Spence* (n 2) 673 [108] (Kiefel CJ, Bell, Gageler and Keane JJ). To review earlier support for the reciprocal operation of the doctrine see *R v Coldham; Ex parte Australian Social Welfare Union* (1983) 153 CLR 297, 313 (Gibbs CJ, Mason, Murphy, Wilson, Brennan, Deane and Dawson JJ).
100 *Cigamatic* (n 15) 378 (Dixon CJ).

an immunity or an immunity that correlates with a restriction on power.[101]   But that view should not be accepted because that which restricts the use of power is different to that which provides immunity.

First, immunity does not necessarily follow a restriction on a power. Whether a subject is immune to some condition depends foremost upon the qualities that it possesses, not on the extent of the power of something else. The Commonwealth's capacity to use its powers may therefore be restricted, but whether the states are immune from certain Commonwealth action ultimately directs attention to the character of the states as bodies politic.

Secondly, neither Commonwealth nor state power can be affected by any Commonwealth or state immunity. As discussed in the previous section, the Commonwealth and the states' powers are distinct from the Commonwealth and the states as bodies politic. An inter-governmental immunity may therefore limit the Commonwealth's and the states' *capacity* to affect one another, but that does not equate to a restriction on their respective powers, which are not touched by any immunity they possess.

Thirdly, because the Commonwealth and the states are distinct political entities with their own constitutional powers, the application of an implied restriction will raise different issues and questions to be addressed depending on whether it is being applied to the Commonwealth or a state. However, the application of an inter-governmental immunity would raise the same issues for consideration regardless of which entity it is

---

101 For example, in *Spence* (n 2) the majority described the doctrine as: '[T]he doctrine of inter-governmental immunities expounded in the *Melbourne Corporation Case* as a limitation on the permissible exercise of State legislative power as well as a limitation on the permissible exercise of Commonwealth legislative power ...' at 673 [108] (Kiefel CJ, Bell, Gageler and Keane JJ), Edelman J described it as 'a constitutional intergovernmental immunity of the States in the sense that it is co-relative to a lack of Commonwealth legal power' at 714 [307], citing Walter Wheeler Cook, 'Hohfeld's Contributions to the Science of Law' (1919) 28 *Yale Law Journal* 721, 726–7.

being applied to because its ultimate concern is always whether some effect upon restrict the Commonwealth or a state is constitutional.

In the light of those three considerations, it is suggested that there is a qualitative difference between that which provides immunity from certain affectations of power and that which restricts power. The question is whether it is better to conceptualise the *Melbourne Corporation* principle as an implied restriction or an inter-governmental immunity.

1. An Implied Immunity

Because power does not form part of the conception of the Commonwealth and the states as bodies politic, a distinction must be drawn between the preservation of the states and the Commonwealth as bodies politic and the preservation of their power.[102] Accordingly, to determine how the *Melbourne Corporation* principle is best conceptualised one must determine whether, at its core, the doctrine is concerned with protecting the Commonwealth and the states as bodies politic or with restricting their power.

The *Constitution* was framed upon the concept of a federal system of government comprised of a central government and separate state governments.[103] The *Constitution* predicates the continued existence of the Commonwealth and the states as independent entities.[104] That, as I explained in an earlier part of this chapter, is the *Melbourne Corporation* principle reduced to a single proposition. It is therefore apparent that the doctrine recognised in *Melbourne Corporation* is concerned primarily with the Commonwealth and the states as political entities,

---

102 See generally Stellios (n 10) 488, discussing *Melbourne Corporation* (n 1) 82 (Dixon J).
103 *Melbourne Corporation* (n 1).
104 Ibid 82 (Dixon J).

more specifically, with preserving their continued independent existence. The *Melbourne Corporation* principle is therefore best conceptualised as an inter-governmental immunity. It is a less extreme version of the immunity that was rejected in the *Engineers' Case*;[105] but an inter-governmental immunity nonetheless. It is true that to the extent that the *Melbourne Corporation* principle operates to protect the Commonwealth and the states, the Commonwealth and the states' *capacity* to affect one another is limited. But as I have endeavoured to explain the Commonwealth and states' *powers* themselves are not affected by the inter-governmental immunity.

IV.   Applying the *Melbourne Corporation* principle

Commonwealth action has been found by the High Court to have infringed the immunity recognised in the *Melbourne Corporation* case on five occasions.[106]   But analysis reveals inconsistencies throughout the jurisprudence about how the principle is to be applied.

A.   Overview of the High Court's application of the doctrine

In *Melbourne Corporation* Rich, Starke and Dixon JJ each expressed different views about the sort of governmental action that will infringe the doctrine.[107] But the doctrine was gradually developed across a number of cases[108] to the point where it was,

---

105 See *Spence* (n 2) 673 [107] (Kiefel CJ, Bell, Gageler and Keane JJ). See also Donaghue and Ernst (n 36) 51.

106 *Melbourne Corporation* (n 1); *Queensland Electricity Commission* (n 5); *Re Australian Education Union; Ex parte Victoria* (1995) 184 CLR 188; *Austin* (n 3); *Clarke* (n 3).

107 See *Melbourne Corporation* (n 1) 66 (Rich J), 75 (Starke J), 79–83 (Dixon J).

108 See, eg, *Bank of New South Wales v Commonwealth* (1948) 76 CLR 1; *Payroll Tax Case* (n 16); *Tasmanian Dam Case* (n 6); *Queensland Electricity Commission* (n 5); *Western Australia v Commonwealth* (1995) 183 CLR 373; *Re Australian Education Union; Ex parte Victoria* (1995) 184 CLR 188.

for a time, basically settled that (1) a Commonwealth law that imposed a special disability on a state was invalid[109] and (2) a law of general application that curtailed a state's ability to function as a government was also invalid.[110]

In *Austin*, however, Gleeson CJ, the plurality and Kirby J (dissenting) rejected what McHugh J described in that case as the 'settled [two rule] doctrine'[111] set out by Mason J in *Queensland Electricity Commission*.[112] The plurality held that Commonwealth legislation that sought to tax the superannuation entitlements of state judges infringed the *Melbourne Corporation* principle,[113] which, according to their Honours, embodies a single limitation.[114] Specifically, their Honours rejected the idea that a Commonwealth law that singles out a state imposes a 'special disability' and therefore necessarily infringes the principle.[115] But despite reaching that conclusion the plurality used the same criteria that 'Mason J ... and other judges ... used when describing the two aspects of the implied immunity'.[116] Specifically, the plurality stated: 'The question presented by the doctrine in any given case requires assessment of the impact of particular laws by such criteria as "special burden" and "curtailment" of "capacity" of the States "to function as governments".'[117] Moreover, and as McHugh J persuasively stated:

> Perhaps nothing of substance turns on the difference between holding that there are two rules and holding that there is one limitation ... If there is a difference

---

109 See, eg, *Queensland Electricity Commission* (n 5).
110 See, eg, *Re Australian Education Union; Ex parte Victoria* (1995) 184 CLR 188.
111 *Austin* (n 3) 281 [223] (McHugh J).
112 Ibid 217 [24] (Gleeson CJ), 249 [124] (Gaudron, Gummow and Hayne JJ), 301 [281] (Kirby J).
113 Ibid 267 [174] (Gaudron, Gummow and Hayne JJ).
114 Ibid 249 [124] (Gaudron, Gummow and Hayne JJ).
115 See *Melbourne Corporation* (n 1); *Queensland Electricity Commission* (n 5). See also Stellios (n 10) 495–6.
116 Stellios (n 10) 495.
117 *Austin* (n 3) 249 [124] (Gaudron, Gummow and Hayne JJ).

> in content or application, it may lead to unforeseen problems in an area that is vague and difficult to apply. If there are no differences, no advantage is to be gained by jettisoning the formulation of Mason J in *Queensland Electricity Commission*.[118]

In *Clarke* the majority followed the plurality's approach in *Austin*.[119] To similar effect in a separate judgment French CJ provided six factors that his Honour considered relevant to the question whether the *Melbourne Corporation* principle has been breached, none of which in isolation would necessarily lead to invalidation.[120]

In *Fortescue* the plurality stated:

> Hence, as the decisions in *Austin* and *Clarke* each demonstrate, the *Melbourne Corporation* principle requires consideration of whether impugned legislation is directed at States, imposing some special disability or burden on the exercise of powers and fulfilment of functions of the States which curtails their capacity to function as governments.[121]

The plurality's decision in *Fortescue* clearly draws inspiration from *Austin* and *Clarke*. However, the above quote from *Fortescue* contains a host of conceptual difficulties.

The way the sentence is drafted, specifically the effect of the comma between 'States' and 'imposing', gives the impression that when applying the doctrine, one need only consider the impact of laws that are directed to the states. But if that is correct then the Court's statement in *Fortescue* effectively reinvigorates the discrimination branch of the immunity rejected in *Austin* and rejects the principle that it requires consideration of laws of general application. Respectfully, it cannot be the case that

---

118 Ibid 282 [224] (McHugh J).
119 *Clarke* (n 3) 306 [65] (Gummow, Heydon, Kiefel and Bell JJ).
120 Ibid 299 [34] (French CJ).
121 *Fortescue* (n 12) 609 [130] (Hayne, Bell and Keane JJ) (citations omitted).

the plurality in *Fortescue* intended to revise the doctrine like this since their Honour's cited *Austin* (and *Clarke*) when they explained how the doctrine is supposed to operate. Another problem with the statement in *Fortescue* is that it does not address the question whether the doctrine applies to exercises of executive as well as legislative power.[122] Lastly, despite observing that 'the perceived vice of the Commonwealth law in [*Austin* and *Clarke*] lay in its impact upon the capacity of a State to fix the terms of its relationships with its judiciary and legislature',[123] the plurality held that the legislation impugned in *Fortescue* '[was] not aimed at the States or their entities as was the legislation considered in each of *Melbourne Corporation, Queensland Electricity Commission, Austin* and *Clarke*'.[124] In the light of these difficulties, it does appear that *Fortescue* 'does not advance our understanding of [*Austin* and *Clarke*]'.[125]

In *Spence*, which at the time of writing is the most recent High Court case to address the principle's application, by 4:3 majority, the High Court, upheld impugned Queensland legislation that prohibited property developers in Queensland from making gifts to political parties and found s 302CA of the *Commonwealth Electoral Act 1918* (Cth) to be beyond Commonwealth power.[126] *Spence* is a noteworthy decision for several reasons. As professor Nicholas Aroney has argued, the Court's decision in *Spence* appears to invoke aspects of 'reserved powers reasoning'.[127] But the decision is also helpful in its elucidation of the *Melbourne Corporation* principle, which, although not relied upon by any of the judges to invalidate the impugned Commonwealth or

---

122 For example, in *Melbourne Corporation* (n 1) Starke J held that the doctrine applied to legislative and executive action: at 75.
123 *Fortescue* (n 12) 610 [135] (Hayne, Bell and Keane JJ).
124 Ibid 611 [137] (Hayne, Bell and Keane JJ).
125 Stellios (n 10) 500.
126 *Spence* (n 2) 653 [5] (Kiefel CJ, Bell, Gageler and Keane JJ).
127 Aroney (n 33) 33. For further discussion see Donaghue and Ernst (n 36).

state legislation,[128] was expounded upon in detail.

The majority in *Spence* reiterated the plurality's approach in *Fortescue*[129] and confirmed that the doctrine operates reciprocally.[130] Their Honours described the nature of the doctrine's application as 'essentially practical',[131] which does not say much because the process of applying anything is practical in nature.[132] Justice Nettle did not decide whether the doctrine operates reciprocally and only applied it in respect of the Commonwealth legislation.[133] Justice Gordon stated: '[I]t is unnecessary to decide whether a reverse *Melbourne Corporation* principle exists, beyond that identified in [*Cigamatic*], because any such doctrine would not be infringed by prohibition of a limited class of political donations.'[134] However, Gordon J's connection of *Melbourne Corporation* to *Cigamatic* should be approached cautiously because of the differences between the principles recognised in those cases, which have already been discussed. Justice Edelman proffered a new method for applying the principle that requires more in-depth analysis.

After discussing the relevant authorities, Edelman J observed that '[a]ll of these formulations can be reduced to a consideration of the magnitude of the burden upon the other polity's capacity to function as a government'.[135] His Honour then explained the application of the principle as follows:

> The magnitude of a burden has dimensions of both *breadth* and *depth*. A burden will be more deeply felt the more that it is targeted at the other polity and

---

128 See Spence (n 2) 673 [109] (Kiefel CJ, Bell, Gageler and Keane JJ), 685 [148]–[151] (Nettle J), 700 [235], 705 [266] (Gordon J), [317]–[319], [365]–[367] (Edelman J).

129 Ibid [108] (Kiefel CJ, Bell, Gageler and Keane JJ), quoting *Fortescue* (n 12) 609 [130].

130 *Spence* (n 2) 673 [107] (Kiefel CJ, Bell, Gageler and Keane JJ).

131 Ibid 671 [100] (Kiefel CJ, Bell, Gageler, Keane JJ).

132 The word "apply" has multiple definitions, one of which is 'to bring to bear; *put into practical operation*, as a principle, law, rule, etc.': *Macquarie Dictionary* (7th ed, 2017) 'apply' (def 2) (emphasis added).

133 *Spence* (n 2) 685 [148]–[151] (Nettle J).

134 Ibid 705 [266] (Gordon J) (citations omitted).

135 Ibid 717 [314] (Edelman J).

the more essential the governmental function that it
curtails is to that other polity. ...

A burden will be wider the more that it curtails the
operation of the governmental functions of the other
polity.[136]

His Honour also opined that if the magnitude of the burden
imposed on the affected polity is relevant to whether the
principle has been breached then so must be the significance of
the impugned law to the enacting polity's capacity to govern.[137]
Respectfully, this is persuasive. If, as it has been argued in this
chapter, the purpose of the *Melbourne Corporation* principle
is to preserve the continued existence of the Commonwealth
and the states as independent entities, then the significance of
the impugned action to the acting polity's capacity to govern
must be relevant because the efficacy of a government and by
extension the polity may depend upon its ability to enact certain
legislation or exercise an executive power.

Justice Edelman's method for applying the doctrine therefore
manifests a principle that can protect the Commonwealth
and the states in two distinct ways. First, because it requires
consideration of the magnitude of the burden imposed by an
impugned exercise of power on an affected polity to preserve that
polity's capacity to govern, the doctrine can *constrain* capacity
to use power. Secondly, because it also requires consideration
of the significance of an impugned exercise of power to the
preservation of the acting polity's capacity to govern, it can
uphold capacity to use power. Such a method demonstrates why
the *Melbourne Corporation* principle should be conceptualised
as an inter-governmental immunity rather than a restriction on
power; if the doctrine can be relied upon to invalidate or uphold
an exercise of power, it cannot only be a restriction on power.

---

136 Ibid 717 [314]–[315] (Edelman J) (emphasis added).
137 Ibid 717 [316].

B.   New approach to the *Melbourne Corporation* principle

The previous section set out to demonstrate that a consistent approach for applying the *Melbourne Corporation* principle remains elusive. In this section a revised approach that accords with the conception of the principle propounded in Part III is offered. A specific method for applying the principle is not proposed. Rather what is suggested is a way of approaching it to guide and facilitate its proper application. As will be seen, the recommended approach is broad and so could work alongside more specific methods for application, such as that propounded by Mason J in the earlier cases or by Edelman J in *Spence*. The suggestion is that the application of the *Melbourne Corporation* principle requires consideration of whether an exercise of power encroaches upon the autonomy of an independent body politic operating in a federal system. The key terms and phrases of that recommendation, namely 'encroaches', 'autonomy', 'independent body politic' and 'federal system' are each considered in turn.

1. *Key Terms*

Autonomy has been debated as a concept underlying both public and private law for centuries.[138] It would be inappropriate to enter that debate here either by endorsing an established conception of autonomy or by trying to suggest something novel. But the meaning of the concept cannot be assumed. Accordingly, what follows is a discussion of a narrow conception of autonomy, useful perhaps only insofar as it aids the present debate.

Because the essence of the *Constitution* is the conception of a federal system of government comprised of the Commonwealth and the states, the *Constitution* predicates the Commonwealth and the states' continued existence as 'independent' political

---

138 See, eg, Joseph Raz, 'Promises in Morality and Law' (1982) 95(4) *Harvard Law Review* 916.

entities.[139] It is suggested that one defining trait of an independent political entity is capacity to self-govern, that is 'autonomy'. But because the Commonwealth and states are independent entities operating in one federal system, even within the confines of their constitutional powers, they cannot have autonomy to operate completely free from interference from one another.[140] This in turn raises conceptual issues to which we must now turn concerning the question how multiple autonomous political entities may operate in the same federal system.

Subject to other terms of the *Constitution*, there seems no reason to assume that the Commonwealth and the states should not be treated even-handedly when applying a principle aimed at assuring their continued capacity to function independently. Application of the *Melbourne Corporation* principle should not result in preferential treatment of the Commonwealth or the states. Commonwealth and state autonomy may therefore be deemed to exist in the abstract on a single spectrum; the autonomy of one body politic ends where the autonomy of the other begins. Accordingly, the proposition the application of the *Melbourne Corporation* principle requires consideration of whether an exercise of power encroaches upon the autonomy of an independent body politic operating in a federal system can be considered in the converse as requiring consideration of whether an exercise of power is a legitimate exercise of the acting polity's right to self-govern. In determining such a question, the 'assessment will be one of "evaluation and degree"'.[141] But in all cases the effect of the impugned exercise of power upon the capacity of both the acting body politic and the affected body politic to govern must be considered.

---

139 *Melbourne Corporation* (n 1) 82 (Dixon J).
140 Besides the *Engineers' Case* (n 15) provides that no immunity of this kind exists in the *Constitution*.
141 *Spence* (n 2) 717 [314] (Edelman J), quoting *Austin* (n 3) 249 [124]; *Clarke* (n 3) 290 [16], 307 [66], 312 [93].

In assessing the impact of impugned action on the capacity of an independent body politic to govern one may turn to the authorities in which the principle has been applied for guidance. An independent body politic must have control of its own banking and accounts and so cannot control the banking arrangements of another independent body politic.[142] It can determine the employment conditions of its senior government officials and so cannot determine the awards of senior government officials of another body politic.[143] It can determine the operation of its organs of government and so cannot determine the operation of the organs of government of another body politic.[144] Several other qualities may also be deemed essential to an independent body politic. Writing in relation to the states, Zines and Stellios observed that essential aspects of government include:

> [A]dvice to ministers by the civil service, the relationship of the Governor to ministers and to Parliament, parliamentary debate and the internal procedures of Parliament, the operation of "responsible government", the freedom of the State judiciary, and the capacity to employ persons and resources necessary to carry out State functions.[145]

Equivalent principles should apply in respect of the Commonwealth.

2. Determining whether an exercise of power encroaches upon the autonomy of an independent body politic operating in a federal system

At the end of the last sub-section some of the qualities that may be considered essential to an independent body politic operating in a federal system were provided by reference to the High

---

142 See *Melbourne Corporation* (n 1).
143 See *Re Australian Education Union; Ex parte Victoria* (1995) 184 CLR 188; *Austin* (n 3); *Clarke* (n 3).
144 See *Austin* (n 3); *Clarke* (n 3); *Fortescue* (n 12).
145 Stellios (n 10) 489.

Court's application of the *Melbourne Corporation* principle and to examples from other commentators. But how should a novel case be decided? To answer that question, the *Melbourne Corporation* principle (as framed in this chapter) will be applied to a hypothetical exercise of Commonwealth power. Specifically, to consider whether an exercise of a Commonwealth power to control New South Wales' internal borders would encroach upon that State's autonomy or, conversely, constitute a legitimate exercise of the Commonwealth's right to govern autonomously.

Fundamental to a sovereign state is capacity to control its borders.[146] Absent express provision to the contrary, that principle should also apply to the internal borders of states that occupy space in a federation. The states' capacity to control their internal borders is limited by the *Constitution*.[147] But it should not be assumed that when the colonies conceded some control over their borders that sovereignty was deferred to the Commonwealth. Moreover, it is difficult to conceive how the capacity to control New South Wales' internal borders could be connected to the Commonwealth's right to self-govern — connected to its autonomy — let alone be necessary to sustain it. There may be exceptions, such as if the Commonwealth needed to take control of a state border to protect the country from invasion.[148] But the situation would have to be severe and unusual. Accordingly, as a general starting position, an exercise of a Commonwealth power to control a state border should be treated as encroaching upon the autonomy of an independent body politic that operates in a federal system.

A similar result would probably be reached by asking the same

---

146 See *Ruddock v Vardalis* (2001) 110 FCR 491, 543 [193] (French J). Sir Harry Gibbs, 'Dinner Address: The Erosion of National Sovereignty' (Conference Paper, Twelfth Conference of The Samuel Griffith Society, 10–12 November 2000).

147 *Constitution* s 92. See *Cole v Whitfield* (1988) 165 CLR 360.

148 For example, it is well-established that the Commonwealth's defence power "waxes and wanes" in accordance with the level of threat: see *Andrews v Howell* (1941) 65 CLR 255, 278 (Dixon J).

questions in the context of the more specific methods for applying the doctrine. The hypothetical action by the Commonwealth would impose a special disability on New South Wales insofar as it isolated it from the general law. It would also curtail New South Wales' capacity to function as a government by depriving it of the commercial and political advantages of being connected to the other states and the territories.[149] Both limbs of Mason J's method would probably be breached by the hypothetical law. Further, the hypothetical exercise would impose a burden of great magnitude. Such a law would target New South Wales and curtail an essential government function, namely border control. The burden would also be wide insofar as it curtailed, either directly or indirectly, 'the range of legislative policy choices of the other polity'.[150] It has already been explained that it is unlikely that such action by the Commonwealth could be necessary to sustain its capacity to function as a government. Accordingly, absent extraordinary circumstances an attempt by the Commonwealth to control a state border would probably infringe the *Melbourne Corporation* principle as conceptualised in this chapter.

3. Discrimination and the *Melbourne Corporation* principle

A final issue is whether an exercise of power by one body politic in a federal system that imposes special disabilities and burdens on another encroaches upon the autonomy of an independent body politic operating in a federal system. That is, whether Commonwealth action that discriminates against a state (or vice-versa) necessarily triggers the *Melbourne Corporation* principle following the conceptualisation of it offered in this chapter.

---

149 Although cf *Permanent Trustee Australia Ltd v Commissioner of State Revenue (Vic)* (2004) 220 CLR 388.
150 *Spence* (n 2) 717 [315] (Edelman J).

It is suggested that the autonomy of an independent polity in a federal system does not include capacity to discriminate against another member of that federal system. Conversely, immunity from discriminatory exercises of power by another member of the federal system is a quality of an independent body politic operating in a federal system. This is because the concept of a federal system assumes the co-operation of its constituent entities. Political entities occupying jurisdictional authority in a shared federal system should therefore be immune to action by one another that is discriminatory.

There is however no need to consider discrimination as a distinct branch of the doctrine. Compartmentalising the doctrine into a two-branch principle may assist, but is not necessary to facilitate, the doctrine's proper application. It need only be recognised that an exercise of power by one constituent body politic in a federal system that discriminates against another encroaches upon the autonomy of any independent body politic that operates in a federal system.

V.   Conclusion

In 1952, upon taking the oath of office as Chief Justice of the High Court, Sir Owen Dixon stated: 'Federalism means a demarcation of powers and this casts upon the Court a responsibility of deciding whether legislation is within the boundaries of allotted powers.'[151] In 2008 the Honourable Ian Callinan stated that '[t]he whole purpose of a federation is to divide power. ... Somebody has to say where the dividing line is, and in this country that body is the High Court.'[152] What we have come to know as the *Melbourne Corporation* principle,

---

151 Dixon (n 23) 247.
152 Ian Callinan, 'Australian Federalism: A Reply to the Thematic Issue' (2008) 31(3) *University of New South Wales Law Journal* 825, 827.

operates constantly in the background whenever the High Court must determine whether an exercise of power crosses that dividing line. A sound conception of and approach for applying it is therefore of paramount importance. The differences between the majority's and Edelman J's respective approaches in *Spence* demonstrates divergence in the High Court about how the principle should be applied. But the debate also offers hope of a clearer principle to come. This chapter has entered that debate. It argued that a clear conception of the doctrine is required to facilitate its proper application. The conception offered is that of an inter-governmental immunity the application of which requires consideration of whether an exercise of power encroaches upon the autonomy of an independent body politic operating in a federal system.

2

The Separation of Powers and the Mineralogy/Palmer Litigation

Anthony Gray

Abstract

In a landmark decision in 1996, a majority of the High Court found that the principle of separation of powers could be effectively drawn down from the *Australian Constitution* so as to be applicable to the state context. The principle is axiomatic as part of constitutional governance, seeking to enshrine checks and balances as a means of limiting the power of the state against individuals. Recently, the Western Australian Parliament passed legislation specifically naming and targeting an individual and organisation, in relation to particular matters in dispute. Effectively, the legislation rendered court proceedings pointless, because it effectively ordered courts not to review or quash government decisions or to provide a remedy in the event it found a law had been breached. The High Court validated the measure. This article argues there were good arguments in favour of the law being held invalid. The decision to validate such measures also imperils the rule of law.

Keywords

Separation of powers, *Kable*, Clive Palmer, Western Australia, usurpation, judicial power, Chapter III, *Australian Constitution*

Introduction

In 2020, the Western Australian Parliament, concerned with possible extensive financial liability to businessman Clive Palmer, passed legislation directed at Mr Palmer and one of his companies, purporting to deny the validity of past arbitral awards made in relation to a dispute between the parties, deny the liability of the state in relation to particular matters, and deny the ability of Mr Palmer to commence legal action in relation to particular matters. Legislation of this kind raises fundamental constitutional issues, including application of the constitutionally enshrined principle of the separation of powers. All members of the High Court upheld the validity of the Western Australian legislation, in the face of the constitutional challenge.[1] This chapter respectfully suggests there were strong arguments supporting Mr Palmer's claim that the legislation offended separation of powers principles.

Background to the litigation

In 2002, Mr Palmer entered into an agreement with the Western Australian government. The agreement is reflected in Schedule 2 of the *Iron Ore Processing (Mineralogy) Pty Ltd Agreement Act* 2002 (WA). The agreement permitted Mineralogy to submit proposals for mining development to the government. In turn, the agreement provided that the government could accept, defer or impose reasonable requirements upon the proposed

---

1 *Mineralogy Pty Ltd v Western Australia* [2021] HCA 30; *Palmer v Western Australia* [2021] HCA 31.

development. A decision was required within two months. Interestingly, there was no express provision for the government to reject a proposed development. If the government made a decision with which the company agreed, it could take the matter to commercial arbitration.

The Western Australian government apparently delayed approving a proposed mining development, before directing amendments to it that may or may not have been reasonable. Mr Palmer took this matter, and others, to arbitration. He was successful. Mr Palmer apparently believed that the delay caused his company to lose a large amount of money, and he proposed to reclaim these monies from the government. As a result, Parliament passed the *Iron Ore Processing (Mineralogy) Pty Ltd Agreement Amendment Act 2020* (WA)*(Amendment Act)*, amending the 2002 legislation.

Outline of Amendment Act

The Amendment Act applies to 'disputed matter', 'relevant arbitrations' and 'protected matter'. Section 7 states that 'disputed matter' includes the Minister's refusal to accept Mr Palmer's proposed mining development, the Minister's delayed response, and the Minister's direction to amend the proposal. 'Relevant arbitrations' includes those relating to disputed matter. 'Protected matter' included actions relating to passage of the Amendment Act.

These definitions are utilised in the following provisions:

. s10 – this states that any relevant arbitration on foot at the time the legislation is passed is invalid, that arbitral awards made between the parties during the years 2014-2019 are of no effect, and are deemed never to have had effect. Further, the arbitration agreement under which those awards were made is deemed not to exist.

. s11 – this states that Western Australia is not liable in respect of any relevant arbitrations or in respect of disputed matter. Such liabilities are 'extinguished'.[2] No action can be taken to enforce such a liability,[3] and any action already commenced is terminated.[4]

. s12 – this states that actions by the Western Australian government related to disputed matter cannot be challenged, quashed, or otherwise called into question, and cannot be the basis of any remedy.

. s18 – applies to protected matters, and likewise directs that none of the Western Australian government's actions can be the basis of an action for commission of a civil wrong, or otherwise form the basis of a remedy.

. s19 – Western Australia has no liability in respect of protected matter.

. s20 – Western Australia's actions in relation to protected matter cannot be challenged, quashed or otherwise called into question, and cannot be the basis of any remedy.

Relevant law – Separation of powers principles

Articulation of the separation of powers principle is typically sourced to the work of French philosopher Montesquieu.[5] It gained partial recognition in the United Kingdom over

---

2 Section 11(2).
3 Section 11(3).
4 Section 11(4).
5 'When the legislative and executive powers are united in the same person, or in the same body of magistrates, there can be no liberty': Charles de Montesquieu *The Spirit of Laws Book XI: Of the Laws Which Establish Political Liberty with Regard to the Constitution* (1748) para 6; see also Sir William Blackstone 1 *Commentaries on the Laws of England* (Clarendon Press, 1765-1769) 269.

time,[6] but has proved most influential in jurisdictions with a written constitution. The United States Supreme Court struck out legislation as being contrary to the separation of powers principle in *United States v Klein*.[7] There the Court denounced legislation passed in order to 'prescribe a rule for the decision of a cause in a particular way', where the Court was being asked to 'allow one party to the controversy to decide it in its own favor'.[8] The idea is that power is separated into the legislature, executive and the judiciary, in order that each can act as a check and balance on the other.

The principle of separation of powers was emphasised in the well-known Privy Council decision of *Liyanage v The Queen*,[9] involving the written *Constitution* of (former) Ceylon. There, parliament passed a special law purporting to deal with conspirators involved in a failed coup-d'etat. It applied retrospectively only to that situation. It provided special features to attend prosecution of those accused of involvement, including arrest without warrant, trial without jury, accused individuals to prove that any confessions were obtained involuntarily, minimum mandatory jail terms for those convicted of wrongdoing, and removed rights to appeal a conviction. Eleven individuals were convicted under the special law. They appealed their convictions to the Privy Council, arguing the law abridged the separation of powers provided for in the country's *Constitution*. Their appeal was unanimously upheld.

The Privy Council discerned the separation of powers principle in the structure of the *Ceylon Constitution*, which was divided into several parts devoted to the legislature, executive and

---

6 For a historical example of lack of judicial independence, see the *Ship Money Case* (R v Hampden (1637) 3 State Tr 826. Judicial independence was improved in the *Act of Settlement 1701* (Eng), mandating that judges could only be removed by the legislature.
7 80 US 128 (1871).
8 146.
9 [1967] AC 259.

judiciary. The Council was hesitant to lay down precise rules as to when a law might offend the separation of powers principles, much depending on the precise facts. However, it concluded that:

> Legislation ad hominem which is thus directed to the courts of particular proceedings may not always amount to an interference with the functions of the judiciary. But in the present case ... there was such an interference ... (that was) the intended effect of the impugned enactments, and that ... is fatal to their validity ... these alterations (to the traditional system of criminal justice) constituted a grave and deliberate incursion into the judicial sphere. Quite bluntly, their aim was to ensure that the judges in dealing with these particular persons on these particular charges were deprived of their normal discretion as respects appropriate sentences ... if such Acts were valid, the judicial power could be wholly absorbed by the legislature and taken out of the hands of the judges.[10]

The Australian High Court accepted the applicability of the separation of powers to the *Australian Constitution* in the landmark decision of *R v Kirby; Ex parte Boilermakers' Society of Australia (Boilermakers')*.[11] The Court recognised that judicial power must in general only be exercised by a judicial body, and that non-judicial power must in general be exercised by a non-judicial body, with narrow exceptions not presently relevant.[12] The Court has been somewhat tentative in defining judicial power,[13] generally preferring to express its characteristics rather than attempting an exhaustive definition. These characteristics

---

10 290-291.
11 (1956) 94 CLR 254 (Dixon CJ McTiernan Fullagar and Kitto JJ; Williams Webb and Taylor JJ dissenting).
12 270.
13 One early example is *Huddart, Parker and Co Pty Ltd v Moorehead* (1909) 8 CLR 330, 357 where Griffith CJ defined judicial power as 'the power which every sovereign authority must of necessity have to decide controversies between the subjects or between itself and its subjects, whether the rights relate to the liberty or property' (with whom Barton J (366) agreed).

include decisional independence,[14] natural justice/due process,[15] finality of decisions,[16] adversarial and accusatorial system,[17] and the settling of disputes about the existence of rights or obligations.[18] Laws which require courts to depart from these characteristics of judicial power are vulnerable to constitutional challenge.[19]

While it is clear that the separation of powers is constitutionally enshrined in the *Australian Constitution*, its applicability to state laws remains somewhat opaque. It was established in the *Builders' Labourers' Federation of New South Wales v Minister for Industrial Relations (BLF)*[20] that there is no formal separation of powers within state constitutions. The case involved a New South Wales government minister cancelling a union's registration. While a union appeal against this action was on foot, the Parliament passed a law effectively validating what the Minister had done. This made the judicial proceedings academic. Upon a hearing challenging the validity of this measure, the New South Wales Court of Appeal held it valid. It reasoned that the law infringed the separation of powers principle; however, it also found that this principle was not enshrined in the *New South Wales Constitution*. Some argue that the High Court decision in *Kable*,[21] which I discuss below,

---

14 *South Australia v Totani* (2010) 242 CLR 1, 20 (French CJ), 66 (Gummow J), 87 (Hayne J), 157 (Crennan and Bell JJ), and 172-173 (Kiefel J).

15 *Wainohu v New South Wales* (2011) 243 CLR 181, 213 (French CJ and Kiefel J) and Gummow Hayne Crennan and Bell JJ (225).

16 *Attorney-General (Qld) v Lawrence* [2013] QCA 364.

17 *X7 v Australian Crime Commission* (2013) 148 CLR 92.

18 *R v Trade Practices Tribunal; Ex parte Tasmanian Breweries Pty Ltd* (1970) 123 CLR 361, 374 (Kitto J), 387 (Menzies J), and 396 (Windeyer J).

19 *Forge v Australian Securities and Investment Commission* (2006) 228 CLR 45, 76 (Gummow Hayne and Crennan JJ); Anthony Gray *Criminal Due Process and Chapter III of the Australian Constitution* (Federation Press, 2016, 78-81).

20 (1986) 7 NSWLR 372; see also *Australian Building Construction Employees' and Builders' Labourers' Federation v Commonwealth* (1986) 161 CLR 88, 96.

21 *Kable v Director of Public Prosecutions* (NSW)(1996) 189 CLR 51.

effectively over-ruled this decision,[22] though the decision has not (yet) been expressly over-ruled.

Laws challenged under the separation of powers principle might usurp judicial power, interfere with judicial power, or do both. A law *usurps* judicial power where it provides for the legislature to step in and effectively act as a court.[23] A law *interferes* with judicial power where it permits courts to act, but greatly constrains the manner in which it can do so. The High Court considered a law that arguably usurped judicial power in *Polyukhovich*.[24] There, the Court held in obiter that a law that provided that a particular person was guilty of an offence would be offensive to the separation of powers principle and unconstitutional. It is appreciated that these statements apply to the criminal context. However, Deane J considered its application to the non-criminal context. He stated that a law directing a verdict for a plaintiff in a civil defamation case of $500,000 would be an example of a civil law that usurped judicial power.[25]

An example of a law interfering with judicial power is found in *Chu Kheng Lim v Minister for Immigration, Local Government and Ethnic Affairs*.[26] There a majority of the Court struck out a provision which had expressly prohibited a court from releasing a person in a particular category from detention. The Court determined this was an attempt to direct the courts as to the manner and outcome of the exercise of its powers, which was offensive to separation of powers principles.[27] The Court suggested parliament might be able to grant or withhold jurisdiction, as opposed to directing the manner and outcome of

---

22 Suri Ratnapala and Jonathan Crowe 'Broadening the Reach of Chapter III: The Institutional Integrity of State Courts and the Constitutional Limits of State Legislative Power' (2012) 36 *Melbourne University Law Review* 175, 176.
23 *Leeth v Commonwealth* (1992) 174 CLR 455, 469-470 (Mason CJ Dawson and McHugh JJ).
24 *Polyukhovich v Commonwealth* (1991) 172 CLR 501.
25 Ibid 608.
26 (1992) 176 CLR 1.
27 Ibid 36-37 (Brennan Deane and Dawson JJ), with whom Gaudron J agreed (53).

the exercise of a court's powers, though subsequent decisions may be at odds with this distinction.[28]

In the landmark *Kable v Director of Public Prosecutions (NSW)(Kable)*,[29] a majority of the High Court struck out as invalid a New South Wales statute that applied only to a named individual. The legislation permitted the Court to order Kable's further incarceration if satisfied, on the balance of probabilities, that he would re-offend if released. The Court side-stepped the *BLF* precedent discussed above, which had held there was no strict separation of powers within state constitutions. It did this by insisting that there was one integrated court structure in Australia, including state courts (at least, those exercising or capable of exercising federal jurisdiction). As part of that integrated structure, state courts were subject to the separation of powers principle, drawn down from the federal level, and inherent in the federal judicial structure of which they were a part. Members of the majority noted the highly anomalous nature of the legislation, expressly targeted at one individual,[30] involved arbitrary abrogation of rights,[31] and reflecting a legislative plan to imprison the accused. The Court was being asked to implement a legislative plan.[32] In doing so, the legislation fatally undermined the court's independence, and was unconstitutional.

Apart from *BLF*, some other cases have considered the validity of legislation affecting matters currently the subject of litigation. An early case rejected a constitutional challenge to Commonwealth legislation purporting to validate past action, in light of a High Court challenge to it. The Court found the validating legislation was itself valid. It is noteworthy that

---

28 *Plaintiff S157/2002 v Commonwealth* (2003) 211 CLR 476.
29 (1996) 189 CLR 51.
30 Ibid 108 (Gaudron J).
31 Ibid.
32 Ibid 124 (McHugh J) and 134 (Gummow J).

this decision was rendered prior to acceptance of separation of powers principles by the High Court in *Boilermakers'*, so should be treated with some caution.

More recently, the High Court considered the matter in *HA Bachrach Pty Ltd v Queensland*.[33] There a party to a decision which had dismissed a challenge to a town planning decision approving a shopping centre appealed it. While the appeal was pending, the Queensland Parliament passed legislation validating the proposed development. That legislation became the subject of constitutional challenge, which was unanimously dismissed.

The High Court noted that town planning decisions were not inherently judicial in nature, in contrast with decisions about criminal guilt, which were. It also distinguished town planning decisions from 'trial of actions for breach of contract and civil wrongs', which involved the 'inalienable exercise of judicial power'.[34] The Court noted here the legislation did not refer to the particular dispute. It did not name individuals or individual companies; thus, it was not ad hominem in nature. It did not merely purport to settle an existing dispute.[35]

The High Court has also considered cases involving a line between alteration of rules of evidence and interference with substantive rights. A good example of this is *Nicholas v The Queen*.[36] There legislation provided that the court should in some cases disregard the fact that law enforcement bodies acquired evidence unlawfully. A majority of the High Court validated the provision. Brennan CJ drew a contrast between laws merely prescribing rules of evidence and those where the legislature directed the judiciary as to the manner in which

---

33 (1998) 195 CLR 547.
34 Ibid 562 (Gleeson CJ Gaudron Gummow Kirby and Hayne JJ).
35 Ibid 564 (Gleeson CJ Gaudron Gummow Kirby and Hayne JJ).
36 (1998) 193 CLR 173.

judicial discretion should be exercised; the former would pose no constitutional difficulty, the latter might.[37]   Brennan CJ added as a reason for validity that the legislation was not targeted at an individual.[38] Toohey J agreed, adding it was not determinative as to whether a particular action would succeed or fail.[39]   Gaudron J agreed that it left ultimate issues for the court to determine,[40] as did Gummow J. Gummow J suggested that laws which deemed facts, upon which guilt or innocence directly turned, might offend constitutional requirements.[41] Hayne J similarly distinguished mere rules of evidence, and matters going to guilt or innocence (which may create separation of powers questions).[42]   Kirby J (dissenting) held that where parliament had prejudged an issue before a court, and required courts to act in accord with that pre-judgment, the law would be unconstitutional.[43] He expressly extended this to the civil context. He added that laws which nullified prior authoritative judicial activity might be invalid,[44] and laws which targeted named individuals would be highly problematic on separation of powers grounds.[45]

In *Duncan v Independent Commission Against Corruption*,[46] the Court rejected a challenge to legislation purporting to validate past executive action that had been declared illegal by the court in another case.   The High Court confirmed that parliament could validly alter substantive rights, though they were the subject of pending court proceedings. The Court noted that the challenged legislation did not withhold a court's jurisdiction or

---

37 Ibid 188.
38 Ibid 192.
39 Ibid 202.
40 Ibid 211.
41 Ibid 236.
42 Ibid 277-278.
43 Ibid 254-255.
44 Ibid 255-256.
45 Ibid 257.
46 (2015) 256 CLR 83.

otherwise dealt with the functions of a court. It did not refer expressly to any court proceeding, and did not direct the court as to particular relief to be granted or not granted.[47]

Summary of relevant principles prior to the *Palmer Case*

. Legislation that targets a named individual is vulnerable to challenge on the basis of separation of powers principles;

. Legislation that targets a particular dispute, as opposed to merely changing the law, is more likely to offend separation of powers principles;

. Legislation that focuses on the judicial process itself, rather than merely changing substantive rights, is more likely to offend separation of powers principles;

. There is an important distinction in this context between mere alterations of rules of evidence, and changes relating to substantive issues for judicial adjudication, the latter being more likely to offend separation of powers principles;

. where the law interferes with the manner of the exercise of judicial power, as opposed to withholding jurisdiction, it is more likely to offend separation of powers principles; and

. where the law causes courts to exercise power in a way that departs from traditional features of judicial process, it is more likely to offend separation of powers principles

I will now turn to apply these principles to the *Amendment Act*.

---

47 Ibid 99 (French CJ, Kiefel Bell and Keane JJ); Nettle and Gordon JJ agreed that the challenged amendment involved a substantive change to the law (102).

Argument that Amendment Act offends separation of powers principles

(a) Legislation targets a particular individual

As discussed above, in cases such as *Liyanage* and *Kable*, the Court noted the fact that legislation is targeted at a particular individual or small number of clearly identified individuals is suggestive of a breach of separation of powers principles. A similar view was taken by Kirby and Hayne JJ in *Nicholas*. This is the antithesis of typical legislation, which applies to a range of unknown individuals, and is of general application. In contrast, targeted legislation suggests the legislature has made a decision about a particular individual or individuals, and seeks to have its decision implemented by others. It is not conclusive, but a factor tending towards invalidity. The *Amendment Act* at issue here names Mr Palmer, and the only individual named is Mr Palmer. This suggests possible invalidity.

(b) Does the legislation target a particular dispute or does it merely change the law?

One of the main reasons that the legislation challenged in the *Bachrach* and *Duncan* cases, noted above, was held valid is that the court determined the legislation merely operated to change the law, and the law was of general application. This was a valid exercise of legislative power.

On the other hand, the Court has viewed more dimly legislation that targets a particular dispute, or at least it has indicated it would view such legislation more dimly. So in *Bachrach*, the joint reasons specifically noted that a trial of an action for breach of contract and/or a civil wrong is an 'inalienable exercise of judicial power'.[48] Surely, this dicta fits very closely the situation presently under consideration. Mr Palmer claimed that the Western Australian government had breached its contract with him, through delays in approvals, imposition of unreasonable conditions etc, contrary to the original agreement. Such claims may well also have a basis in negligence. The joint reasons in *Bachrach* stated very clearly that the resolution of such a dispute was an inalienable exercise of judicial power. However, the Western Australian government has boldly sought to alienate this power to itself, by deciding the controversy in its favour. The Western Australian government has not sought to generally amend the law relating to contract, tort or other legal remedy. It has not made a general change to the law. Rather, it has purported to resolve a dispute in which it is a party in its favour. According to the precise wording of five justices in *Bachrach*, such an attempt would (should) be unconstitutional.

(c) Does the law focus on the judicial process itself or does it simply alter substantive rights?

In some precedent cases where courts have validated amending laws that pertain to an ongoing dispute, one line of reasoning has been that the law simply alters substantive rights, which is constitutionally permissible, as opposed to focussing on the judicial process itself, which would be constitutionally impermissible. One example of this is the High Court's reasoning in *Duncan*, where the Court, in validating the law, stated that it

> [d]oes not operate as an impermissible direction to the judicature: it is not concerned with the functions or jurisdiction of courts; it does not refer to court proceedings either specifically or generally; and it

---

48 *H A Bachrach Pty Ltd v Queensland* (1998) 195 CLR 547, 562 (Gleeson CJ Gaudron Gummow Kirby and Hayne JJ).

does not direct the courts as to the giving of relief.[49]

The contrast with the *Amendment Act* in this case could not be stronger. The *Amendment Act* is very much concerned with the functions of courts – it directs a court that it effectively cannot review conduct of the Western Australian government in relation to disputed matter and protected matters. Such conduct cannot be 'appealed, reviewed, challenged, quashed or called into question'. Similarly, a court cannot find that the State has been engaged in a civil wrong, or be liable to a remedy, in relation to disputed and protected matters. In contrast to the legislation in *Duncan*, the *Amendment Act* is specific in relation to the parties to whom it relates. The *Amendment Act* does direct the courts as to the giving of relief – effectively directing it not to do so.

(d) **Does the law merely alter rules of evidence or does it relate to ultimate issues for judicial resolution?**

In *Nicholas v The Queen*,[50] the Court purported to distinguish between legislation which merely altered rules of evidence, which would not be objectionable, and laws which impacted the ultimate issues for judicial resolution. As it was, the legislation in that case was only held valid by five of seven justices. Of this majority, Toohey, Gaudron and Gummow JJ noted the challenged legislation was not determinative of the dispute between the parties. This was critical in their determination that the law there was valid. Though they dissented in the application of this sentiment on the facts, Hayne and Kirby JJ clearly agreed with the principle.

Of course, it is not known how these judges would decide a challenge to the *Amendment Act*. However, their reasoning in

---

49 *Duncan v Independent Commission Against Corruption* (2015) 256 CLR 83, 99 (French CJ Kiefel Bell and Keane JJ).
50 (1998) 193 CLR 173.

Nicholas suggests they would find it invalid. In contrast to the provision in *Nicholas*, the provisions in the *Amendment Act* are determinative in terms of the dispute between the parties – Mr Palmer is effectively declared to have no remedy against the Western Australian government in relation to the dispute, regardless of the actual merits of any claim. According to the High Court judgment in *Nicholas*, it is submitted that the law would be invalid.

(e) Does the law withhold jurisdiction or interfere with the manner of its exercise?

The joint reasons of Brennan, Deane and Dawson JJ in *Chu Kheng Lim* drew a distinction between, on the one hand, laws which grant or withhold jurisdiction and, on the other hand, laws which purport to direct courts as to the manner and outcome of the exercise of their jurisdiction. Laws of the former category did not raise constitutional objection; laws of the latter category would. It will be recalled that, in *Chu Kheng Lim*, a majority of the High Court struck out as constitutionally invalid a legislative provision which sought to preclude a court from ordering a particular category of person to be released from detention. The Court found this to be an impermissible intrusion into the exercise of a court's discretion.

It is submitted that the *Amendment Act* contains a similarly egregious intrusion into the exercise of a court's discretion. It directs a court not to provide Mr Palmer with a remedy in relation to a particular dispute, no matter what its view might be as to the legality of the state's actions. This is considered to be a serious interference in the exercise of a court's discretion, which offends the separation of powers principle enshrined in the *Australian Constitution*, and applicable to Western Australian courts through the *Kable* reasoning discussed above.

(f) Does the law interfere with traditional characteristics of judicial process?

As explained above, the High Court has discerned numerous characteristics of judicial process. A law that causes a court to depart from these characteristics is vulnerable to constitutional challenge on the basis of a breach of separation of powers principles. Three examples here are legislation which effectively removed a court's discretion, making it a mere vessel in the implementation of a legislative judgment,[51] legislation which prevented a court from giving reasons for its decisions,[52] and legislation which required a court to proceed to make final determinations on an ex parte basis.[53] In each case, the High Court found the legislative mandate caused a court to depart so substantially from what traditionally characterised judicial process as to be constitutionally invalid. While at one time the High Court stated the principle uniting these cases was legislation that undermined public confidence in the independence of the judiciary,[54] it has become more common to refer to legislation as impairing the institutional integrity of the court. The fact that public confidence in the judiciary has been undermined is an indicia, but not the touchstone, of invalidity.[55] The principle was succinctly stated in *Forge v Australian Securities and Investment Commission*:

> The relevant principle is one which impinges upon maintenance of the defining characteristics of a court ... it is to these characteristics that the reference to institutional integrity alludes. That is, if the institutional integrity of a court is distorted, it is because the body no longer exhibits in some relevant

---

51 *South Australia v Totani* (2010) 242 CLR 1.

52 *Wainohu v New South Wales* (2011) 243 CLR 181.

53 *International Finance Trust Co Ltd v New South Wales Crime Commission* (2009) 240 CLR 319.

54 *Grollo v Palmer* (1995) 184 CLR 348, 365 (Brennan CJ Deane Dawson and Toohey JJ).

55 *Fardon v Attorney-General (Qld)*(2004) 223 CLR 575, 618 (Gummow J); *Northern Australia Aboriginal Justice Agency v Northern Territory* (2015) 256 CLR 569, 595 (French CJ Kiefel and Bell JJ).

> aspect those defining characteristics which make a
> court apart from other decision making bodies.[56]

I will now consider the extent to which the *Amendment Act* undermines fundamental characteristics of a court.

One relevant characteristic is *decisional independence* – It is axiomatic that a key characteristic of a judicial process is that there is decisional independence from other arms of government. As five members of the High Court noted:

> A legislature which imposes a judicial function or an adjudicative process on a court, whereby it is essentially directed or required to implement a political decision or a government policy without following ordinary judicial processes, deprives that court of its defining independence and institutional impartiality.[57]

With respect, one would have thought that the *Amendment Act* seriously undermined a court's decisional independence. It mandated that no remedy should be granted to a claimant. It mandated that a court not hear a matter. If the High Court found that a court had been denuded of decisional independence in *International Finance Trust* because it was directed to hear a matter ex parte, it is hard to see how a court directed not to hear a matter at all, and not to grant a party any remedy, retains any decisional independence.

Another way in which courts have described decisional independence is by insisting that courts not be conscripted into the execution of a plan by other arms of government. In so doing, the High Court drew from the statement of principle of the United States Supreme Court decision in *Mistretta v United States* that the court must not be borrowed by other arms of

---

56 (2000) 228 CLR 45, 76.
57 *Attorney-General (NT) v Emmerson* (2014) 253 CLR 393, 426 (French CJ Hayne Crennan Kiefel Bell and Keane JJ).

government to 'cloak their work in the neutral colors of judicial action'.[58]   When this principle has been applied, the courts have been drawn into a plan to do something – in *Kable*, the plan was clearly to keep Mr Kable locked up, and the court was asked to make the order; in *Totani*, the plan was to effectively prevent meetings of members of motorcycle clubs that the government had determined to have criminal purposes, and the court was asked to make a control order to carry this into effect. In both cases, the court's decisional independence was fatally undermined. It was effectively a puppet in the implementation of a government plan.

It is respectfully submitted that a similar theme is evident in the *Amendment Act*. However, this time the court's role in the 'plan' is not active – it is passive. It is ordered not to do something it otherwise would (or might) have done. It is not to hear a matter. It is not to order a remedy. The nature of the court's role is different but the underlying problem is the same – the court is effectively being ordered how to deal with a particular dispute. Respectfully, I would have thought this fatally undermined the independence of the Western Australian court.

Another relevant characteristic of a judicial process is that it involves the *quelling of a dispute*. In *R v Trade Practices Tribunal; Ex parte Tasmanian Breweries Ltd*,[59] Kitto J stated that judicial power involved 'a decision settling for the future as between defined persons or classes of persons a question as to the existence of a right or obligation'.[60] Menzies J took a similar position, defining judicial power as involving 'the determination and enforcement of existing rights or liabilities of parties'.[61] Windeyer J stated judicial power involved application of existing legal principles 'in the application of disputes

---

58 488 US 361, 407 (1989), quoted in *South Australia v Totani* (2010) 242 CLR 1, 172 (Kiefel J).
59 (1970) 123 CLR 361.
60 Ibid 374.
61 Ibid 387.

between particular parties'.[62] Kiefel J in *Totani* reflected on judicial power in terms of 'quelling ... controversies and ... ascertainment and determination of rights and liabilities'.[63]

The result of the *Amendment Act* is that the court's role in quelling a dispute has been removed. It does not quell the dispute. The legislature has effectively quelled the dispute. It is hard to see how this is not an attempted arrogation by the legislature of the exercise of judicial power. It should not be countenanced, if the separation of powers principle is to have any substance.

Other scholars have created models to determine whether or not legislation infringes separation of powers principles. Professor Gerangelos suggested three major indicia and two minor indicia of invalidity.[64] The major indicia were (a) legislation relates to a particular individual; (b) legislation is specific to a particular dispute; and (c) the government is a party to the proceedings. In relation to these three indicia of invalidity, the Amendment Act clearly meets each one. It refers to Mr Palmer, refers to a particular dispute, and the Western Australian government is a party to the proceedings.

Sir Anthony Mason expressed similar sentiments:

> *Liyanage* seems to have been consigned to perennial distinction. That is because it was an extreme case. But ... cases not as extreme as *Liyanage* will involve unconstitutional interference with judicial process. They would generally involve retrospective legislation, affecting pending litigation which targets individuals, departs in some significant respect or respects from normal processes and amounts to a direction on a crucial issue in the case, the direction being confined to the litigation which is the target of

---

62 Ibid 396.
63 (2010) 242 CLR 1, 162.
64 'The Separation of Powers and Legislative Interference in Pending Cases' (2008) 30 *Sydney Law Review* 61, 92-93; *The Separation of Powers and Legislative Interference in Judicial Process* (Hart Publishing, 2009) 177-180.

the legislation.[65]

Sir Anthony's comments are particularly apt to the *Amendment Act*. It is retrospective in nature, applying to a dispute which arose several years prior to its passage, affects pending litigation, targets an individual, and is highly irregular, effectively precluding a court from hearing a matter, and granting a remedy. The provisions apply only to a particular dispute.

Neither Professor Gerangelos' nor Sir Anthony Mason's learned comments were referred to in the High Court decision on the legislation, to which I now turn. There were in fact two decisions, *Mineralogy Pty Ltd v Western Australia*[66] and *Palmer v Western Australia*,[67] but almost all of the material relevant for this article is in the former decision. I will focus most discussion on the separation of powers questions, though other constitutional issues were briefly discussed.[68]

Mineralogy Pty Ltd v Western Australia

It is imperative in understanding the High Court's decision in this litigation to understand its extremely narrow ambit. The High Court was clearly not satisfied with the way in which the case was presented to the Court. It expressed dissatisfaction with the special case presented by the parties. In expressing its dissatisfaction, it emphasised the need to provide a statement of

---

65 Sir Anthony Mason 'Comment' (2008) 30 *Sydney Law Review* 95, 99.
66 [2021] HCA 30.
67 [2021] HCA 31.
68 Once again, appeals to the High Court concerning the 'rule of law' were unavailing. Readers may be aware that, 70 years ago, Sir Owen Dixon referred to the rule of law as an 'assumption' underlying the *Constitution: Australian Communist Party v Commonwealth* (1951) 83 CLR 1, 193. In *Kartinyeri v Commonwealth* (1998) 195 CLR 337, 381 Gummow and Hayne JJ observed the occasion was 'yet to arise' for full consideration of the possible consequences of such an assumption. The current High Court is apparently not enthusiastic to provide this full consideration. All members of the Court in the companion case *Palmer v Western Australia* [2021] HCA 31, [8] flatly denied that the rule of law could be utilised as a basis for constitutionally invalidating a law (Kiefel CJ Gageler Keane Gordon Steward and Gleeson JJ).

facts which makes it necessary to answer the questions raised by the parties, that the High Court does not deal in hypotheticals or render advisory opinions.[69] It is evident that the High Court did not believe that a sufficient statement of facts had been made, with respect to most of the claims of invalidity. As a result, the High Court only considered separation of powers issues in respect of ss 9 and 10 of the Act. This is most unfortunate, since most of the real objections to the legislation arise from later sections, as explained above. Section 9 states that neither of the proposals submitted by Mr Palmer are deemed to have contractual effect, and s 10 states that relevant arbitrations currently on foot are terminated, and an arbitral award already made and the arbitral agreement to which it relates, are nullities.

Joint Reasons

The joint reasons noted that the plaintiffs had commenced a proceeding seeking damages for breach of contract and other remedies in the Federal Court against the Western Australian government on 12 August 2020.[70] A day earlier than this, the Western Australian Parliament had first considered the Amendment Act, and a day after it, the legislation passed the upper house and received royal assent. The joint reasons stated it was not known whether the Western Australian government would rely on the Amendment Act in defending the proceedings commenced on 12 August. The proceeding had been adjourned, pending resolution of the High Court decision on validity. This led the joint reasons to fundamentally narrow consideration of the *Amendment* Act to only ss 9 and 10. This is a great pity, with respect. Large constitutional issues were in play. Respectfully, it seems extremely likely the Western Australian government

---

69 *Mineralogy Pty Ltd v Western Australia* [2021] HCA 30, [61].
70 Ibid [65](Kiefel CJ Gageler Keane Gordon Steward and Gleeson JJ).

was going to rely on the *Amendment Act* to defend itself from the action commenced on 12 August. Otherwise, with respect, there would have been no point in passing it. The Western Australian government was very clear in media reports that this was the intent. See for example, the Western Australian Attorney-General John Quigley, in an article in *The Australian Financial Review* on 20 August 2020 entitled 'The Law Stacks Up Against Palmer'. Respectfully, the High Court might have taken judicial notice of this. In the alternative, it might have adjourned the matter until the Western Australian government filed its defence in the Federal Court. If it had done so, it is very likely that any arguments about 'advisory opinions' and 'insufficient detail' would evaporate.

Having constrained the matters to be determined within extremely narrow limits, the joint reasons then determined that ss 9 and 10 amounted merely to an alteration of substantive legal rights, and did not involve an exercise of judicial power.[71] Respectfully, the reasoning was extremely brief, largely avoiding engagement in the material discussed above. The joint reasons cited a large paragraph from the *Bachrach* decision in reaching this conclusion, and justifying the distinction between a (constitutionally valid) mere alteration of substantive rights, and an unacceptable infringement of judicial power. The joint reasons did not cite that part of the joint reasons in *Bachrach* which stated that 'the trial of actions for breach of contract and for civil wrongs are inalienable exercises of judicial power'.[72] Respectfully, this was relevant to the *Mineralogy* dispute.

As indicated, the joint reasons relied on *Bachrach* to support its

---

71 Ibid [84]. Of course, it is not known whether, if the previous decisions had been judicial in nature rather than arbitration decisions, the outcome would have been different. For differences between judicial and arbitral determinations, see *R v Kirby; Ex parte Boilermakers' Society of Australia* (1956) 94 CLR 254, 281-282 (Dixon CJ McTiernan Fullagar and Kitto JJ).

72 *Bachrach Pty Ltd v Queensland* (1998) 195 CLR 547, 562 (Gleeson CJ Gaudron Gummow Kirby and Hayne JJ).

position. However, it should be noted that part of the reasoning in favour of validity in *Bachrach* was that the legislation was general in nature; it did not refer or relate to a particular individual, company or dispute. Of course, this is in sharp contrast with the factual scenario in *Mineralogy*, a distinction to which the joint reasons in *Mineralogy* did not allude when those reasons cited and purported to apply principles from *Bachrach*.

The joint reasons stated there was no occasion to determine the 'large question' of whether Chapter III of the *Constitution*, and the separation of powers which it represents, precluded the exercise of judicial power by a state parliament.[73]

This raises an interesting question. As the separation of powers principle has been expounded in recent years, the focus has been on the role of courts, and whether courts are being asked to exercise powers that are non-judicial in nature, or whether their institutional integrity is being impaired. The type of legislation typically being challenged is legislation which alters the way in which courts traditionally go about resolving matters. While the focus has been on this pattern of legislation, other issues have remained unresolved. The High Court expressed the 'large question' whether state parliaments could exercise judicial power. This is not within the pattern of cases such as *Kable*, *Totani*, *Wainohu* or *International Finance Trust*.

It is beyond the scope of this chapter to comprehensively answer the question raised by the joint reasons. It should be acknowledged in this discussion that the High Court has sometimes utilised the 'chameleon doctrine' in this context, pursuant to which a power can take its nature from the body in which it is reposed.[74] It can only be hoped that this doctrine is not expanded, with respect, given its potential to undermine a

---

73 *Mineralogy Pty Ltd v Western Australia* [2021] HCA 30, [87].
74 *Thomas v Mowbray* (2007) 233 CLR 307, 326-327 (Gleeson CJ) and 425-428 (Kirby J).

principled separation of powers position.

That having been said, it is submitted that it would be an egregious breach of separation of powers principles for a legislature to exercise judicial power. It would undermine and betray the separation of powers doctrine espoused by a majority of the High Court in *Boilermakers*. As four judges concluded in that case:

> Chapter III (of the Australian *Constitution*) does not allow the exercise of a jurisdiction which of its very nature belongs to the judicial power of the Commonwealth by a body established for purposes foreign to the judicial power.[75]

References to the 'judicial power of the Commonwealth' are now understood to refer to state courts, as discussed above. We have an integrated court hierarchy in Australia.[76] A state legislature is an example of a body 'established for purposes foreign to the judicial power'. As such, simply it must not exercise judicial power. Consider the consequences if the High Court now were to permit state parliaments to exercise judicial power. The 'exclusively' judicial function of determining and punishing criminal guilt[77] would suddenly be in play. If this were allowed, the spectre of state parliaments determining the guilt or innocence of individuals, and ordering their incarceration, would become real. It is difficult to think of an action that would more seriously betray the separation of powers principles upon which our constitutional system fundamentally resides. Frankly, it must never be permitted.

---

75 (1956) 94 CLR 254, 296 (Dixon CJ McTiernan Fullagar and Kitto JJ).
76 *Kable v Director of Public Prosecutions* (NSW)(1997) 189 CLR 51.
77 *Chu Kheng Lim v Minister for Immigration* (1992) 176 CLR 1, 27 (Brennan Deane and Dawson JJ).

Edelman J

In a separate judgment, Edelman J agreed with the narrow confining of the case in the joint reasons. That said, he indicated some more sympathy with Mr Palmer's arguments:

> There are features of the (*Amendment Act*) that, in combination, provide significant support for the plaintiffs' submissions that those provisions amount to a direction to the courts or an exercise of judicial power. First, there is the ad hominem nature of the provisions. Secondly, and in circumstances where "trials or actions for breach of contract are inalienable exercises of judicial power" (citing *Bachrach*) the provisions are expressed as declarations of law about the effect or application of contractual provisions … if the (*Amendment Act*) had been enacted whilst litigation was pending in the courts concerning the same parties and the same subject matter then there may have been forced, even at the level of state courts, in the plaintiff's submission to the effect that the legislation would have undermined the assignment of judicial power to judges … but the effect of (a) the absence of any extant legal proceedings to which the *Amending Act* was directed at resolving and (c) the purpose of the *Amending Act* being to provide cascading layers of protection for the financial position of the State of Western Australia rather than to resolve a judicial dispute, is that the (*Amendment Act*) bear(s) the character of provisions which extinguish rights of the plaintiffs.[78]

Some comments are appropriate by way of respectful response. At least, it may be said that Edelman J was more sensitive to the potential separation of powers issues raised by the legislation.

That acknowledged, I respectfully disagree with some of the sentiments expressed in this passage. Firstly, there were in fact proceedings on foot – Mr Palmer had commenced a

---

78 [157]-[159].

proceeding in the Federal Court. The timing of the Western Australian *Amendment Act*, in the same few days, was clearly no coincidence. The Western Australian Attorney-General himself made the connection known between the legislation and the impending court case in a newspaper article. Logically, of course the Western Australian government was going to rely on the defences in the *Amendment Act*. Otherwise, there would have been no need to pass it. It was passed extremely quickly. If it were the case that the *Amendment Act* had not (yet) been raised in documentation relating to the Federal Court proceeding, in particular the state's defence to the action, the High Court could have adjourned this matter until that documentation had been filed. Respectfully, it seems too convenient for members of the High Court to rely on this technicality. Fundamentally important issues were engaged in the litigation. Respectfully, they required adjudication and resolution from an authoritative body, not left to wait another day.

Secondly, of course legislation can have more than one purpose. It need not be an either/or proposition. Clearly, the *Amendment Act* did have the purpose of defending the state's financial position. However, it was sought to achieve this by resolving a judicial dispute. Respectfully, it is considered highly artificial to separate them and treat them as distinct purposes, asserting that one, but not the other, was engaged. The Western Australian government sought to achieve one purpose (extinguishment of a dispute), which would lead to achievement of the other purpose (preserving its financial position). Of course, all would agree that it would be unacceptable judicial reasoning to assert that because the enacting legislature had the honourable motivation of preserving the state's financial position, this rendered what would otherwise be unconstitutional in fact constitutional.

Conclusion

The outcome of the Mineralogy/Palmer challenge to the Western Australian *Amendment Act* was, in my respectful view, very disappointing. My reading of the precedents suggested strong arguments as to the invalidity of legislation clearly targeted at 'resolving' a particular dispute without it going to court, effectively preventing a court from giving a remedy to a party, if it found that a cause of action existed. The judiciary's role should be as the third arm of government, independently exercising judicial power, and acting as a check and balance on the other two arms of government. This was supposedly enshrined and protected by the separation of powers principle for which Sir Owen Dixon fought to obtain constitutional recognition. It is in peril when parliaments can effectively 'resolve' civil disputes that are before the courts and arbitrarily deprive citizens of rights and remedies.

Members of the High Court largely did not engage in discussion of the fundamentally important constitutional issues in play. The judges relied on a technical ground, that in their view the special case was not formed sufficiently in order for most of the claims to be ventilated, and the Western Australian government had not (at the time of challenge) relied on most of the *Amendment Act* which Mr Palmer sought to challenge. However, the conclusion is surely irresistible that the Western Australian government would rely on the *Amendment Act*. It was passed by one House of Parliament the day before, and the other House of Parliament the day after, Mr Palmer launched his challenge. The Western Australian Attorney-General was on the record claiming his government's legislation had dealt with the Palmer issue. Respectfully, another way of dealing with this issue, if the High Court were minded to deal with the fundamentally important constitutional issues at stake, would have been to adjourn the High Court challenge until, at least, the Western Australian government had filed its defence to Mr Palmer's challenge, which almost certainly would have relied on the Act. This would then have permitted the High Court to fully consider the fundamentally important constitutional questions involved in many sections of the Act, not limiting the case to a couple of the more minor provisions.

The determination of the joint reasons, with which Edelman J agreed, that what was involved was a mere alteration of substantive legal rights is also open to question. The joint reasons clearly relied on the *Bachrach* precedent to support this view, citing a large paragraph from it before reaching this conclusion. The joint reasons omitted to include reference to the statement of five justices in *Bachrach* that the trial of actions for breach of contract and civil wrongs was an 'inalienable' exercise of judicial power. This was surely relevant. And it similarly failed to mention that *Bachrach* involved legislation that was general in nature, not focused on a particular individual, organisation and dispute, as was the legislation at issue in *Mineralogy*. That these important distinctions were ignored is, in my respectful view, troubling.

More concerning is the message that the outcome of this case sends to parliaments, perhaps emboldening them to attempt ever greater incursions on what was traditionally judicial power, and relying on technicalities to see off any challenge based on substance. Further, I respectfully disagree with the assertion that the purpose of the *Amendment Act* was not to resolve a judicial dispute. Mr Palmer had commenced legal action against the Western Australian government. The effect of the *Amendment Act* was to prevent the court from hearing his claims, and from awarding him a remedy if they believed, based on legal principles, he was entitled to one. A dangerous precedent has been set. The settled legal principle reflected in the *Boilermakers'* decision no longer seems so secure.

3

National Emergency Powers in Australia – the current constitutional limits.

Mrs Lorraine Finlay

Abstract

Recent emergencies in Australia – most notably the COVID-19 pandemic and the 2019-20 Black Summer bushfires – have focused attention on the question of Australia's emergency management framework and, in particular, the powers of the Commonwealth government in emergency situations. The introduction of the *National Emergency Declaration Act 2020* (Cth) was designed to establish a national legislative framework for declaring national emergencies, and to strengthen the role of the Commonwealth Government in dealing with a national emergency. This paper considers the question of national emergency powers from the perspective of Australia's constitutional framework, and in light of recent emergency situations. Despite the introduction of the *National Emergency Declaration Act 2020* (Cth), it concludes that there remains a gap in Australia's emergency management framework. A substantive national emergency law would be desirable both to ensure a single, coordinating emergency response authority mandated under law at the national level and clearer lines of responsibility between the different levels of government.

Keywords

National emergency powers, *Constitution*, nationhood power, external affairs power, defence power, referral of state powers, constitutional amendment

Introduction

In recent years Australia has faced a series of significant national emergencies, most notably the COVID-19 pandemic and the 2019-20 Black Summer bushfire season. These emergencies have focused attention on the question of Australia's emergency management framework and, in particular, the powers of the Commonwealth government in emergency situations. This question is particularly critical in a federal system (such as Australia) where the absence of clear lines of responsibility between various levels of government can potentially have serious consequences in an emergency.

These issues were highlighted by the then Prime Minister in his address to the National Press Club on 29 January 2020 when he reflected on the Black Summer bushfires. Prime Minister Morrison observed that there was now 'a clear community expectation that the Commonwealth should have the ability to respond in times of national emergency and disasters'[1] and that he had 'been very conscious of testing the limits of constitutionally defined roles and responsibilities during this bushfire season'.[2] When subsequently announcing the establishment of the Royal Commission into National Natural Disaster Arrangements

---

1 Prime Minister of Australia, 'Address, National Press Club' (Speech, National Press Club, ACT, 29 January 2020).
2 Ibid.

('Royal Commission') the Prime Minister observed:[3]

> During the Black Summer bushfires, we entered a
> constitutional grey zone by directly initiating defence
> force deployments, utilising the first ever compulsory
> call out of Reservists, with over 6,500 ADF personnel
> serving in support of state and territory response
> efforts. But we did that without clear rules.

The subsequent Royal Commission recognised the importance
of clear rules when it comes to emergency management. The
final Report made eighty recommendations in total, including a
series of recommendations designed to improve both the national
emergency response capability and national coordination
arrangements. These included a specific recommendation that
national legislation should be introduced to allow the Australian
government to declare a state of national emergency.[4]

This was followed by the introduction of the *National
Emergency Declaration Act 2020* ('NED Act'), which was
passed by the Australian Parliament in December 2020. The
NED Act is designed 'to recognise and enhance the role of the
Commonwealth in preparing for, responding to, and recovering
from emergencies that cause, or are likely to cause, nationally
significant harm'.[5] To this end, the NED Act establishes
a national legislative framework for declaring national
emergencies, which then trigger the potential exercise of various
powers and functions at the national level. The NED Act was
introduced in response to Recommendation 5.1 of the Royal

---

3 Prime Minister of Australia, *National Royal Commission into Black Summer bushfires established*
(Media Release, 20 February 2020) <National Royal Commission into Black Summer
bushfires established | Prime Minister of Australia (pm.gov.au)>.
4 Royal Commission into National Natural Disaster Arrangements, *Report*, 28 October
2020, Recommendation 5.1 <Royal Commission into National Natural Disaster Arrangements Report>.
5 *National Emergency Declaration Act 2020* (Cth), s. 3(1).

Commission Report[6] and was designed to strengthen the role of the Commonwealth government in dealing with a national emergency.

The introduction of the NED Act took place against the background of the COVID-19 pandemic, which has again highlighted the importance of effective emergency management frameworks and the challenges of coordinating emergency responses amongst various levels of government in a federal system. Two key features of Australia's pandemic response are particularly relevant when considering the overall effectiveness of Australia's emergency management framework. The first is the (sometimes vastly) different policies adopted by various national, state and territory governments with respect to key issues such as border closures, quarantine arrangements, lockdown restrictions and vaccination mandates. The second is the lack of clear lines of responsibility in terms of which level of government is ultimately accountable for making key decisions, and implementing and funding particular aspects of the pandemic response. The National Cabinet represents one attempt to address this, being designed as a forum intended to facilitate collaboration between the Prime Minister and State and Territory Premiers and Chief Ministers. However, as an intergovernmental forum with no constitutional or legal powers of its own, its utility is entirely dependent on the goodwill and cooperation of its participants.

This paper will consider the question of national emergency

---

6 Recommendation 5.1 was entitled 'Make provision for a declaration of a state of emergency', and provided:The Australian Government should make provision, in legislation, for a declaration of a state of national emergency. The declaration should include the following components: the ability for the Australian Government to make a public declaration to communicate the seriousness of a natural disaster processes to mobilise and activate Australian Government agencies quickly to support states and territories to respond to and recover from a natural disaster, and the power to take action without a state or territory request for assistance in clearly defined and limited circumstances.

powers from the perspective of Australia's constitutional framework, and in light of both recent emergency situations and the introduction of the *NED Act*. That is, what powers does the Commonwealth government actually have in an emergency situation, what are the current constitutional limits, and is there a need for legal or constitutional reform in this area. The conclusion that is ultimately reached is that a substantive national emergency law (that goes beyond the declaration mechanism provided for in the *NED Act*) would address an existing gap in Australia's emergency management framework and would allow for the clearer delineation of responsibilities between the national and state levels of government. The most constitutionally secure way of achieving this would be through either a referral of state powers using s. 51(xxxvii) of the *Constitution* or constitutional amendment under s 128, although there are significant practical and political challenges attaching to both of these options.

The existing emergency management framework

The primary responsibility for emergency management in Australia currently lies with the state and territory governments.[7] Each state and territory jurisdiction has implemented overarching emergency management legislation,[8] has designated a relevant

---

7 Royal Commission into National Natural Disaster Arrangements, *Report,* 28 October 2020, [11] – [15]. See also *Australian* Institute for Disaster Resilience, 'Australian Emergency Management Arrangements' (Department of Home Affairs, 2019), 4; Michael Eburn, 'Coordination of federal, state and local disaster management arrangements in Australia: Lessons from the UK and the US' (Strategic Insights, Australian Strategic Policy Institute, 2017), 4; Michael Eburn, 'Legal preparedness for international disaster response in Australia: Laws, Policies, Planning and Practices' (Strategy 2020, International Federation of Red Cross and Red Crescent Societies, 2010), 13; Michael Eburn, 'Managing 'civil contingencies' in Australia' (2014) 18(2) *International Journal of Human Rights* 143, 146; Anthony Bergin, 'Nothing federal about disasters', *The Australian,* 7 February 2020.
8 See *Emergencies Act 2004* (ACT); *State Emergency and Rescue Management Act 1989* (NSW); *Emergency Management Act 2013* (NT); *Disaster Management Act 2003* (Qld); *Emergency Management Act 2004* (SA); *Emergency Management Act 2006* (Tas); *Emergency Management Act 1986* (Vic); *Emergency Management Act 2013* (Vic); *Emergency Management Act 2005* (WA).

Minister with portfolio responsibilities for emergency responses and management,[9] and has established emergency response agencies. As the International Federation of Red Cross and Red Crescent Societies has observed:[10]

> The arrangements for disaster response are relatively similar across the Australian jurisdictions. Each State and Territory has detailed disaster management legislation that provides for disaster planning at State, regional and local levels. When events require a coordinated and ongoing response, there is provision for a declaration of a State of Alert, Emergency or Disaster (the terms vary across jurisdictions). Once a formal declaration has been made, the functions and powers to be exercised by the emergency controllers charged with the responsibility of managing the response to a disaster are set out.

Indeed, the Royal Commission observed that there were 'compelling reasons for state and territory governments to continue to be responsible for disaster management',[11] and further noted that while there was constitutional scope for the Commonwealth Government to play a complementary or supporting role, 'disaster management is not a matter expressly assigned to the Commonwealth in the Australian Constitution'.[12] The *Australian Constitution* does not include emergency powers within the list of enumerated legislative powers granted to the Commonwealth under s 51 and, until the passage of the *NED Act* in December 2020, the Commonwealth government did not have the power to declare a national emergency.

---

9 Minister for Police and Emergency Services (ACT); Minister for Police and Emergency Services (NSW); Minister for Police, Fire and Emergency Services (NT); Minister for Police, Emergency Services and Correctional Services (SA); Minister for Police, Fire and Emergency Management (Tas); Minister for Police and Emergency Services (Vic); Minister for Fire and Emergency Services (Qld); Minister for Emergency Services (Western Australia).
10 Michael Eburn, 'Legal preparedness for international disaster response in Australia: Laws, Policies, Planning and Practices' (n 8), 2-3.
11 Royal Commission into National Natural Disaster Arrangements (n 5), [14].
12 Ibid [15].

Traditionally, 'the role of the Commonwealth has been limited in responding to natural disasters ... to responding to requests for assistance from state governments'.[13] For example, Michael Eburn observed in response to demands that the Prime Minister declare a national emergency over the 2019-20 Black Summer bushfires (which occurred prior to the passage of the *NED Act*):[14]

> The answer is that the Commonwealth has no overarching emergency management legislation. There is no power to declare a 'national emergency' and the declaration, if made, would have no legal effect or impact. Unlike a declaration at state level it would not trigger any extraordinary powers or authority or release any emergency funds. The declaration, if made, would at best be symbolic.

That is not to say that the Commonwealth government did not, and does not continue to, have specific powers under specific laws that may be invoked in response to emergency situations (over and above the new powers under the *NED Act*). For example, while disasters or emergencies aren't included in the list of legislative powers of the Parliament outlined in s 51 of the *Constitution*, this does not mean that the Parliament was entirely unable to respond to disasters prior to the passage of the *NED Act*. A number of the enumerated powers listed under s 51 concern topics that are undoubtedly important in emergency management, including the power to make laws with respect to (for example) 'postal, telegraphic, telephonic, and other like services'[15], insurance,[16] and various forms of social security benefits,[17] and other constitutional powers such as the grants

---

13 Prime Minister Scott Morrison (n 2).
14 Michael Eburn, 'What is a "national emergency"?', *Australian Emergency Law* <https://emergencylaw.wordpress.com/2019/12/25/what-is-a-national-emergency/>.
15 *Australian Constitution*, s 51(v).
16 *Australian Constitution*, s 51(xiv).
17 *Australian Constitution*, ss 51(xxiii) and (xxiiiA).

power.[18] Further, as Michael Eburn has observed:[19]

> The Commonwealth Parliament has the power to
> make laws with respect to how Commonwealth
> agencies will behave, and Commonwealth services
> will be provided and maintained during a disaster.
> The parliament could provide that the Minister
> for Immigration may waive visa requirements
> in an emergency as an exercise of the legislative
> power with respect to aliens and immigration; the
> Commonwealth has the power to make laws with
> respect to various social security benefits so the
> Commonwealth can, and does, make laws with
> respect to how those benefits will be delivered
> during an emergency. Commonwealth agencies
> have offices and staff and provide services around
> the nation. Commonwealth staff and buildings will
> be affected by catastrophic events and the agencies
> need to plan how they will deal with the disruption
> and damage caused by a natural hazard. They will
> need to respond to the disaster to ensure that federal
> services are maintained and people who need and are
> eligible for Commonwealth assistance can receive it.
> It follows that the Commonwealth has constitutional
> authority to legislate for the emergency response by
> Commonwealth agencies and to legislate how the
> Commonwealth will respond to disasters.

Eburn goes on to note that this has been done to some extent, with various laws including provisions that allow ministers in specific areas to make emergency declarations and take particular actions once an emergency has been declared. However, he goes on to note that '[w]ithout a single, coordinating authority, each minister must make their declaration rather than a single declaration of a national emergency being sufficient to activate all the emergency provisions'.[20]

---

18 *Australian Constitution*, s 96.

19 Michael Eburn, 'Natural Disasters and the Need for Commonwealth Legislation' (2011) 10(3) *Canberra Law Review* 81, 85.

20 Ibid 86.

This is something that the Commonwealth government has sought to address through both the *NED Act,* and other responses to the Royal Commission recommendations. The *NED Act* now allows for a single declaration of a national emergency, which has the effect of activating specified powers or functions, waiving red tape requirements, and compelling Commonwealth entities to report on information relevant to the emergency. The establishment of the National Recovery and Resilience Agency is a further example of attempts to strengthen emergency coordination at the national level.

It is also important to note that – even prior to the passage of the *NED Act* – the Commonwealth government had an emergency management framework in place.[21] The Department of Home Affairs has primary responsibility for emergency management at the national level, and this is coordinated through a group within the Department, known as Emergency Management Australia ('EMA').[22] The Department's own website acknowledges that '[i]n Australia, state and territory governments have primary responsibility for protecting life, property and environment within their borders'[23] but states that the role of EMA is to 'lead the Australian Government disaster and emergency management response'.[24]

This is done pursuant to the Australian Government Crisis Management Framework ('AGCMF') which underpins a range of other crisis plans that explain how the Australian government

---

21 Note that this paper reflects the emergency management framework in place at the time of writing, namely prior to the federal election held in May 2022
22 *Administrative Arrangements Order* (Cth) (18 March 2021) <Administrative Arrangements Order made on 18 March 2021 with effect from18 March 2021 (pmc.gov.au)>.
23 'Emergency response plans', *Department of Home Affairs* <Emergency response plans (homeaffairs.gov.au)>.
24 'Emergency Management', *Department of Home Affairs* <Emergency management (homeaffairs.gov.au)>

will coordinate responses in various emergency situations.[25] These include the Australian Government Disaster Response Plan 2020 (COMDISPLAN) and the Australian Government Overseas Disaster Assistance Plan 2018 (AUSASSISTPLAN). The Minister with portfolio responsibility in this area immediately prior to the 2022 federal election was the Minister for Emergency Management and National Recovery and Resilience.[26]

There is also an agreed framework modelling coordination between national and state governments in emergency situations. Until recently this consisted of the National Strategy for Disaster Resilience and the National Disaster Risk Reduction Framework, which were developed through the Council of Australian Governments. The COVID-19 pandemic has driven significant changes in this area, primarily seen in the implementation of the National Coordination Mechanism ('NCM'). The NCM is now embedded within the AGCMF and 'brings together relevant Australian Government, state and territory government and private sector representation for coordination, communication and collaboration during response and recovery to domestic crises'.[27] The mechanism is designed to facilitate cooperation, but it is expressly noted on the Department of Home Affairs website that it 'is not a mechanism for command and control'.[28]

The key point to note, however, is that while there is an emergency management framework in place, it is a framework that – even following the passage of the *NED Act* – relies to a significant

---

25 Department of Prime Minister and Cabinet, *Australian Government Crisis Management Framework* (Version 3.1), December 2021 <Australian Government Crisis Management Framework (pmc.gov.au)>.

26 'Second Morrison Ministry', *Department of the Prime Minister and Cabinet* <Ministry List as at 8 October 2021 - Second Morrison Ministry (pmc.gov.au)>.

27 Department of Prime Minister and Cabinet, *Australian Government Crisis Management Framework* (Version 3.1), December 2021, 33 <Australian Government Crisis Management Framework (pmc.gov.au)>.

28 'National Coordination Mechanism', *Department of Home Affairs* < National Coordination Mechanism (homeaffairs.gov.au)>.

degree on cooperation and goodwill rather than reflecting a clear legal mandate. This is particularly the case in terms of coordination between national, state and territory governments. While a declaration under the *NED Act* is designed to activate a range of existing Commonwealth emergency powers it 'will not automatically trigger the operation of these powers',[29] and the *NED Act* does not appoint an overall coordinating body to manage the government response to a declared national emergency. While the *NED Act* allows the Commonwealth government to make a public declaration of a state of national emergency, it does not establish at the national level a legislated emergency management framework that is equivalent to that existing at the state and territory levels. For example, it remains the case that the EMA – which the departmental website proclaims to be 'Australia's National Disaster Management Organisation'[30] – does not have the legal authority to compel either other national government agencies, or state and territory governments, to take particular actions in preparing for or responding to an emergency, and its emergency coordination role is not grounded in any specific legal authority.

This has been recognised as a potentially significant limitation in Australia's emergency management framework. It would always be hoped that government agencies at both the state and national levels would work together cooperatively in response to a national disaster, even without this being required by law. However, even if the highest levels of cooperation and goodwill are present, an emergency situation is clearly not the best time to be trying to clarify roles or to deal with disputes about areas of responsibility. The lack of substantive national emergency management legislation (that is, a law extending

---

29 Commonwealth, *Parliamentary Debates,* House of Representatives, 3 December 2020, 10420 (Christian Porter, Attorney General).
30 'Emergency management', *Department of Home Affairs* <About emergency management (homeaffairs.gov.au)>.

beyond a declaration mechanism to include broader emergency coordination powers) means that 'the Australian Government's authority to act during times of national crisis can be, and has been, challenged,'[31] and that 'there is ample room for complication, duplication and confusion at a time when such confusion must be avoided'.[32] As was observed by Michael Eburn:[33]

> The failure of the Commonwealth to legislate in this area has, to date, not inhibited Australia's responses to natural hazards or other civil emergences, but it does leave gaps in the country's emergency arrangements that may, in due course, be revealed as vulnerabilities and which have been dealt with in other jurisdictions.

Existing constitutional powers

If the lack of substantive national emergency management laws is considered to be a gap in Australia's emergency arrangements, could the Commonwealth Parliament rectify this by introducing such a law? Such a law would go beyond the existing power under the *NED Act* to declare an emergency, and would include both emergency coordination powers that operate as a result of that declaration, and the specification of areas over which the Commonwealth claims responsibility under an emergency declaration.

This part of the paper will consider the powers currently provided under the *Constitution* to determine whether such a law would be constitutionally valid. These constitutional issues were considered by the Royal Commission in the context of the legislative framework required to establish a national declaration

---

31 Michael Eburn, 'Coordination of federal, state and local disaster management arrangements in Australia: Lessons from the UK and the US' (n 8), 1.
32 Michael Eburn, 'Legal preparedness for international disaster response in Australia: Laws, Policies, Planning and Practices' (n 8), 45.
33 Michael Eburn, 'Managing 'civil contingencies' in Australia' (n 8), 146.

mechanism. The Royal Commission concluded that there was 'a sound constitutional basis for introducing a declaration mechanism through legislation'.[34] The key conclusion was that the existing suite of Commonwealth legislative powers under s 51 of the *Constitution* would provide sufficient constitutional authority, with the Royal Commission expressing the view 'that given the extensive scope of the combined powers, and the wide ranging potential impact of natural disasters, it would be difficult to encounter a situation that is not relevantly connected to the subject matter of a head of power'.[35]

These are threshold questions worth considering in detail. This is particularly the case if what is being considered is not simply providing the Commonwealth government with the power to make a largely symbolic national emergency declaration, but a more substantive revision of Commonwealth emergency management powers and their interaction with existing state government powers in this area. The constitutional powers that will be specifically considered in this part of the paper are the executive and nationhood powers,[36] external affairs power,[37] defence power,[38] and referrals power.[39] The conclusion that is drawn is that while each of these may provide constitutional support for aspects of a national emergency law, for the most part they do not provide clear and comprehensive support for such a law in its entirety. The exception is potentially the referrals power; however, this presents its own practical complexities as it relies upon agreement being reached between the Commonwealth and each of the states.

---

34 Royal Commission into National Natural Disaster Arrangements (n 8), [5.42].
35 Royal Commission into National Natural Disaster Arrangements (n 8), [5.52].
36 *Australian Constitution*, ss 61 and 51(xxxix).
37 *Australian Constitution*, s 51(xxix).
38 *Australian Constitution*, s 51(vi).
39 *Australian Constitution*, s 51(xxxvii).

The executive and nationhood powers

The executive power has been described as an 'elusive beast'[40] whose scope has 'often been discussed but never defined.[41] Under s 61 of the *Constitution* the executive power 'extends to the execution and maintenance of this Constitution, and of the laws of the Commonwealth'. This does not, however, encapsulate the full extent of the power and capacities of the executive government. In *Williams v Commonwealth* French CJ said that the executive power referred to in s 61 extends to: 'powers necessary or incidental to the execution and maintenance of a law of the Commonwealth', 'powers conferred by statute', 'powers defined by reference to such of the prerogatives of the Crown as are properly attributable to the Commonwealth', 'powers defined by the capacities of the Commonwealth common to legal persons', and 'inherent authority derived from the character and status of the Commonwealth as the national government'.[42]

The idea of executive powers incorporating some form of emergency powers is well established. For example, H.P. Lee has suggested that 'a special or emergency prerogative lies dormant in the fabric of executive powers. Such a prerogative awaits activation in the face of extreme necessity'.[43] Similarly, in *Burmah Oil Co (Burma Trading) Ltd v Lord Advocate,* Viscount Radcliffe recognised the existence of a prerogative power 'exercisable by the Crown in circumstances of sudden and extreme emergency which put that safety in peril', and which could potentially be invoked not only in response to 'the imminence or outbreak of war' but also to respond to

---

40 Matt Harvey et al, *Constitutional Law (LexisNexis Study Guide)* (LexisNexis Butterworths; 2010), [3.14]
41 *Davis v Commonwealth* (1988) 166 CLR 79, 92 (Mason CJ, Deane and Gaudron JJ) (*'Davis'*). See also *Pape v Federal Commissioner of Taxation* (2009) 238 CLR 1, 62 [131] (French CJ) (*'Pape'*).
42 *Williams v Commonwealth* (2012) 248 CLR 156, 184-185 [22] (French CJ).
43 H.P. Lee, *Emergency Powers* (Law Book Co, 1984), 322.

circumstances such as 'riot, pestilence and conflagration'.[44]

These types of emergency powers in Australia have been described as being based upon the combined effect of the executive power under s 61 and the incidental power under s 51(xxxix) of the *Constitution*,[45] with broader interpretations also drawing on implications that can 'be deduced from the existence and character of the Commonwealth as a national government'.[46] This has been described by some as an implied nationhood power, conferring on the Commonwealth Government the power 'to engage in enterprises and activities peculiarly adapted to the government of a nation and which cannot otherwise be carried on for the benefit of the nation',[47] and discussed variously as a component of executive power, legislative power, or some combination thereof.[48] The core idea underpinning the implied nationhood power is 'that there exist uniquely national problems that are beyond the capacities of the States, because they extend beyond the boundaries of a State or involve logistical problems that the States are not well adapted to solve'.[49]

This was seen in *Pape v Commissioner of Taxation* where a majority in the High Court held that the *Tax Bonus for Working Australians Act (No 2) 2009* (Cth) – which authorised the Commonwealth government to appropriate money from consolidated revenue to make stimulus payments to individual

---

44 [1964] UKHL 6; [1965] AC 75, 115 (Viscount Radcliffe).

45 Section 51(xxxix) gives the Parliament the power to make laws with respect to 'matters incidental to the execution of any power vested by this Constitution in the Parliament or in either House thereof, or in the Government of the Commonwealth, or in the Federal Judicature, or in any department or officer of the Commonwealth'.

46 *Victoria v Commonwealth and Hayden* (1975) 134 CLR 388, 397 (Mason J) ('*AAP Case*'); *Pape* (n 41) 60 [127] (French CJ), 83 [214-215] (Gummow, Crennan and Bell JJ); *Davis* (n 30) 93 (Mason, Deane and Gaudron JJ), 103 (Wilson and Dawson JJ), 111 (Brennan J); *Ruddock v Vadarlis* (2001) 110 FCR 491, 542 [191] (French J).

47 *AAP Case* (n 46) 397 (Mason J); *Davis* (n 41), 107, 111 (Brennan J).

48 For a discussion about the various expressions that have been given to the nationhood power in the case law see *Pape* (n 41) [487]-[546] (Heydon J).

49 H.P. Lee (n 43) 204.

taxpayers in response to the Global Financial Crisis – was constitutionally valid. The majority found that the law in question was validly enacted under s 51(xxxix) of the *Constitution*, being incidental to the exercise of the executive power under s 61.

In their joint judgment, Gummow, Crennan and Bell JJ suggested that 'determining that there is the need for an immediate fiscal stimulus to the national economy' in the circumstances of a global financial and economic crisis was analogous to 'determining a state of emergency in circumstances of a natural disaster.[50] In these types of circumstances, they stated:[51]

> The Executive Government is the arm of government capable of and empowered to respond to a crisis be it war, natural disaster or a financial crisis on the scale here. This power has its roots in the executive power exercised in the United Kingdom up to the time of the adoption of the Constitution but in form today in Australia it is a power to act on behalf of the federal polity.

There are broadly defined limits to this nationhood power, primarily in that 'the exigencies of "national government" cannot be invoked to set aside the distribution of powers between Commonwealth and States and between the three branches of government for which this Constitution provides, nor to abrogate constitutional prohibitions'.[52]   However, as Anne Twomey has observed:[53]

> The greatest difficulty with ascertaining the internal limits on the nationhood power is that the source of that power remains unclear. If one follows the chain of reasoning and authority, one discovers that, like the rope in the Indian rope trick, the nationhood power is floating free, because it is no longer tied to, or can

---

50 *Pape* (n 41) 89 [233] (Gummow, Crennan and Bell JJ).
51 Ibid, 89 [233] (Gummow, Crennan and Bell JJ).
52 Ibid, 60 [127] (French CJ).
53 Anne Twomey, 'Pushing the Boundaries of Executive Power – Pape, the Prerogative and Nationhood Powers' (2010) 34(1) *Melbourne University Law Review* 313.

no longer be supported by, the originally identified
sources of power.

The foundations and scope of the nationhood power are not,
however, without controversy or entirely settled. For example,
the result in *Pape* was reached by a slim majority, with three
judges dissenting and there being different views expressed
about all aspects of the nationhood power. The danger here is
that whilst the result in *Pape* suggests that the Commonwealth
government has broad constitutional authority to respond to
national emergencies (potentially in terms of both executive and
legislative powers), the precise contours of this authority are far
from certain. As a result:[54]

> there may be challenges as to whether the power
> exists, and whether it extends to allow the measures
> that the government proposes. Leaving the matter
> up to a court to determine when and how the
> Commonwealth may act in an emergency would not
> be appropriate when such powers are required as a
> matter of urgency.

To begin with, it is not clear when the threshold of a national
emergency is reached so as to invoke the nationhood power. In
their joint judgment in *Pape,* Hayne and Kiefel JJ noted that
'words like "crisis" or "emergency" do not readily yield criteria
of constitutional validity'.[55] They further cautioned that if it
was left to the Executive to decide when the threshold of a
national emergency is reached, 'then the Executive's powers in
such matters would be self-defining'.[56]

The potential for a vague and imprecise nationhood power to be
relied upon to support a significant expansion of Commonwealth
powers was outlined by Heydon J in his dissenting judgment in

---

54 Michael Eburn, 'Managing 'civil contingencies' in Australia' (n 8) 151.
55 *Pape* (n 41) 122 [347] (Hayne and Kiefel JJ).
56 Ibid, 123 [353] (Hayne and Kiefel JJ).

Pape:[57]

> The truth is that the modern world is in part created by the way language is used. Modern linguistic usage suggests that the present age is one of 'emergencies', 'crises', 'dangers' and 'intense difficulties', of 'scourges' and other problems. They relate to things as diverse as terrorism, water shortages, drug abuse, child abuse, poverty, pandemics, obesity, and global warming, as well as global financial affairs. In relation to them, the public is endlessly told, 'wars' must be waged, 'campaigns' conducted, 'strategies' devised and 'battles' fought. Often these problems are said to arise suddenly and unexpectedly. Sections of the public constantly demand urgent action to meet particular problems. The public is continually told that it is facing 'decisive' junctures, 'crucial' turning points and 'critical' decisions. Even if only a narrow power to deal with an emergency on the scale of the global financial crisis were recognised, it would not take long before constitutional lawyers and politicians between them managed to convert that power into something capable of almost daily use. The great maxim of governments seeking to widen their constitutional powers would be: 'Never allow a crisis to go to waste'.

It is also not clear exactly what actions the *Constitution* would allow as part of an appropriate Commonwealth government response to an emergency under the nationhood power. One potential limitation is the question of whether the nationhood power is able to be exercised in a coercive manner. This is potentially a particularly significant limitation in the context of emergency laws that may well contain coercive elements and seek to restrict individual rights in an effort to prioritise community safety and ensure quick and decisive responses. The nationhood power is fundamentally facultative in nature, and it has been suggested that it cannot be used in a coercive manner

---

57 Ibid, 193 [551] (Heydon J).

to impair individual freedom or liberty[58] or, at the very least, that any coercive exercise of the power must be reasonably and appropriately adapted to an objective that lies within the scope of the power.[59]

These potential limits have not been fully explored by the courts to date, although French CJ suggested in *Pape* that future questions about the coercive application of these constitutional powers 'are likely to be answered conservatively'.[60] In doing so, he recalled the 'cautionary words' of Dixon J in the *Communist Party Case*:[61]

> History and not only ancient history, shows that in countries where democratic institutions have been unconstitutionally superseded, it has been done not seldom by those holding the executive power. Forms of government may need protection from dangers likely to arise from within the institutions to be protected.

A further limitation creating uncertainty about the potential scope of Commonwealth government emergency responses under the nationhood power is the uncertain impact of the final thirteen words of what has been referred to as 'Mason J's test', namely the words 'and which cannot otherwise be carried on for the benefit of the nation'.[62] Their inclusion suggests that 'expanded meanings of "executive power" to include a "nationhood power" cannot disturb "the broad division of responsibilities between the Commonwealth and the States achieved by the distribution of legislative powers" in the Constitution'.[63] The fact that the state governments all have well established emergency management laws in place, that

---

58 *Commonwealth v Tasmania* (1983) 158 CLR 1, 203-4 (Wilson J) (*'Tasmania Dam Case'*); *Davis* (n 41) 112-13 (Brennan J).
59 *AAP Case* (n 46) 397 (Mason J).
60 *Pape* (n 41) 24 [10] (French CJ).
61 *Australian Communist Party v Commonwealth* (1951) 83 CLR 1, 187 (Dixon J).
62 *AAP Case* (n 46) 397 (Mason J).
63 *Pape* (n 41) 188-189 [537] (Heydon J) quoting *AAP Case* (n 46) 398 (Mason J).

history shows state government has been able to effectively respond to natural disasters, and that a cooperative framework between state and Commonwealth governments currently exists in Australia, are all factors weighing against the suggestion that the nationhood power would support a broad Commonwealth take-over of emergency management responsibilities. The federal division of responsibilities between state and national governments is a factor that is of constitutional relevance when considering the potential reach of any nationhood power.

The end result here is that both the executive and legislative arms of the Commonwealth Parliament appear to have a recognised constitutional capacity to respond to national emergencies through the combined application of the executive power, incidental power and nationhood power (in whatever form that takes). It is important, however, to recognise that the precise scope and limits to these powers have not been clearly identified. In itself, this is a strong argument for the introduction of a specific emergency power for the Commonwealth government under the *Constitution*. Such a power would assist in providing significant guidance towards removing the current confusion around what the threshold is for allowing the Commonwealth government to act, and what the limits are. It would also avoid trying to navigate these complexities during an emergency situation, at a time when confusion or disagreement about roles and responsibilities can have potentially disastrous consequences.

External Affairs Power

There are other constitutional heads of power that would potentially provide support for aspects of any national emergency management legislation. One obvious example is the external affairs power under s 51(xxix) of the *Constitution*. This has been interpreted as giving the Commonwealth Parliament the power to make laws with respect to Australia's management of relations with other countries,[64] matters physically external to Australia (known as the 'geographic externality principle'),[65] and the implementation of international agreements.[66]

This would be relatively straightforward in terms of potentially supporting, for example, laws with respect to responding to emergencies occurring overseas, or dealing with foreign assistance for emergencies originating in Australia. The use of the external affairs power would be more contentious, however, if it was attempted to be used to support laws dealing with the domestic response to a domestic emergency. There may potentially be international agreements that could provide some support to particular laws, but they would not currently appear to provide comprehensive support to an overarching national emergency management law and a number of constitutional restrictions would need to be kept in mind.

With respect to the implementation of international agreements, it is important to note that the external affairs power 'does not provide the Parliament with a blank cheque'.[67] A domestic law will only be able to rely on this aspect of the external affairs power for constitutional support if the international agreement is *bona fide*,[68] and meets a specificity requirement in that the domestic law 'must prescribe a regime that the treaty itself has defined with sufficient specificity to direct the general course to

---

64 R v Sharkey (1949) 79 CLR 121; Kirmani v Captain Cook Cruises Pty Ltd (No. 1) (1985) 159 CLR 351.

65 Polyukhovich v Commonwealth (1991) 172 CLR 501; XYZ v Commonwealth (2006) 227 CLR 532.

66 Tasmanian Dam Case (n 58); Victoria v Commonwealth (1996) 187 CLR 416 ('Industrial Relations Act Case').

67 Lorraine Finlay, 'The Constitutional Limitations & Implications of a Religious Freedom Act' in Iain T. Benson, Michael Quinlan and A. Keith Thompson (eds.), Religious Freedom in Australia – a New Terra Nullius? (Shepherd Street Press, 2019).

68 R v Burgess; Ex parte Henry (1936) 55 CLR 608, 687 (Evatt & McTiernan JJ); Koowarta v Bjelke-Petersen (1982) 153 CLR 168, 200 (Gibbs CJ).

be taken by the signatory states'.[69] The domestic law must also sufficiently conform to the terms of the treaty, meaning that it is 'capable of being reasonably considered to be appropriate and adapted to give effect to the treaty'.[70]

Australia is signatory to a number of international agreements that concern specific types of emergencies,[71] or outline emergency cooperation commitments with respect to specific countries.[72] There is, however, no overarching international treaty addressing emergency management which, given the number of international agreements in the modern age concerning an ever-growing range of topics 'represents an anomaly in comparison to other areas of law'.[73]

This may change in the future noting, for example, that the International Law Commission has developed *Draft Articles on the Protection of Persons in the Event of Disasters* that aims to 'facilitate the adequate and effective response to disasters, and reduction of the risk of disasters, so as to meet the essential needs of the persons concerned, with full respect for their rights'.[74] The International Law Commission adopted the final text of the Draft Articles in 2016 and recommended to the United Nations General Assembly 'the elaboration of a convention on the basis

---

69 *Industrial Relations Act Case* (n 66) 486 (Brennan CJ, Toohey, Gaudron, McHugh and Gummow JJ).

70 Ibid 487 (Brennan CJ, Toohey, Gaudron, McHugh and Gummow JJ); *Richardson v Forestry Commission* (1988) 164 CLR 261.

71 See, for example, *Convention on Assistance in the Case of a Nuclear Accident or Radiological Emergency*, opened for signature 26 September 1986, 1457 UNTS 133 (entered into force 26 February 1987); *Protocol on Preparedness, Response and Co-operation to Pollution Incidents by Hazardous and Noxious Substances*, adopted 14 March 2000, 2003 ATNIF 9 (entered into force 14 June 2007).

72 See, for example, *Agreement between Australia and the Republic of Indonesia on the Framework for Security Cooperation*, Australia-Indonesia, signed on 13 November 2006, [2008] ATS 3 (entered into force 7 February 2008).

73 Giulio Bartolini, *A universal treaty for disasters? Remarks on the International Law Commission's Draft Articles on the Protection of Persons in the Event of Disasters* (International Review of the Red Cross, No. 906, April 2019), 1104.

74 International Law Commission, *Report of the International Law Commission: Sixty-Eighth Session (2 May – 10 June and 4 July – 12 August 2016)*, UN Doc. A/71/10, 2016, 14 (Article 2). <https://legal.un.org/ilc/reports/2016/english/a_71_10.pdf>

of the draft articles on the protection of persons in the event of disasters'.[75] On 9 December 2021 the General Assembly adopted a resolution noting the draft articles and establishing a working group to report to the United Nations General Assembly Sixth Committee[76] 'with a view to the Committee making a recommendation to the Assembly as to any further action to take in respect of the draft articles'.[77] The working group is currently scheduled to report to the Sixth Committee in 2023, which serves to highlight that any final adoption of the *Draft Articles* still remains – at best – years into the future.

Whether the *Draft Articles* could potentially support the introduction of a national emergency management law under the external affairs power would depend on whether Australia ultimately ratified any convention that was developed, and the types of obligations that were included within that instrument. It does, however, point to the possibility that an international treaty could, at some point in the future, provide constitutional support for a broadening of Commonwealth emergency management powers.

At present, however, the closest thing to an international framework in this area is the *Sendai Declaration* and *Sendai Framework for Disaster Risk Reduction (2015-2030)*,[78] which builds on the *Hyogo Framework for Action 2005-2015*. The *Declaration* and *Framework* were first adopted at the Third United Nations World Conference on Disaster Risk Reduction in 2015 and were endorsed by the United Nations General Assembly

---

75 Ibid 13 [46].

76 The United Nations General Assembly Sixth Committee is the Legal Committee, and is one of the six Main Committees established under Rule 98 of the *Rule of Procedure of the General Assembly*. The Sixth Committee 'is the primary forum for the consideration of legal questions in the General Assembly': see <https://www.un.org/en/ga/sixth/index.shtml>.

77 *Protection of persons in the event of disasters*, GA Res 76/119, UN Doc A/RES/76/119 (17 December 2021, adopted 9 December 2021).

78 *Sendai Framework for Disaster Risk Reduction 2015-2030*, GA Res 69/283, UN Doc A/RES/69/283 (23 June 2015, adopted 3 June 2015).

in Resolution 69/283 in the same year.[79]   The Framework has been endorsed by Australia 'and guides Australia's approach to disaster risk reduction'.[80]   It informs and is referenced in, for example, the *Australian Disaster Preparedness Framework*[81] and the *National Disaster Risk Reduction Framework.*[82]   The Framework is based around four priority areas and seven global targets, but is a non-binding or 'soft-law' instrument.[83]   It is doubtful that it would provide constitutional support for a national emergency law in its current form, particularly in terms of satisfying both the specificity and conformity requirements.

Defence Power

Another constitutional power with relevance here is the defence power under s 51(vi) which allows the Commonwealth Parliament to make laws with respect to 'the naval and military defence of the Commonwealth and of the several States, and the control of the forces to execute and maintain the laws of the Commonwealth'.

The defence power is a purposive power, whose range is elastic depending on the surrounding factual circumstances.   As was explained by Dixon J in *Andrews v Howell:*[84]

> unlike some other powers its application depends upon facts, and as those facts change so may its actual operation as a power enabling the legislature

---

79 Ibid.
80 'Disaster risk reduction and resilience', *Department of Foreign Affairs and Trade* <https://www.dfat.gov.au/aid/topics/investment-priorities/building-resilience/drr/Pages/disaster-risk-reduction-and-resilience>.
81 Department of Home Affairs, *Australian Disaster Preparedness Framework* (October 2018) <https://www.homeaffairs.gov.au/emergency/files/australian-disaster-preparedness-framework.pdf>.
82 Department of Home Affairs, *National Disaster Risk Reduction Framework* (2018) <https://www.homeaffairs.gov.au/emergency/files/national-disaster-risk-reduction-framework.pdf>.
83 Giulio Bartolini (n 73), 1105.
84 (1941) 65 CLR 255, 278 (Dixon J).

> to make an actual law. The existence and character of hostilities, or a threat of hostilities, against the Commonwealth are facts which will determine the extent of operation of the power.

It has been given a broader scope in modern times, with it being confirmed in *Thomas v Mowbray* that the defence power is not limited to protecting against external threats, but is instead 'concerned centrally with the defence of the Commonwealth and the several States as bodies politic'.[85]

When considering whether the defence power would extend to supporting laws designed to defend the nation against natural disasters, the second part of s 51(vi) becomes particularly relevant, namely the power to make laws with respect to 'the control of the forces to execute and maintain the laws of the Commonwealth'. This was intended to allow the use of armed forces 'when some sudden emergency renders it necessary, in order to maintain the public peace'.[86] The section 'was designed to give Parliament the power to pass legislation to govern the circumstances and procedures of a call-out of forces to deal with threats to public order'.[87]

There are, however, limits to the use that should be made of defence powers and forces in the civil context. For example, Justice Hope has observed:[88]

> Use of the military other than for external defence, is a critical and controversial issue in the political life of a country and the civil liberties of its citizens. 'An armed disciplined body is in its essence dangerous

---

85 *Thomas v Mowbray* (2007) 233 CLR 307, 458 [440] (Hayne J).

86 Sir John Quick and Sir Robert Garran, *The Annotated Constitution of the Australian Commonwealth* (Legal Books 1976, reprint 1901 ed) 565.

87 Hugh Smith, 'The use of armed forces in law enforcement: Legal, constitutional and political issues in Australia' (1998) 33(2) *Australian Journal of Political Science* 219, 227.

88 R. M. Hope, 'Protective Security Review' (Parliamentary Paper No. 397/1979, Parliament of Australia, 15 May 1979) 142, quoting Edmund Burke. See also Elizabeth Ward, 'Call Out the Troops: an examination of the legal basis for Australian Defence Force involvement in 'non-defence' matters (Research Paper 8 1997-98, Parliament of Australia).

to Liberty: undisciplined, it is ruinous to Society'.
Given that there must be a permanent Defence Force,
it is critical that it be employed only for proper
purposes and that it be subject to proper control.

This caution was similarly reflected by Justice Kirby in *Thomas
v Mowbray*:[89]

> For the purposes of s 51(vi), I will therefore accept that
> there need not always be an external threat to enliven
> the power. However, the threat, in whatever way it is
> characterised, must be directed at the bodies politic.
> This is the characteristic that lifts the subject-matter
> of s 51(vi) of the Constitution to a level beyond that
> of particular dangers to specific individuals or groups
> or interests *within* the bodies politics so named. It
> is a vital constitutional distinction. Its origin is
> found in the text. But it is reinforced by the strong
> constitutional history involving the strictly limited
> deployment of defence personnel in domestic affairs
> which was the background (and shared assumption)
> against which the constitutional text was written and
> intended to operate. This Court should maintain and
> uphold that historical approach. It should do nothing
> to undermine it. Any departure invites great danger,
> as the constitutional history of less fortunate lands,
> including some that once shared our tradition, has
> repeatedly demonstrated.

It has been suggested this power should be exercised only when
vital Commonwealth interests are seriously threatened, however
a clear difficulty here is that 'the extent of such interests … has
not been tested in law'.[90] Determining the threshold at which the
constitutional power will be engaged may prove contentious, as
the distinction between a local emergency and one that threatens
vital Commonwealth interests will not necessarily be precise or
clear at any given point in time.

---

89 *Thomas v Mowbray* (n 85), 395 [251] (Kirby J).
90 Hugh Smith (n 87), 227.

It would also be important in this context to consider the impact of s. 119 of the *Constitution*, which provides that:[91]

> The Commonwealth shall protect every State against invasion and, on the application of the Executive Government of the State, against domestic violence.

With respect to protection 'against domestic violence' s 119 requires a prior request for assistance from the State Government and "does not authorise unilateral action by the Commonwealth Government".[92] In *Thomas v Mowbray* Kirby J suggested that this section was instructive when considering the ambit of the defence power as it 'assumes that, ordinarily, the reach of federal legislative power, including the defence power, excludes areas of civil government and matters usual to "police powers", including those of the States'.[93] As a consequence, '[t]o permit s 51(vi) to extend to the protection of all persons and all property would therefore sit uncomfortably with s 119'.[94]

From the above it can be seen that the defence power may well provide constitutional support for some aspects of a national emergency law. Its use will, however, become increasingly contestable the further the emergency law extends beyond providing for a direct response to an immediate emergency, and moves instead into the realm of longer-term prevention and preparation.

The Referral of State Powers

An important option to be considered here, from both a constitutional and practical perspective, is the use of the referral power under s 51(xxxvii) of the *Constitution*. This placitum

---

91 *Australian Constitution*, s 119.
92 Elizabeth Ward (n 88).
93 *Thomas v Mowbray* (n 85) 394 [248] (Kirby J).
94 Ibid, 394-395 [249] (Kirby J).

allows the Commonwealth Parliament to make laws with respect to 'matters referred to the Parliament of the Commonwealth by the Parliament or Parliaments of any State or States, but so that the law shall extend only to States by whose Parliaments the matter is referred, or which afterwards adopt the law'. The power has previously been used to facilitate reforms in a number of significant policy areas, including anti-terrorism measures, corporations law, and aspects of family law.

The referral power has received comparatively little judicial or academic consideration over the years, and yet it has been described as potentially providing a simpler and more certain approach to co-operative federalism.[95] Andrew Lynch outlined the 'accepted wisdom' on s 51(xxxvii) as including:[96]

- Use of the power in s 51(xxxvii) may result in a law of general application or one limited only to those States making the reference or subsequently adopting the Commonwealth Act;

- The power may be used in connection to a referral of subject-matter or specific legislative text;

- Regardless of form, the referral is of a "matter" over which the States enjoy legislative capacity, not State legislative power itself;

- The referral may be conditional and expressed to determine after a specified period or on the occurrence of some event. However ... it has not been authoritatively settled whether a State may revoke the referral nor what consequences would follow from such an action;

95 Daryl Williams, 'Making Federalism Work: A New Frame of Reference', *Australian Association of Constitutional Law Seminar* (Perth, 22 May 2002), quoted in Justice Robert S. French, 'The Referrals Power' (2003) 31 *Western Australian Law Review* 19, 30.

96 Andrew Lynch, 'After a Referral: The Amendment and Termination of Commonwealth Laws Relying on s 51(xxxvii)' (2010) 32(2) *Sydney Law Review* 363, 371.

- The referral must be made by legislation enacted by
  the Parliament of the relevant States and cannot be
  delegated.

The advantage of using the referral power over other existing s
51 powers is that it can avoid a patchwork approach, whereby
existing constitutional powers with limited scope are used in
combination to attempt to provide comprehensive coverage.
The provision of a clear and certain source of constitutional
power would be a particular advantage in this context, with
uncertainty and confusion being particularly undesirable when
dealing with emergency situations. This was a key advantage
recognised by the Royal Commission, which concluded that
a referral of power by the states 'could provide a strong and
unequivocal basis to enable the Australian Government to
implement a declaration'.[97]

A second potential advantage is that the states can qualify any
referral, and include safeguards in an attempt to control the
scope and use of the referred power by the Commonwealth
government. As Andrew Lynch has observed, '[t]he States will
only be willing to hand over areas to Commonwealth control if
they can be confident that sufficient safeguards are in place to
prevent over-reaching or misuse of those powers by the national
legislature'.[98] In particular, a referral grants concurrent powers
to the Commonwealth Parliament,[99] with the result that states
retain the capacity to legislate with respect to the matters that
are referred. It will be important in this context to ensure
that existing state emergency management frameworks are
considered, and that potential inconsistency issues that might
arise under s 109 of the *Constitution* are taken into account
when framing any referral.

---

97 Royal Commission into National Natural Disaster Arrangements (n 5), [5.45].
98 Andrew Lynch (n 96), 364.
99 *Graham v Paterson* (1950) 81 CLR 1.

Another important consideration here will be whether the states retain the ability to revoke a referral of legislative power in the future. This question has not been authoritatively determined. In *R v Public Vehicles Licensing Appeal Tribunal (Tas); Ex parte Australian National Airways Pty Ltd* the High Court suggested that this was possible, observing that:[100]

> it must be remembered that the paragraph is concerned with the reference by the Parliament or Parliaments of a State or States. The will of a Parliament is expressed in a statute or Act of Parliament and it is the general conception of English law that what Parliament may enact it may repeal.

However, the Court in that case also noted that the question 'forms only a subsidiary matter' and expressly[101] stated that they 'do not therefore discuss it or express any final opinion upon it'.

Interestingly, contrary views were expressed when the clause was debated at the third session of the Federal Convention in Melbourne in 1898. For example, Isaac Isaacs disagreed that there was a power of revocation, suggesting that '[i]f a State refers a matter to the Federal Parliament, after the Federal Parliament has exercised its power to deal with that matter, the State ceases to be able to interfere in regard to it.'[102] Alfred Deakin also adopted this view when considering the referral power:[103]

> Another difficulty of the sub-section is the question whether, even when a State has referred a matter to the federal authority, and federal legislation takes place on it, it has any – and, if any, what – power of

---

100 (1964) 113 CLR 207, 226 (Dixon CJ, Kitto, Taylor, Menzies, Windeyer and Owen JJ). See also Luke Beck, *Australian Constitutional Law: Concepts and Cases* (Cambridge University Press, 2020), 53.

101 Ibid, 226 (Dixon CJ, Kitto, Taylor, Menzies, Windeyer and Owen JJ).

102 *Official Report of the National Australasian Convention Debates*, Melbourne, 27 January 1898, 223. See also Justice Robert S. French (n 95) 27.

103 J A La Nauze (ed), *Federated Australia: Selections from Letters to the* Morning Post *1900-1910* (Melbourne University Press, 1968) 217, quoted in Justice Robert S. French (n 95) 26.

> amending or repealing the law by which it referred
> the question? I should be inclined to think it had
> no such power, but the question has been raised and
> should be settled. I should say that having appealed
> to Caesar, it must be bound by the judgment of Caesar
> and that it would not be possible for it afterwards to
> revoke its reference.

It is difficult, however, to reconcile this view with the underlying concepts of parliamentary sovereignty and co-operative federalism that inform Australia's constitutional design. As Luke Beck has concluded:[104]

> The idea that a State could not revoke a referral of
> legislative power is inconsistent with the idea that
> the States possess plenary legislative power and can
> make *and unmake* any law they want.

The key hurdles to using the referral power in these circumstances appear to be practical and political, rather than legal. An obvious hurdle is that state governments may not themselves agree to refer these issues to the Commonwealth government. A number of state governments quickly expressed opposition to the expansion of Commonwealth constitutional powers that was proposed by the Prime Minister in his National Press Club address back in 2020 in the context of the Black Summer bushfires. For example, the West Australian Premier, Mark McGowan, expressed the view that the Defence Force should continue to only be deployed with state permission.[105] The subsequent tensions evident between state and national governments during the COVID-19 pandemic with respect to issues such as border closures and responsibility for quarantine arrangements have bought into sharp focus the clear risk that

---

104 Luke Beck, *Australian Constitutional Law: Concepts and Cases* (Cambridge University Press, 2020), 53.

105 John Kehoe, 'States resist bushfire royal commission, oppose expansion of powers', *Australian Financial Review*, 14 January 2020 <https://www.afr.com/politics/federal/states-resist-bushfire-royal-commission-oppose-expansion-of-powers-20200114-p53r9l>.

any proposed expansion of Commonwealth powers in this area will be firmly opposed by at least a number of state governments.

Secondly, any law made under the referral power only extends to those states by whose Parliaments the matter is referred. The use of the referral power raises the prospect of a 'Swiss cheese Commonwealth law'[106] that applies in certain states, but not in others. This would be a particularly undesirable outcome in relation to a national emergency law, with natural disasters not being known for the respect that they show to man-made jurisdictional boundaries.

Amending the *Constitution*

A final option would be to formally amend the *Constitution* to provide the Commonwealth Parliament with the power to legislate with respect to national emergencies, or to constitutionalize a national emergency law by inserting an emergency provision into the *Constitution* itself. Both of these would have the advantage of providing a level of clarity, but the latter in particular would require broad agreement to be reached about the details of such a power, such as the threshold for an emergency declaration, what powers could be exercised in an emergency, who would be responsible for exercising those powers, and what safeguards are necessary to protect against misuse. These are all difficult questions in their own right, and attracting the level of agreement and support needed to successfully navigate the amendment process set out in the *Australian Constitution* is a significant practical hurdle that should not be under-estimated.

The process for amending the *Constitution* is set out in s 128. In short, the proposed amendment must be passed by an absolute majority of each House of Parliament, and then approved by

---

106 Justice Robert S. French (n 95) 34.

the electors at a national referendum. A 'double majority' requirement applies at the national referendum, requiring the proposed amendment to be approved by not only an overall majority of electors at the national level, but also by a majority of voters in a majority of states. As I have previously noted:[107]

> The amendment process under s. 128 is not an easy one, as shown by the fact that only 8 out of 44 proposed amendments have ever been approved. Of course, the fact that an amendment process sets a high threshold should not discourage a government from pursuing important constitutional reforms. But it does highlight the importance of taking a practical approach when assessing potential reforms, and the desirability of seeking a broad consensus when formulating reform proposals.

Conclusion

Both the Black Summer bushfires that occurred in 2019-20 and the COVID-19 pandemic response have bought into sharp focus questions about Australia's existing emergency management arrangements. The *NED Act* has sought to strengthen the role of the Commonwealth government in dealing with a national emergency, specifically through the introduction of the power to make a NED. However, there is still no single, coordinating emergency response authority mandated under law at the national level, and the lines of responsibility between the national and state levels of government remain unclear in important respects. Fortunately, it has been the case to date that 'such omission has not rendered the Commonwealth or the States impotent in the face of crises'.[108] Recent events have highlighted, however, the desirability of considering this question *before* another

---

107 Lorraine Finlay, Submission No. 51 to Joint Standing Committee on Electoral Matters, *Inquiry into matters relating to Section 44 of the Constitution* (9 February 2018) 6.
108 H.P. Lee (n 43), 261.

emergency situation arises, and in a manner that is proactive rather than reactive.

The Commonwealth government currently has a range of constitutional powers available to it that would support aspects of a national emergency management framework. These include the executive and nationhood powers, external affairs power and defence power, although there are important limitations and uncertainties that arise with respect to each of these. To ensure both completeness and clarity the most constitutionally secure way of introducing an overarching, substantive national emergency management law would be through a referral of state powers using s 51(xxxvii). The other alternative would be to formally amend the *Constitution*, but this is an option that faces even greater practical and political hurdles than the use of the referral power.

When dealing with an emergency situation it is vital that a government is able to act decisively, that there is a clear demarcation of responsibilities, and that there is no confusion surrounding the legal framework. A substantive national emergency law would assist in this regard, and would be particularly useful in the federal context in helping to define the respective roles of the Commonwealth, state and territory governments. Just as importantly, clearly providing for a single, coordinating emergency authority at the national level and clearly outlining the powers that this body could exercise in an emergency situation would be helpful in ensuring not only the effectiveness of any emergency response, but would also allow the limits of those powers to be expressly stated, provide for clear lines of accountability and allow for appropriate safeguards to be inserted to protect against misuse.

A substantive national emergency law (that goes beyond the declaration mechanism provided for in the *NED Act*) is desirable to ensure that the Commonwealth government can act quickly and decisively to protect Australians in a national emergency. However, equally as important is ensuring that the law is strictly limited to emergencies and is crafted in a way that does not undermine our broader democratic freedoms and principles in the longer term.

4

No More Than Legal Fiction?
A Critical Evaluation of the Implied Freedom of Political Communication in Australia

Augusto Zimmermann

Abstract

This article provides a general account of the numerous instances in Australia in which freedom of political communication has become no more than a legal fiction. Australian governments have a long history of suppressing speech that is critical of the prevailing values of the ruling elites. Although the nation's highest court has acknowledged an implied, constitutional freedom of political communication, this freedom remains remarkably unprotected insofar as the systematic suppression of dissenting voices is concerned. Whilst enjoying full speech due to the privileges of their office, our elected politicians often deny the enjoyment of these same freedoms to those who have elected them and see no reliable protection whatsoever. Some Australians have found themselves at the receiving end of expensive legal action, especially if they dare to hold traditional views that are no longer accepted by the nation's ruling elites.

Keywords

Freedom of speech, implied freedom of political communication, protection of free speech, elite suppression of free speech, traditional views

1. First considerations

I am writing this article in order to expose attempts to stigmatise as illegitimate the speech of my fellow citizens whose only real 'offence' is straying from the ruling elites' approved range of opinions. In fact, much speech that is criticised in Australia as 'hate speech' is no more than a fair response to the protected speech by others. This is about people in a supposed democracy being denied their basic right to publicly manifest political opinions due to their traditional values contradicting the so-called 'progressive' values of the ruling elites (politicians, the mainstream media, big corporation bosses, and leading academics).

Although the nation's highest court has acknowledged an implied, constitutional freedom of political communication, far too many Australians feel uncomfortable to express their opinions in public, particularly if they are dissenting from the prevailing elitist orthodoxy. Labels such as 'racist', 'sexist' and 'homophobe' are routinely applied in order to demonise persons and deligitimise their argument if they dare to utter a word that does not faithfully support the ideological agenda of the ruling elites. Of course, allowing certain forms of speech to be protected while censoring different opinions is profoundly unfair and undemocratic. This allows the proponents of viewpoints that are favoured by the status quo to *fight freestyle* while requiring dissident voices to observe *The Marquis of Queensbury Rules*.[1]

---

1 E.H. Lipsett, 'Case Comment: Saskatchewan (Human Rights Commission) v Whatcott, 2013 SCC 11' (2013) *Manitoba Law Journal* <http://robsonhall.ca/mlj/sites/default/files/articles/Whatcott%20-%20Blog%20Post%20Version_0.pdf>.

2.   Freedom of speech: History and importance

The history of free speech can be traced back to the ancient Greeks. The Greek word for free speech is *parrhesia*, which implies one's ability to express his or her views without fear of reprisal. In classical times, *parrhesia* was regarded as essential to the equalitarian nature of the Greek democracy.[2] The Greeks believed that only slaves could not speak freely, although all free citizens could.[3] What made the trial of Socrates so unusual is that this was 'the only case in which we can be certain that an Athenian was legally prosecuted not for an overt act that directly harmed the public or some individual – such as treason, corruption or slander – but for alleged harm indirectly caused by the expression and teaching of ideas'.[4]

Naturally, absolute free speech under all circumstances can never be a possibility. There are easily demonstrable exceptions whereby reasonable limits to free speech can be created. Within the boundaries of speech that should enjoy protection, certain limited categories have lower value, most notably sexually explicit speech that falls short of obscenity. Moreover, violence is never acceptable and direct attacks on the physical integrity of another person can never be tolerated.

---

2 Anthony Gray, *Freedom of Speech in the Western World – Comparison and Critique* (London: Lexington Books, 2019), 6.

3 Chris Berg, *In Defence of Freedom of Speech: From Ancient Greece to Andrew Bolt* (Melbourne/Vic: IPA & Mannkal, 2012), 8.

4 'According to Plato's *Apology*, the vote to convict Socrates was very close: had 30 of those who voted for conviction cast their ballots differently, he would have been acquitted. (So he was convicted by a majority of 59. Assuming, as many scholars do, that the size of his jury was 501, 280 favoured conviction and 221 opposed it). It is reasonable to speculate that many of those who opposed conviction did so partly because, however little they cared for what Socrates thought and how he lived, they cherished the freedom of speech enjoyed by all Athenians and attached more importance to this aspect of their political system than to any harm Socrates may have done in the past or might do in the future. The Athenian love of free speech allowed Socrates to cajole and criticize his fellow citizens for the whole of his long life but gave way – though just barely – when it was put under great pressure' – 'The Athenian Ideal of Free Speech', *Encyclopaedia Britannica* <http://www.britannica.com/EBchecked/topic/551948/Socrates/233637/The-Athenian-ideal-of-free-speech>.

The ruling elites have a vested interest in preserving the status quo by legally suppressing any reasonable dissent. They are willing to suppress any opinion that might threaten their prevailing orthodoxy. An example of this occurred in 1621, when the members of the English House of Commons boldly reminded the king of their ancient birthright to freely speak about any subject whatsoever. As a result, King James tore out the page of the parliamentary journal that contained such statement, and then he dissolved the Parliament once again. James also imprisoned several leading parliamentarians deemed disloyal to him, including Sir Edward Coke.

It is worthwhile to indicate the prevalence of social contract theory from the seventeenth to the mid-nineteenth centuries. Concern for free speech fits well within this sort of political theory. In this context, the theory of the English philosopher John Locke was especially relevant because he envisaged the constitution of a government which creates laws that are protective of inalienable rights, in particular rights to life, liberty and property. The failure of government to protect these rights leads to an erosion of political legitimacy. Social contract theory, as noted by Anthony Gray, could accommodate notions that the right of individuals to freedom of speech had not been ceded to the elected legislature. The people had not agreed to relinquish their right to speak, and to hear a range of views. One view of such a consensual view of government actually contemplated broad protection for freedom of speech. The people had to speak, and to have the opportunity to hear a range of views, in order to properly determine how their representative government should be comprised.[5]

The *Bill of Rights 1689* (Eng) guaranteed the protection of free speech, albeit in limited form and only to the sphere of

---

5 Gray, (n 2), 18.

parliamentary debate. Still, the English were known for their strong feelings about free speech and the protective elements of English constitutionalism.[6] In this context, Fox's *Libel Act of 1792* created the power of juries to determine all matters in dispute, including whether any particular material was in fact libellous. A few years later, on 25 November 1795, Charles James Fox, a Whig leader in the House of Commons, spoke in Parliament against the *Treason and Sedition Bills* introduced for 'better securing' the King's person and government. There he made a classic case for freedom of speech, which is worth quoting in part:

> [I]t is not the written law of the constitution of England, it is not the law that is to be found in books, that has constituted the true principle of freedom in any country, at any time. No! it is the energy, the boldness of a man's mind, which prompts him to speak, not in private, but in large and popular assemblies, that constitutes, that creates, in a state, the spirit of freedom. This is the principle which gives life to liberty; without, the human character is a stranger to freedom. If you suffer the liberty of speech to be wrested from you, you will then have lost the freedom, the energy, the boldness of the British character...
>
> So if this bill passes you may for a time retain your institution of juries and the forms of your free Constitution, but the substance is gone, the foundation is undermined – your fall is certain and your destruction inevitable. As a tree that is injured at the root and the bark taken off, the branches may live for a while, some sort of blossom may still remain; but it will soon wither, decay, and perish: so take away the freedom of speech or of writing, and the foundation of all your freedom is gone. You will then fall, and be degraded and despised by all the world for your weakness and your folly, in not taking

---

6 Ibid.

care of that which conducted to all your fame, your
greatness, your opulence, and prosperity.[7]

These are powerful words but legal positivism then became
the prevalent philosophy of the late nineteenth century. Rather
than upholding the inalienable rights of the individual, legal
positivism espoused a concept of parliamentary sovereignty
which presumed that everything Parliament does is legally valid.
As a result, the courts would no longer be authorised to question
and potentially overthrow any legislation passed in Parliament.
This approach did not support the notion of inalienable rights,
including the notion of free speech. To the contrary, such
positivism would even be prepared to sacrifice our freedoms if
it eventually led to a 'safer' society overall.

Fortunately, our founding fathers in Australia generally
endorsed the traditional common law approach to individual
rights protection. This approach starts with the individual's full
enjoyment of basic rights to life, liberty and property, with these
fundamental legal rights being subject only to a few limitations
that are established by legislation. Accordingly, our legal system
inherited from England recognised these rights of the individual,
including free speech, as common law rights that not even the
Parliament should abrogate. As noted by Gray, 'free speech is
necessarily inherent in a democratic nation which our founding
fathers clearly intended Australia to be. The founders viewed
freedom of speech as a common law right'.[8]

Of course, the ruling elites have a particular desire to suppress
any speech that might represent a threat to their hegemonic
discourse. The exercise of free speech threatens the status quo
as it risks exposing the agenda of the ruling elites. The focus
of these elites may be not necessarily on legally protecting

---

7 Charles James Fox, 'The Spirit of Liberty - House of Commons, 25 November 1795',
    in Brian MacArthur, *The Penguin Book of Historic Speeches* (Penguin Books, 1996), 148-49.
8 Gray, (n 2), 119.

everyone but only a few selected groups. That being so, free speech can provoke a real embarrassment to privileged groups, especially when a political agenda has been advanced that is contrary to the best interests of the community at large. This makes some political rulers especially inclined to suppress the speech of dissenting voices.[9] It goes without saying that if the political ruler is considered superior to everybody else, as being by the nature of their position allegedly better than others, it follows that it automatically becomes 'wrong' to criticise them openly.

3. The trouble with anti-discrimination laws

It is not difficult to understand why the ruling elites appear so anxious to reduce any threat to their hegemonic discourse. To preserve their vested interests, such individuals are naturally tempted to establish the means by which our basic rights to free speech can be abrogated. These privileged individuals might be driven not so much for a desire to advance the common good, but rather by a desire to obtain undue advantages and secure legal distinctions which today normally take the form of 'affirmative action' and anti-discrimination laws.

There is enough evidence to assume that our elected politicians are advancing policies that are based not on merit but on a person's political, religious or biological characteristics. These laws benefit a few favoured groups at the expense of everybody else. Some targeted groups are especially discriminated against. Accordingly, whereas the *Sex Discrimination Act* is invariably used against men, the *Racial Discrimination Act* is invariably used against white people. These individuals are made to pay for authentic or imaginary 'past discriminations' which they

---

9 Wojciech Sadurski, *Freedom of Speech and its Limits* (Boston: Kluwer International Publishers, 1999), 28

have not personally committed.

The idea of providing preferential treatment solely on grounds of genetic attributes is grossly discriminatory and unfair. However, some laws prevent some individuals from succeeding in their chosen fields on the sole basis of gender and/or colour of skin.[10] Of course, if the person is excluded on the basis of race, gender or sexual orientation, then the democratic principle of equality before the law is profoundly compromised.

The ruling elites are imposing severe sanctions on those who dare to expose an idea or express an opinion that may be deemed 'offensive' to a more favoured group.[11] Of course, there is nothing more undemocratic than preventing someone from expressing his or her political opinions. An authentic democracy requires freedom of political speech for all. By contrast, writes Tammy Bruce, a self-described American 'lesbian feminist advocate',

> The spiral down and away from individual liberty can be traced directly to the rejection of the rights of each persona in favor of the rights of the group. This group-rights mentality is nothing new; it derives from the "progressive" concept that the individual must submit to what is best for everyone else. This concept, however, stems not from the ideal of civil rights but from the well of socialism, the foundational model of the Far Left.[12]

Bruce completes her insightful argument by reminding us that, 'once we accept group theory, it comes not only easier

---

10 Gabriël A. Moens, *Affirmative Action: The New Discrimination* (Sydney: Centre for Independent Studies, 1985), 32-52.

11 See, for instance, Chris Berg, *In Defence of Freedom of Speech: From Ancient Greece to Andrew Bolt* (Institute of Public Affairs, 2012), 177-217; Augusto Zimmermann, 'The State of Freedom of Speech in Australia: Universities, the Media and Society in General', *in* Grzegorz Blicharz (ed.), *Freedom of Speech: A Comparative Law Perspective* (Warsaw: IWS, 2019), 217-278.

12 Tammy Bruce, *The New Thought Police: Inside the Left's Assault on Free Speech and Free Minds* (New York/NY: Three Rivers Press, 2001), 4-5.

to reject individual rights (such as freedom of expression) but also actually essential that we do so'.[13] Another American commentator, Dinesh D'Souza (an Indian, who came to the United States as an exchange student in the late 1970s) argues that affirmative action policies that favour some groups at the expense of others may actually aggravate ethnic and racial conflicts. Apparently, members of groups which benefit under such a policy will be envied by outsiders who will view their achievements solely as the products of preferential treatment. D'Souza concludes that racial division may become the natural consequence of principles that exalt group differences above individual justice.[14]

Gabriël A. Moens AM shares a similar opinion. He argues that affirmative action policies undermine social equality and fairness by submerging individuals 'into whole groups and subject them to certain prophylactic politics which often harm their interests'.[15] Back in the 1990s he started to perceive 'an increasing number of attempts, by governments of both persuasions around Australia, to restrict the right of Australians to freely express their opinion'. Moens then concluded that even if some Australians spoke on issues of concern to them, their views would be ridiculed and not taken seriously by our leaders. Moens also prophetically warned us that we as a nation were 'developing into a society where governments, policymakers and trendsetters seek to impose their view on others, thereby effectively impeding the right of others to express their views with impunity from punishment'.[16]

Unfortunately, all jurisdictions across the nation have now

---

13 Ibid.
14 Dinesh D'Souza, *Illiberal Education: The Politics of Race and Sex on Campus* (New York/NY: The Free Press, 1991), 51.
15 Gabriël A. Moens, *Enduring Ideas: Contributions to Australian Debates* (Connor Court, 2020), 127.
16 Ibid.

developed policies and enacted laws that engender gender-based or ethnic-based discrimination, especially against white males. These laws put an unreasonable burden on free speech. Because they were enacted to give special protections to select constituencies, some individuals are afforded more rights (privileges) than others in the eyes of the law. If we accept the argument of advocates of 'positive discrimination', then we must also accept that some people, including women and homosexuals, are unusually more sensitive to strong criticism. Therefore, any comment that might affect them more than it does others is deemed important enough to be prohibited by law. Not only is this deeply condescending towards these two groups but also an insult to those within these selected groups who are confident enough to not require any form of legal protection to succeed in their own personal lives.

Despite the 1992 cases recognising an implied freedom of political communication,[17] there remains 'a wealth of legislation and practices which impede attempts by Australians to speak out about controversial issues'.[18] Indeed, the political elite arrogantly assumes that they know what is best for the people. Those who dare to question the prevailing orthodoxy are mercilessly ostracised, harassed and even brought to the courts. In Tasmania, the state anti-discrimination law now bans any conduct that 'offends, humiliates, intimidates, insults or ridicules' on the basis of sexual orientation or gender identity.[19]

17 The implied freedom of political communication is a constitutional principle recognised by the High Court in 1992, which effectively prevents the government from dispropor-tionately restricting freedom of political expression. 'The principle is based primarily on an understanding of our system of representative (and responsible) government, which therefore requires that the people and their representatives must be able to communicate in a free and open manner about political matters'. – Johnny Sakr and Augusto Zimmer-mann, 'Judicial Activism and Constitutional (Mis)Interpretation: A Critical Appraisal' (2021) *University of Queensland Law Journal* 119,

18 Ibid. 132.

19 *Anti-Discrimination Act 1998* (Tas), s 17.

In New South Wales,[20] Queensland,[21] and the ACT[22] laws have been enacted to prohibit some forms of discrimination based on conduct that may incite 'hatred', 'serious contempt' or 'severe ridicule'. And South Australia and Western Australia have banned real or perceived discrimination on similar grounds in the workplace, education and other spheres of society.

In 1989, the state of New South Wales, under a Liberal-National Government, enacted its *Anti-Discrimination (Racial Vilification) Amendment Act*, providing for criminal sanction on those whose speech on the grounds of race may incite not only hatred but also 'serious contempt' or 'severe ridicule'. What is most problematic about this is that a person can be punished even if they had no intention to incite hatred, because the legislation does not require that intent be proved. Indeed, all that is required is simply a likelihood that 'hatred' might be stirred up as a result of the comments made. Thus the law overlooks the fact that hatred may be actually 'the product of a totally unreasonable and irrational response on the part of listeners'.[23]

The uncertainty caused by these vague notions ('offend, humiliate, intimidate, insult, or ridicule') creates a chilling effect on individuals and organisations, religious or not. It does so by imposing an unreasonable burden on anyone who wishes to engage in well-meaning discussion concerning public policy. What is more, under the existing laws judges are often instructed to approach the conduct not by community standards but by the standards of the alleged victim group.[24] Testing to the standard of the 'reasonable victim' lowers an already minimal harm threshold, adding further imprecision and uncertainty potential

---

20 *Anti-Discrimination Act 1977* (NSW), s 22A.
21 *Anti-Discrimination Act 1991* (QLD), s 120.
22 *Discrimination Act 1991* (ACT), s 58.
23 Moens, (n 15), 133.
24 Anna Chapman, 'Australian Racial Hatred Law: Some Comments on Reasonableness and Adjudicative Method in Complaints Brought by Indigenous People' (2004) 30 *Monash University Law Review* 27, at 31-32.

to the provisions' deleterious impact on speech.[25]

These laws have become a dangerous means of censoring ideas that are unacceptable to the intellectual orthodoxy. Of course, the ruling elites rely on politicians to enact legislation that censors any speech that might be perceived as 'bigoted' or 'racist' or 'sexist'. According to Eugene Volokh, a UCLA law professor who is known for his elaborated opinions on free speech and religious freedom, 'all it takes to be called a racist is to express skepticism about immigration or to express plausible concerns about, for example, the spread of Islam throughout the world and the like'.[26] He notes that some groups are often trying to silence the others – a dynamic described by him as 'dangerous for freedom'.[27]

A few examples may be used to confirm these statements. In October 2011, Toowoomba GP Dr David van Gend was forced to appear before Queensland's *Anti-Discrimination Commission*, to respond to a complaint about an article that he wrote for *The Courier-Mail* arguing against any change to marriage laws. The complainant, a homosexual activist and serial litigator from New South Wales, claimed the entire point of that article amounted to vilification because he didn't like the doctor's point of view. He stated: 'The lack of a general statement with regards to all families with only a parent of one sex shows how vilifying the statement is towards same-sex families and also fails to recognise the structure of modern families and the involvement of the community around those families in raising children'.[28]

In the letter sent to Dr van Gend the Commission argued that

25 Peter Kurti, 'The Forgotten Freedom: Threats to Religious Liberty in Australia', *CIS Policy Monograph* N.139, *The Centre for Independent Studies*, 2014, 12.
26 Eugene Volokh, in discussion with Billy Hallowell, 15 August 2016. Quoted from: Billy Hallowell, *Faulty Line: How a Seismic Shift in Culture Is Threatening Free Speech and Shaping the Next Generation* (Lake Mary/FL: Frontline, 2017), 136.
27 Ibid.
28 Angela Shanahan, 'Discrimination Police Indulging in Gay Abandon', *The Australian*, October 15, 2011.

its decision to accept the complaint 'does not indicate that the complaint has merit'. The complainant did not even have to appear before the Commission and would suffer no penalty for his non-appearance. His complaint was ultimately withdrawn, but not before the doctor was forced to appear before the Commission and spend a few thousand dollars on legal fees. In Dr van Gend's own words, 'It costs you time, legal expense and anxiety, and although in my case there was very little of any... [O]ther people would not enjoy the experience'.[29]

As another example, conservative political activist Bernard Gaynor has been the subject of 28 complaints during a 24-month period—all lodged by one homosexual person. So far, none of the complaints has been substantiated but Gaynor must head back into costly legal fights that are also part of a strategy to allow laws in one state to be used against those living in another. Gaynor has spent more than $200,000 fending off the legal complaints and has been forced to sell his house fending off the unsuccessful complaints.[30] He correctly believes the system strongly encourages anti-free-speech activists to lodge complaints.[31]

Another notorious example happened with Julian Porteous, the Catholic Archbishop of Tasmania. He was brought to a state commission due to the distribution of a booklet entitled 'Don't mess with Marriage' to parents of Catholic school students in sealed envelopes and in churches.[32] It is hard to overstate how

29 Ibid.
30 Nicola Berkovic, 'Prolific Litigator Garry Burns in Plea for Costs Help', *The Australian*, 4 July 2018. <https://www.theaustralian.com.au/business/legal-affairs/pro-lific-litigator-garry-burns-in-plea-for-costs-help/news-story/5bfc62a6bb3b-24fab6588e1e86055d17>.
31 Nicola Berkovic, 'Tongue-tied by the Thought Police', *The Weekend Australian*, 28 November 2015, 19.
32 Author Unknown, 'Anti-discrimination Complaint an Attempt to Silence the Church Over Same-Sex Marriage, Hobart Archbishop says', *Australian Broadcasting Corporation*, 28 September 2015. <http://www.abc.net.au/news/2015-09-28/anti-discrimination-com-plaint-an-attempt-to-silence-the-church/6810276>.

moderate that booklet was. It was a calm explanation of a major position on a prominent political policy issue.[33] In this carefully written booklet, the church merely expressed its respect for the dignity of homosexuals while promoting the goodness of a man-woman marriage and why children would be affected if they missed out on a mother and father.

Porteous' chief accuser was the Greens candidate for the federal seat of Franklin. She took a complaint to the Tasmanian Anti-Discrimination Commissioner arguing that the booklet 'does immeasurable harm to the wellbeing of same-sex couples and their families across Tasmania'. According to her, the booklet's content breached a section of Tasmania's *Anti-Discrimination Act* that made it illegal to insult, offend or humiliate a person or group on the basis of a listed attribute.[34] In lodging this complaint the plaintiff claimed that the language used in the booklet somehow implied that homosexuals engage in criminal activity because the words 'messing with kids', in her own opinion, can be used as 'a code for sexual abuse or paedophilia'.[35]

Although the accuser withdrew her complaint apparently for tactical reasons ('My primary reason is the tribunal process is a very long and drawn out process and during that time the message of this booklet is going to continue to be spread,' she told AAP), it is deeply disturbing that a Catholic archbishop was dragged to an anti-discrimination authority for merely expressing a traditional view on the subject that until recently was shared by both the major political parties as well as a large segment of the population.

This leaves religious organisations open to attack from outsiders and leaves their practices and beliefs unguarded. Increasingly,

---

33 Chris Berg, 'Same-Sex Marriage: When Did Dissent Become Discrimination', *The Age*, 22 November 2015.
34 Ibid.
35 Above n 30.

homosexual activists are using anti-discrimination laws to prevent dissenting voices from expressing their views in the public square. Their 'take no prisoners' approach means that exceptions in the legislation are likely to be tenuous and narrow, even when such laws might allow 'religious exceptions'. In their view, freedom of speech has always to give way to a higher moral commitment.

Apparently, anyone who dares to criticise the 'homosexual agenda' can be subject to harsh legal treatment. These infringements of free speech are deemed morally right and, what makes it all the more astonishing, perfectly justifiable on grounds of advancing 'tolerance' and 'diversity'.[36] Christian commentator Bill Muehlenberg points out the irony:

> The group that shouts the most about tolerance is the least tolerant... The group that shouts the most about bigotry is the most bigoted... The group that shouts the most about hate is the most hateful. [37]

4. Freedom of political communication and popular sovereignty

Some judges referred to notions of popular sovereignty in the landmark 1992 decisions concerning the implied freedom, in contradiction to the suggestions of parliamentary sovereignty and the idea of politicians having the power to legislate even on the suppression of free speech. This implied freedom would be based not on a notion of parliamentary sovereignty, but rather on the idea of popular sovereignty, which then acknowledges

36 Tom Switzer, 'The Marriage Equality Movement and the New Intolerance', *The Sydney Morning Herald*, 4 September 2017. <http://www.smh.com.au/comment/the-marriage-equality-movement-and-the-new-intolerance-20170902-gy9hyq.html>.

37 Bill Muehlenberg, 'This is How Homosexual Activists 'Debate' – And This is How Democracy Dies', *CultureWatch*, 17 September 2016. <https://billmuehlenberg.com/2016/09/17/homosexual-activists-debate-democracy-dies/> . See also: Bill Muehlenberg, 'Let Me Explain Hate to You', *CultureWatch*, 29 January 2016. <https://billmuehlenberg.com/2015/01/29/let-me-explain-hate-to-you/>

that members of Parliament represent the people and derive their power from their consent.

To exercise their sovereign role, Australians must have their freedom of political communication constitutionally recognised. This freedom must be protected against any Act of Parliament. Accordingly, citizens must enjoy a democratic right to adopt a language that might even induce significant anger, outrage, resentment, hatred, or disgust. Any protection from strong criticism is not a legitimate end compatible with democratic participation.[38] Indeed, no Parliament should be allowed to enact legislation which prevents people from expressing their political opinions freely as this would be incompatible with our system of representative government.[39]

Anthony Gray, one of the nation's leading constitutional law academics, explains how the concept of popular sovereignty should protect free speech from parliamentary interference.[40] As he points out, the High Court should regard as constitutionally invalid any legislation that takes away our freedom of speech to discuss government and political matters. These notions of sovereignty, writes James Weinstein,

> create a very powerful right of free speech. If the people are the ultimate source of political authority, they must be able to speak to each other about all matters within the scope of this authority, that is, on all matters of public concern. If, to the contrary, the government were able to prohibit speech on the ground that it will persuade the populace to formulate erroneous public policy, then that government, not the people, would be the ultimate sovereign. As James Madison argued over two centuries ago, a logical consequence of a commitment to popular sovereignty is that 'the censorial power is in the people over

---

38 Gray, (n 2), 138.
39 *Monis v The Queen* (2013) 249 CLR 92, 134 (French CJ) and 139 (Hayne J).
40 Gray, (n 2), 128.

the government and not in the government over the people.[41]

Australians must be entirely free to talk about political matters. If Australians are a sovereign people, then no government has the power to prevent us from freely and robustly discussing these matters, even when this discussion involves issues which are controversial in the eyes of a privileged minority, and the employment of language may be considered offensive and insulting. Political communication is critical to democratic law-making, and to holding the executive and legislature branches democratically accountable to the people.[42] In *Attorney-General (SA) v Corporation of the City of Adelaide* (2013) Chief Justice French stated:

> Freedom of speech is a long-established common law freedom…linked to the proper functioning of representative democracies and on that basis has informed the application of public interest considerations to claimed restraints upon publication of information.[43]

The extent to which political speech can be offensive was considered by the High Court in *Roberts v Bass*.[44] During the course of judgment (which dealt with untrue allegations made against a member of the South Australian Parliament), Justice Kirby commented that the constitutionally implied freedom protects insults, abuse, and ridicule made in the process of the political communication: 'Political communication in Australia is often robust, exaggerated, angry, mixing fact and comment and commonly appealing to prejudice, fear and self-interest',

---

41 James Weinstein, 'Extreme Speech, Public Order and Democracy: Lessons from The Masses', *in* Ivan Hare and James Weinstein, *Extreme Speech and Democracy* (Oxford University Press, 2009), 26.
42 *Unions NSW* (2013) 252 CLR 530 [28]-[29] (French CJ, Hayne, Crennan, Kiefel and Bell JJ); *ACTV* (1992) 177 CLR 106, 138 (Mason CJ).
43 *Attorney-General (SA) v Corporation of the City of Adelaide* (2013) 249 CLR 1 [43].
44 *Roberts v Bass* (2002) 212 CLR 1.

he said.[45]

This argument was further expanded in *Coleman v Power*.[46] There the majority argued that a law, to be consistent with the implied freedom, cannot prohibit speech of an insulting nature without significant qualifications. Thus McHugh J informed that 'insults are a legitimate part of the political discussion protected by the Constitution'[47] and that, insofar as the insulting words are used in the course of political debate, 'an unqualified prohibition on their use cannot be justified as compatible with the implied freedom'.[48] Justices Gummow and Hayne concurred and added that 'insult and invective have been employed in political communication since the time of Demosthenes'.[49] Justice Kirby then reminded us that Australia's politics has always included 'insult and emotion, calumny and invective', and that the implied freedom must allow for all this.[50] The natural implication of *Roberts v Bass* and *Coleman v Power* is that provisions like s 18C of the *Racial Discrimination Act 1975* (Cth) unreasonably result in a dramatic limitation of free speech in the context of political discussion, and do effectively infringe the implied freedom of political communication.[51]

Preserving freedom of speech is essential to protect a healthy and functioning democracy. However, as seen above, there are numerous legal restrictions which conflict with the implied freedom of political communication. Of course, the most notorious example is s18C making it unlawful to do an act in public that, due to the person's race, colour or national and

---

45 Ibid 63 [171] (Kirby J).
46 *Coleman v Power* (2004) 220 CLR 1
47 Ibid.
48 Ibid per McHugh J [54].
49 Ibid per Gummow and Hayne JJ,[78].
50 Ibid per Kirby [91].
51 The conclusion that the low harm threshold under s 18C establishes a disproportionate 'overreach' that is problematic from the perspective of the implied right to freedom of political communication under the *Australian Constitution* is examined in more detail in, for example, Asaf Fisher, 'Regulating Hate Speech' (2006) (8) *UTS Law Review* 43–5.

ethnic origin, is likely to insult, offend, intimidate or humiliate such a person. Section 18C has, however, survived for over two decades without being challenged in the High Court of Australia.

Under the *Australian Constitution*, sovereignty ultimately resides in the Australian people.[52] Since Australians are sovereign, it is wrong to assert that members of Parliament may speak outrageously but the people in whom sovereignty resides *cannot* speak freely. If anything, a sovereign people shall remain free to speak the unspeakable about political matters.[53] The concept of representative and responsible government is a constitutional imperative intended 'to make the legislature and executive branches of the Commonwealth ultimately answerable to the Australian people'.[54] As sovereign, the people must be free to communicate about government and political matters fully and frankly. This communication is critical to holding the executive and legislature accountable,[55] and to resolving controversial issues at the ballot box.

No society can ever be authentically democratic if only a few privileged individuals can determine how others must participate in public debate and discourse. However, it is possible to state that 'democracy' in Australia has become no more than an elitist competition between privileged members of a small ruling 'elite', with the average citizen serving only as a convenient tool to produce government by means of the occasional vote.[56]

---

52 *Unions NSW* (2013) 252 CLR 530, 548 [17] (French CJ, Hayne, Crennan, Kiefel and Bell JJ). See also *McCloy* (2015) 257 CLR 178 [45] (French CJ, Kiefel, Bell and Keane JJ), [215] (Nettle J), [318] (Gordon J).
53 *Australian Capital Television Pty Ltd v The Commonwealth* (1992) 177 CLR 106, 137-8 (Mason CJ) ('*ACTV*').
54 *Wills* (1992) 177 CLR 1, 47 (Brennan J). Brennan J did note that the intention for representative and responsible government was 'imperfectly effected': see ibid.
55 *Unions NSW* (2013) 252 CLR 530, 551 [28]-[29] (French CJ, Hayne, Crennan, Kiefel and Bell JJ); *ACTV* (1992) 177 CLR 106, 138 (Mason CJ).
56 Yari Wildheart, 'The Last in Line: Implied Association and Literary-Artistic Expression in the Australian Constitution', Thesis Submitted for the Award of Doctor of Philosophy (PhD), *University of Southern Queensland*, 2020, 100.

Given that politicians need to address controversial matters, it is reasonable to accept they must be shielded from claims by parliamentary privilege.[57] This is necessary because of their engagement in robust debate, particularly on controversial issues. What is not reasonable is that the citizens of this nation are not equally free to discuss political matters frankly and robustly, even if they may offend someone in the process. After all, our freedom of political communication is critical for the people to hold their government accountable.

In reality no democratic system is authentic if free speech is interpreted so narrowly as to become mostly non-existing.[58] If Australians are truly sovereign, then free speech 'should be secured in order to protect their political life, and consequently their ability to hold the government accountable'.[59] However, Australia has a long history of suppressing speech and freedom of association. Although members of the government can indulge in unadulterated free speech, the same level of protection is not afforded to the 'sovereign' people in far too many circumstances.

It is not difficult to observe how free speech and freedom of association are intrinsically linked. Freedom of association is an integral part of freedom of political communication. Their goals are undeniably similar, namely the participation and dissemination of ideas and opinions essential to a free and democratic society. Some people associate in order to communicate more effectively. To form an association with a political message should always be fully recognised. In a broader sense, the ability to discriminate on the basis of an organisation's core commitments and values is central to the democratic freedoms of our nation.

---

57 See, for example, *Commonwealth Constitution* s 49; *Parliamentary Privileges Act 1987* (Cth) s 16; *Parliamentary Privileges Act 1891* (WA) s 1.
58 Wildheart, (n 54), 107.
59 Ibid 72.

In a true democracy, freedom of association is central to the ability of electors to hold their government accountable. If citizens cannot be freely associated and exposed to others also freely associating amongst themselves, then a fundamental avenue by which citizens can identify themselves (and find their place in society) is absent.[60] However, in our present political environment censorship is rampant and freedom of association commonly abrogated. Indeed, an analysis of Australia's free-speech jurisprudence would show regular judicial attempts to increase the power of the state at the expense of the powers of the citizen. Over the past two decades the High Court has dropped reference to democracy and its interpretative approach has gradually become more literalistic and detached from the democratic nature of the *Australian Constitution*. With a few exceptions, the Court remains largely uninterested in ongoing legislative attacks on free speech and freedom of association.[61]

As a consequence, free speech and freedom of association are not properly protected. The jurisprudence of the Court needs to be reformed in order to be accompanied by a robust recognition that 'the current system of speech regulation in Australia is impractical and ... not an authentic system for protection of the people's sovereignty'.[62] Of course, it is not just federal law that negatively affects freedom. By censoring legitimate manifestations of political ideas, state-level laws also undermine freedom in a variety of significant ways. If the Court sought to protect the sovereignty of the people, as well as the legitimacy of the legal-institutional framework, then its members would embrace a new jurisprudential approach to the protection of fundamental freedoms, including free speech and freedom of association.[63]

---

60 Ibid 110.
61 Ibid 193.
62 Ibid 164.
63 Ibid 191.

5. *Racial Discrimination Act 1975* (Cth), Section 18C

Under s 18C of the *Racial Discrimination Act 1975* (Cth) (*'RDA'*) it is unlawful for a person to do an act (other than in private) if the act 'is reasonably likely, in all the circumstances, to offend, insult, humiliate or intimidate' a person where the act is done 'because of the race, colour or national or ethnic origin of the other person or of some or all of the people in the group'.[64]

This is an extremely broad prohibition and it represents an extraordinary limitation of freedom of speech. Such a *hurt feelings* test is far below the defamation threshold which applies when a person has been brought into 'hatred, ridicule or contempt'.[65] Rather, the key words used in s 18C –'offend, insult, humiliate'– are imprecise and largely subjective in nature. Indeed, attempts to define them have become 'a circular and question-begging exercise'.[66] The courts have always struggled to provide a sufficiently certain standard for decisively identifying 'insulting' speech, with Lord Reid concluding in *Brutus v Cozens* that 'there can be no [such] definition'.[67]

Although s 18D of the Act provides for a range of exceptions to s18C, with the overriding qualification that the acts in question must have been 'said or done reasonably and in good faith', such qualifications are 'ambiguous terms of art a judge could use to decide whether some speech on political, social, or cultural topics didn't actually qualify for the exemption'.[68] Without clear and defined legislative terms, a judge may exercise an excessive level of personal discretion, thus passing entirely

64 *Racial Discrimination Act 1975* (Cth), Section 18C.
65 David Flint and Jai Martinkovits, *Give us Back our Country: How to Make the Politicians Accountable* (Ballarat/Vic: Connor Court, 2013), 177.
66 Dean Meagher, 'So Far So Good? – A Critical Evaluation of Racial Vilification Laws in Australia' (2004) 32 *Federal Law Review* 225.
67 *Brutus v Cozens* [1972] 2 All ER 1297, 1300.
68 Chris Berg, 'Politics Stands in the Way of a Full 18C Repeal', *The Drum*, 25 March 2014. <http://www.abc.net.au/news/2014-03-25/berg-rda/5344302>.

subjective judgements on the value, morality, or ethics of any statement.

To make it worse, the courts have been instructed to approach the conduct in question not by community standards but by the standards of the alleged victim group.[69] Testing to the standard of the 'reasonable victim' *lowers* an already minimal harm threshold, adding further imprecision and uncertainty to the provision's potential chilling effect on free speech. The result is a remarkable expansion of governmental powers, from the protection of special groups to the protection of specific activities.

Here in this country anyone can be punished for simply voicing comments perceived as 'offensive' by a legally protected group, with such laws creating a more divisive society by fostering an environment of fear and intimidation around those who simply desire to express their opinions. Of course, this should provide enough reason for amending or repealing the provision. However, on 30 March 2017, the Senate rejected proposed changes to s 18C that replaced the phrase 'offend, insult, and humiliate' with the slightly better threshold of *'harass'*. Such change would provide an incipient re-orientation towards the legal protection of free speech.[70] Remarkably, any attempt to remedy this anti-democratic provision was voted down by Labor together with the Greens and a couple of crossbenchers.

Naturally, the low threshold set by the inclusion of the words 'offend, insult, humiliate' raises real questions as to whether this

---

69 Anna Chapman, 'Australian Racial Hatred Law: Some Comments on Reasonableness and Adjudicative Method in Complaints Brought by Indigenous People' (2004) 30 *Monash University Law Review* 31-32.

70 Augusto Zimmermann, 'Failure to Repeal 18C Ignores our Right to Free Speech', *The Australian*, 21 April 2017, <http://www.theaustralian.com.au/business/legal-affairs/failure-to-repeal-18c-ignores-our-right-to-free-speech/news-story/d29feb-6be1e94e595f617b2ba6ffa1de>.

section would be supported by the *Australian Constitution*.[71] Under the *Australian Constitution*, citizens must be able to freely discuss controversial political and governmental matters, including those involving race, colour, ethnicity, or nationality. Such discussions may at times involve employing language that someone may find potentially offensive. As mentioned, in *Coleman* the majority of the High Court held that a law cannot, consistently with the implied freedom, prohibit speech of an insulting nature without significant qualifications. [72]

Between 2010 and 2016 alone, there were more than 800 complaints lodged under s 18C before the Australian Human Rights Commission.[73] This is not a law that is rarely used, but one that is having a significant impact on freedom of speech. Above all, we should never lose sight of the need to reform s 18C or any similar legislation enacted by the Australian states, even despite the rejection of proposed changes to the federal legislation in March 2017. Of course, such an appalling provision is having a very detrimental impact on free speech without having a corresponding positive impact on eliminating racial discrimination. This is self-evident given the secrecy that seems to surround the conciliation process. What follows are a few high-profile cases decided in accordance with s 18C.

---

71 For a detailed constitutional analysis of s 18C, see: Joshua Forrester, Lorraine Finlay and Augusto Zimmermann, *No Offence Intended: Why 18C is Wrong* (Brisbane/Qld: Connor Court, 2016). Our book considers whether s 18C of the *Racial Discrimination Act* is constitutionally valid. We consider both the external affairs power and the implied freedom of political communication in detail, concluding that s 18C in its current form would be vulnerable to a constitutional challenge.

72 *Coleman v Power* (2004) 220 CLR 1.

73 Simon Breheny, *Racial Discrimination Act: Turnbull Should Revisit 18C Repeal Case*, The Australian, April 29, 2016,   <https://www.theaustralian.com.au/business/legal-affairs/racial-discrimination-act-turnbull-should-revisit-18c-repeal-case/news-story/03037ee74deee25572fe2fd41bccf721>.

5.1.   *Eatock v Bolt* **[2011] FCA 1103**

In September 2011, *Herald Sun* columnist Andrew Bolt lost an
action brought in the Australian Federal Court in which he was
accused of contravening s 18C of the *RDA*. At issue was his
assertion in articles published in August 2009 that the applicants
had chosen to identify themselves as Aboriginal in order to access
grants, prices and career advancement, despite their apparently
fair skin and mixed heritage. The applicants submitted that
any criticism of their lack of Aboriginal appearance was 'an
offensive attack on the genuineness of their Aboriginal identity
and the identity of Aboriginal people with light skin'.[74]   By
contrast, the defendants argued that the articles referred to

> an undesirable social trend by which persons of mixed
> heritage identified as exclusively Aboriginal and
> thereby gained access to benefits, some of which were
> publicly funded. It was claimed that this argument
> involved no disparagement of Aboriginal people. On
> the contrary, it was said, the argument was directed
> towards achieving a less racially divided society.[75]

Justice Bromberg decided that Bolt had contravened s 18C
of the Act. He stated that 'fair skinned Aboriginal people (or
some of them) were reasonably likely, in all the circumstances,
to have been offended, insulted, humiliated or intimidated by
the imputations conveyed in the newspaper articles'. Bromberg
went on to find (in para 424) *that* '[e]ven if I had been satisfied
that the s 18C conduct was capable of being a fair comment, I
would not have been satisfied that it was said or noted by Bolt
reasonably and in good faith'.[76]

In other words, this federal judge made it very clear that if you
write something that may offend someone on grounds of race,

---

74 Adrienne Stone, 'The Ironic Aftermath of Eatock v Bolt' (2015) 38 *Melbourne University Law Review* 929.
75 Ibid.
76 *Eatock v Bolt* [2011] FCA 1103 [424].

even if you do so in good faith and assuming that your argument is perfectly reasonable, this is not a necessarily valid defence and you can still be found to have breached s 18C. In reaching the conclusion that Bolt's conduct lacked 'objective good faith', Justice Bromberg relied upon Bolt's apparent 'lack of care and diligence demonstrated by the provocative and inflammatory language and the inclusion of gratuitous asides'. Ironically, however, during the course of the hearing, Bolt's writings 'were painted as being akin to a "eugenics approach" and similar to the writings that led to the Holocaust'. Bolt subsequently protested against such remarks as 'highly offensive', and 'an unforgivable travesty'.[77]

Bolt described the case as 'two years of worry, two weeks in court, and hundreds of thousands of dollars in legal costs'.[78] The newspaper issued this statement after the decision: 'We maintain that the articles were published as part of an important discussion on a matter of public interest. We defended the action because we believe that all Australians ought to have the right to express their opinions freely, even where their opinions are controversial or unpopular'.[79] However, both Bolt and the publisher decided not to appeal. They complied with the judicial decision to run a prominent corrective notice on the opinion page views within a fortnight in a 'position adjacent' to Bolt's regular column. Justice Bromberg also awarded costs against the publisher in favour of the applicant. According to Jonathan Holmes, presenter of ABC TV's *Media Watch*, the conclusion to be reached after this decision is that s 18C

> sets a disturbingly low bar... So it never seemed to

---

77 Michael Bodey, 'Andrew Bolt Loses Racial Vilification Court Case', *The Australian*, September 28, 2011. <https://www.theaustralian.com.au/business/media/andrew-bolt-x-racial-vilification-court-case/news-story/3c920f44a5d5e4bf26fd3119588c3fb2>.

78 Jonathan Holmes, 'Bolt, Bromberg, and a Profoundly Disturbing Judgment', *ABC - The Drum*, 30 September 2011. <http://www.abc.net.au/news/2011-09-29/holmes-bolt-bromberg-and-a-profoundly-disturbing-judgment/3038156>.

79 Bodey, (n 75).

most observers likely that a court wouldn't find that the columns were unlawful under section 18C. In my view, that is why section 18C shouldn't be in a part of the act which claims in its heading to be about the "Prohibition of offensive behaviour based on racial hatred". Whatever you think of Bolt's columns, they were clearly not based on or motivated by racial hatred ... [T]his judgement reinforces all the concerns that its opponents had when the [federal] government added Part 2A to the Racial Discrimination Act in 1995. It creates one particular area of public life where speech is regulated by tests that simply don't apply anywhere else, and in which judges – never, for all their pontifications, as friends of free speech – get to do the regulating.[80]

5.2.   *Prior v QUT* [2016] FCCA 2853

The case involving Cindy Prior, a Queensland University of Technology lecturer, provides another compelling example of the impact of s 18C on freedom of speech. Prior made a claim under s 18C for slightly less than AU$250,000 against a staff member and a couple of students. She also sued QUT and two other staff members under separate provisions of the *RDA*.[81]

Prior filed a complaint on the basis of comments made following her decision to eject three students from an indigenous-only computer lab, in 2013. On 28 May 2013, Alex Wood and two other students were using a QUT computer lab when Prior asked them whether they were indigenous. They replied they weren't. Prior then asked them to leave. She said the room was an indigenous space for Aboriginal and Torres Strait students,

---

80 Holmes, (n 76).
81 See: Lorraine Finlay, Augusto Zimmermann and Joshua Forrester, 'Section 18C is Too Broad and Too Vague, and Should Be Repealed', *The Conversation*, 31 August 2016 <https://theconversation.com/section-18c-is-too-broad-and-too-vague-and-should-be-repealed-64482>; see also: Augusto Zimmermann, Joshua Forrester and Lorraine Finlay, '18c May Render All Speech Inoffensive', *Newsweekly*, 26 March 2016, 12-3

only.

Later that day, on the *QUT Stalkerspace* Facebook page, Wood posted: 'Just got kicked out of the unsigned Indigenous computer room. QUT stopping segregation with segregation…?' Many people commented. Jackson Powell posted 'I wonder where the white supremacist computer lab is…' and a number of subsequent related comments. Prior alleged that Callum Thwaites posted 'ITT niggers'. [82] A claim that Thwaites has always categorically denied.[83] Prior's action also cited a student writing on the Facebook page: 'My Student and Amenity fees are going to furbish rooms in the university where inequality reigns supreme? … All this does is encourage separation and inequality.'

The tone and content of the comments by the students varied considerably. Most were mild; some weren't. However, all concerned a matter that is clearly one of public concern: whether publicly-funded universities should have separate facilities for certain racial groups. Naturally, the very fact that a claim can be made on the basis of these facts in the first place highlights the problems with the low harm threshold established by s 18C. In many respects, 'the process is the punishment', particularly in a context where an allegation of racism inevitably carries with it special opprobrium in the community. There is no way to accurately measure the indirect 'chilling effect' that such ill-conceived provisions may have, when legal action can be commenced based on occurrences that fall well short of the types of serious and egregious examples of racial hatred that the community would ordinarily view as justifying intervention by the state.

Prior complained to the university administration about these

---

82 Finlay et al., (n 81).
83 Hedley Thomas, 'Offer to Drop QUT Race "Slur" Case for $5000', *The Australian*, 4 February 2016.

comments, which were promptly removed. However, she was unhappy with QUT's handling of the matter and lodged a complaint against ten respondents (including the three students) in the Australian Human Rights Commission ('AHRC'). Curiously, a fellow lecturer, Dr Sharon Hayes, was also accused in Prior's claim for stating that 'it seems a bit silly' to evict students from a computer lab for not being indigenous when there are computers not being used in the room. She suggested that Prior may have been in breach of the QUT anti-discrimination policy by asking whether the students were indigenous. Prior claims that she felt 'sick, furious and distraught' after Dr Hayes's comments.

Above all, Prior argued that these comments were racist and that they caused her to suffer 'offence, embarrassment, humiliation and psychiatric injury'. She didn't feel safe and was worried about being verbally abused or physically assaulted. QUT's equity director, Mary Kelly (one of the other staff members being sued in Prior's legal action) reviewed the matter. She removed some of the Facebook posts, and told Prior that three students had personally taken down their material. In a further meeting, she told Prior: 'With the small amount of contact I've had with the students, it is clear that these students aren't racist'.[84]

Unfortunately this was not considered to be good enough. Prior advised that she was still going to complain about their comments to the AHRC. The AHRC conciliated Prior's complaint. However, it did not contact the students directly about the complaint or the conciliation conference. Instead, it left this task to QUT, who ended up not knowing about Prior's complaint until after the conciliation conference.[85]

---

84 Finlay et al., (n 81).
85 H. Thomas, *Watchdog Kept 18C Respondent in the Dark About QUT Complaint*, The Australian, February 7, 2016, <https://www.theaustralian.com.au/national-affairs/indigenous/watchdog-kept-18c-respondent-in-the-dark-about-qut-complaint/news-story/b5aa4706ba62548bd20353bd1682f31b>.

Conciliation failed and so Prior commenced proceedings in the Federal Circuit Court. The AHRC determined in August 2015 that there was 'no reasonable prospect of the matter being settled by conciliation', resulting in Prior filing her claim in the Federal Circuit Court. She argued that the Facebook posts were 'reasonably likely to offend, insult, humiliate or intimidate her'. Her claim was for $247,570.52 included lost wages from 29 May 2013 to 6 September 2015.

Fortunately, in November 2016 the Federal Circuit Court dismissed Cindy Prior's case against QUT students Alex Wood, Callum Thwaites, and Jackson Powell. Because Judge Jarrett held that Prior's claim had no reasonable prospect of success, one might say that decisions like this prove that the system works: an unmeritorious claim was dismissed at an early stage.

However, this case in fact highlights significant problems with the provision.[86] First, the process itself is the punishment. A summary dismissal application involves the filing of pleadings, affidavits and submissions, and appearance in court. There are significant costs in time, money, and stress. Indeed, the cost to defendants may run into hundreds of thousands of dollars. Most people cannot afford to defend themselves, and legal aid is unavailable.[87] Hence, it is unsurprising that other QUT students settled their cases with Prior for $5,000,[88] even though they probably could have successfully defended themselves.

In addition to the costs in time and stress, and despite being 'cleared', the QUT students' reputations have suffered enormously. The stain of being an alleged racist will be hard

86 See: J. Forrester, A. Zimmermann, and L. Finlay, *QUT Discrimination Case Exposes Human Rights Commission Failings*, The Conversation, November 7, 2016, <https://the-conversation.com/qut-discrimination-case-exposes-human-rights-commission-failings-68235#comment_1124894>.
87 A. Morris, *There Will Never Be Winners Under Section 18C As It Stands*, The Australian, August 24, 2016 <https://www.theaustralian.com.au/opinion/there-will-never-be-winners-under-section-18c-as-it-stands/news-story/1bacb30956b99217e34116f222196ff2>.
88 Thomas, (n 85).

to remove. One of the defendants abandoned becoming a schoolteacher because parents or students may Google his name and find he was accused of racism.[89] Finally, the dismissal of this case by a federal judge raises the question as to why the AHRC did not initially reject Prior's complaints. By failing to do so, the AHRC seriously misled the complainant into believing she had any chance of winning a frivolous case in which she had no chance of succeeding. That the AHRC proceeded to conciliation may have given Prior false hope that her case had merit.

5.3.   *Dinnison v Leak* [2016] AHRC

The AHRC's investigation into cartoonist Bill Leak was triggered by Melissa Dinnison, an Australian Caucasian who lived in Germany at the time her complaint was lodged. She claimed to have experienced 'racial hatred' as a result of a cartoon which depicted an Aboriginal police officer, presenting a wayward child to his father, saying, 'You'll have to sit down and talk to your son about personal responsibility', to which the father replies, 'Yeah righto, what's his name then?'

Dinnison, a self-described 25-year-old "Indigenous student", said the cartoon was 'humiliating' and that she has 'no sympathy' for Leak.[90] By claiming to have felt deeply offended by the cartoon, she submitted from Germany (where she was completing a university exchange) a complaint to the AHRC. Curiously, on the same day the cartoon was published, the AHRC's Race Discrimination Commissioner (Tim Soutphommasane) used social media to urge people to lodge complaints about it with

---

89 H. Thomas, *Section 18C Teaching: Cases Can End Dreams*, The Australian, August 24, 2016, <https://www.theaustralian.com.au/higher-education/section-18c-teaching-cases-can-end-dreams/news-story/dee28734e8ead0efd89243ed4e471caf>.

90 Ange McCormick, 'I Felt Degraded, Humiliated: Meet the Woman Who Took Bill Leak's Cartoon to the Human Rights Commission', *ABC – Triple J Hack*, 16 November 2016 <http://www.abc.net.au/triplej/programs/hack/why-i-took-bill-leak-cartoon-to-the-human-rights-commission/8030268>.

the AHRC.

Leak complained that his life was 'thrown into utter chaos' during the process. He said this about the complainant: 'She has put me through a month or so of incredible stress. As a consequence my life has been thrown into utter chaos. I've got News Corp backing me legally. But if I was a private citizen, this would have cost me an absolute fortune'. But Leak also said 'he was coping and still had the strength for the fight'.[91] In his submission to the federal *Parliamentary Joint Committee* on 'Freedom of Speech in Australia', Leak commented:

> The cartoon in question was drawn in the context of a raging debate about aboriginal issues that had been triggered by a Four Corners Program about conditions inside a juvenile detention centre in the Northern Territory. My intention was to try to draw attention to the fact that the high level of parental neglect and abuse of children in many Aboriginal communities is one of the underlying reasons why the disproportionally high number of 97% of the inmates in the detention centre were indigenous.[92]

Unfortunately, on 10 March 2017 Bill Leak died of a massive heart attack after being dragged through the AHRC.[93] In the words of Keith Windschuttle, '[he] was the greatest cartoonist of his era... We were lucky to live in a country made so much better by his dedication to its deepest ideals'.[94] A few days

---

91 Roger Franklin, 'Bill Leak and His Persecutors', *Quadrant*, 10 March 2017 <https://quadrant.org.au/opinion/qed/2017/03/bill-leak-persecutors/>.

92 Bill Leak, 'Bill Leak's Full Submission to 18C Parliamentary Inquiry', *The Australian*, 12 March 2017 <https://www.theaustralian.com.au/national-affairs/bill-leaks-full-submission-to-18c-parliamentary-inquiry/news-story/41472906b6842d0ba81cdb08b4f-40b8a>.

93 James Allan, 'If Only Turnbull Had Bill Leak's Spine', *Quadrant*, 10 March 2017 <https://quadrant.org.au/opinion/qed/2017/03/turnbull-bills-principles-spine/>.

94 'Bill Leak was the greatest cartoonist of his era and deserves comparison with David Low, the greatest cartoonist of his era, from the First World War to the 1950s. Both initially made their names on *The Bulletin* magazine in Sydney as left-of-centre satirists but eventually went on to become the most powerful foes of left-wing authoritarianism in all its forms'. – Keith Windschuttle, 'Bill Leak and David Low', *Quadrant*, 10 March 2017 <https://quadrant.org.au/opinion/qed/2017/03/bill-leak-david-low/>.

before he passed away, Leak commented:

> I find it difficult to believe a complaint under 18C
> had been filed against me and I was subject to
> an investigation by the Australian Human Rights
> Commission because a cartoon I had drawn was
> deemed likely to 'offend' on basis of race. Far from
> seeking to malign indigenous people on the basis
> of their race, my cartoon aimed to expose the truth
> about the appalling levels of violence endured by
> Aboriginal women and children. It was nothing
> more, and nothing less than an entirely reasonable,
> and considered, expression of a view on a subject of
> intense public interest and yet, incredibly, it resulted
> in me not only being publicly vilified as a racist by
> anonymous 'social justice warriors' on social media
> but also being persecuted by an agency of the state.[95]

A few more cases could be provided but I hope this gives a good idea of what is happening. Of course, it should also be noted that it is hard to see how s 18C is supposed to educate people about what they can and cannot say when the vast majority of complaints before the AHRC do not even make it into the public arena. Most complaints do not make it to court and are settled behind closed doors, so people would not even be aware of how often the provision has been invoked. However, even when a complaint is not upheld, there are two particularly serious consequences that arise. Firstly, those complained against are required to expend considerable resources defending themselves regardless of whether that complaint is ultimately upheld or not; and, secondly, Australians increasingly fear discussing certain topics because they know that laws like s18C can make what they say unlawful.

---

95 Leak, (n 94).

6. Final considerations

The Greek philosopher Socrates became a martyr for the cause of free speech when he was put to death for posing a threat to the established order.[96] Ever since, free speech has been acknowledged as a fundamental right of every free individual. Accordingly, democracy demands the constitutional protection of free speech. This right of the citizen works as a mechanism to avoid not only the free exchange of ideas but also the concentration of power in the hands of a few.[97]

Despite a supposed implied, constitutional freedom of political communication, many Australians have found themselves at the receiving end of expensive legal action for merely expressing opinions that are no longer accepted by the ruling classes. Allowing the speech of some while prohibiting the speech of others unfairly favours one side of the debate over another. This goes against the democratic principle of equality before the law.[98]

In a democracy all power emanates from the people, who exercise it by means of elected representatives or more directly, as provided by the law. These representatives must be accountable to the people they are serving, having the obligation to take their views into account. Since the members of Parliament are free to discuss political matters on behalf of their electorate, this same freedom should be automatically extended to all those who have elected them to exercise power on their behalf. This would allow us to discuss political issues without risking punitive lawsuits based on laws that contradict the most elementary principles of democracy and the rule of law.

---

96 Gray, (n 2), 5.

97 Alexander Tsesis, 'Free Speech Constitutionalism' (2015) (3) *University of Illinois Law Review* 1021, 1042-43.

98 Lipsett, (n 1).

5

The importance of Gageler and Gordon JJ's continuing dissent against structured proportionality

Thomas Boyle

Abstract

In 2021 a majority of the High Court applied structured proportionality – an analytical tool used since 2013 in implied freedom of political communication cases – to a constitutional challenge under s 92. This evidenced the Court's willingness to extend the use of structured proportionality to other aspects of Australian constitutional law. It also confirmed a common thread in the cases which considered structured proportionality which is that Justices Gageler and Gordon do not believe it an appropriate tool of analysis for constitutional questions.

Rather than make an argument on the merits of any proposed alternative, this chapter places their Honours' objections in the context of broader constitutional jurisprudence. This reveals two bases to the rejection of structured proportionality. First, it does not conform with the legalist tradition of the High Court and the tradition of the common law. Second, the strictness and rigidity of structured proportionality does not leave enough room for judicial deference and risks the Court making a value judgment as to the merits of proposed legislation. These are not superficial grounds for dissent and explain the continuing opposition of the two justices and firm ground for prediction that their dissent will not soon abate.

Keywords

Constitutional law, implied freedom of political communication, section 92, proportionality, structured proportionality, legalism, separation of powers

Introduction

In the context of rights and freedoms, proportionality has been used in many jurisdictions to determine whether the legislative arm of government has gone too far. In Australia, however, the use of the test is in its infancy. To decide that a sovereign government has gone further than the law (*Constitution*) allowed was always going to be difficult for judges trained in deference to legislative authority, like those in Australia. Justice Isaacs, in 1926, framed this tension as a serious and responsible duty of the High Court:

> It is always a serious and responsible duty to declare invalid, regardless of consequences, what the national Parliament, representing the whole people of Australia, has considered necessary or desirable for public welfare...Unless, therefore, it becomes clear beyond reasonable doubt that the legislation in question transgresses the limits laid down by the organic law of the Constitution it must be allowed to stand as the true expression of the national will.[1]

---

1 *Federal Commissioner of Taxation v Munro* (1926) 38 CLR 153, 180 approved by the Privy Council in *Shell Company of Australia Ltd v Federal Commissioner of Taxation* (1930) 44 CLR 530.

Although this was new territory, the Supreme Court of the United States had pioneered the process.[2] But US Supreme Court jurisprudence did not answer all the questions; unlike the *Australian Constitution* the *US Constitution* entrenched a Bill of Rights which vested in US Supreme Court judges more power to overrule their legislature. Further, American jurisprudence was restricted in its application by Australian judges after the *Amalgamated Society of Engineers v Adelaide Steamship Co Ltd* (*'Engineers' Case'*) decision.[3]

So, how were Australian judges to give due deference to the legislative arm of government while ruling that they had overstepped in a respectful and predictable way that accorded with the rule of law? Both of these ideas found their way into the High Court of Australia's jurisprudence when s 51(vi) of the *Constitution* had to be interpreted during and after a major war.[4] The issue became even more pressing when the Court found the implied freedom of political communication in the words and structure of the *Constitution* in 1992.[5] Now, Australian laws could be deemed invalid if they were considered by the High Court to unnecessarily and unjustifiably burden this new implied freedom. Consequently, the following questions required resolution:

1   How   were   lower   judges   to   decide   whether   a

---

2 See, eg, *Near v Minnesota*, 283 US 697 (1931); Geoffrey R Stone, 'Restrictions of Speech Because of Its Content: The Peculiar Case of Subject-Matter Restrictions' (1978) 46 *University of Chicago Law Review* 81; Kenneth L Karst, 'Equality as a Central Principle in the First Amendment' (1975) 43 *University of Chicago Law Review* 20; Frederick Schauer, 'Codifying the First Amendment: *New York v Ferber*' [1982] *Supreme Court Review* 285.

3 *Amalgamated Society of Engineers v Adelaide Steamship Co Ltd* (1920) 28 CLR 129 ('*Engineers' Case*') 'But we conceive those American authorities, however illustrious the tribunals may be, are not a secure basis on which to build fundamentally with respect to our own Constitution. While in secondary and subsidiary matters they may, and sometimes do, afford considerable light and assistance, they cannot…be recognised as standards whereby to measure the respective rights of the Commonwealth and States under the Australian Constitution.' at 146 (Knox CJ, Isaacs, Rich and Starke JJ).

4 See, eg, *Stenhouse v Coleman* (1944) 69 CLR 457.

5 *Australian Capital Television Pty Ltd v Commonwealth* (1992) 177 CLR 106 ('*ACTV*'); *Nationwide News Pty Ltd v Wills* (1992) 177 CLR 1 ('*Nationwide*').

Commonwealth or state law intruded too far into the freedom of political communication?

2   What interpretive tests were to be used?

3   How were lawyers to advise their clients about the impact of this new implied freedom?

Without clear guidance, Professor Adrienne Stone observed that accurate interpretation or prediction may become a matter of assessing the values of the High Court judges who decided a particular case.[6]

As the jurisprudence of the implied freedom has developed, the Court has continued to explore the standard of review it should apply. This resulted in a method of analysis called structured proportionality. A majority of the High Court settled its usage, in the context of the implied freedom of political communication, in *McCloy v New South Wales* (*'McCloy'*).[7] The Court's two newest members, Steward and Gleeson JJ, seemingly agree.[8] However, Gageler and Gordon JJ continue to reject its usage.

A   The significance of proportionality

An early example of proportionality testing as a means of determining legislative overstep is seen in Dixon J's 1933 judgment *Williams v Melbourne Corporation*.[9] There, his Honour said that the question was whether the impugned law went 'beyond any restraint which could reasonably be adopted' for the

---

6 See, Adrienne Stone, 'The Limits of Constitutional Text and Structure: Standards of Review and the Freedom of Political Communication' (1999) 23(3) *Melbourne University Law Review* 668. 'Thus, reasoning about the freedom of political communication *will* involve reference to values that are external to the *Constitution* and the High Court can only choose whether to express those values in rules or whether to allow them to remain unexpressed through the use of an incompletely theorised test.' at 704.
7 *McCloy v New South Wales* (2015) 257 CLR 178,193-195 [2], 217 [79] (*'McCloy'*).
8 *LibertyWorks Inc v Commonwealth of Australia* [2021] HCA 18 [44] (Kiefel CJ, Keane and Gleeson JJ); [298] (Steward J) (*'LibertyWorks'*).
9 *Williams v Melbourne Corporation* (1933) 49 CLR 142,155-156.

specific purpose it intended.[10] Since *McCloy,* a majority of the High Court have accepted the use of structured proportionality to assess whether a piece of legislation impermissibly burdens the implied freedom of political communication.[11] Justice Edelman has said that it is unsurprising that a structured proportionality analysis has been adopted by 'virtually every effective system of constitutional justice in the world'.[12] Additionally, the introduction of structured proportionality to answer questions concerning the freedom of interstate trade, commerce and intercourse under s 92 was recently seen in *Palmer v Western Australia ('Palmer').*[13]

Gageler and Gordon JJ have, however, persistently dissented against the use of the test.[14] This dissent is important to understand because it reveals an underlying tension in the High Court. The significance of this tension was highlighted by Steward J in the recent *LibertyWorks v Commonwealth* (*'LibertyWorks'*) decision:

> The divergence of views in this Court concerning the test for the application of the implied freedom perhaps may illustrate the tenuous nature of that implication. If the content of the implied freedom cannot even now be agreed upon, then, for my part,

---

10 Ibid 156.

11 *LibertyWorks* (n 8), 18 [48] (Kiefel CJ, Keane and Gleeson JJ) citing *Brown v Tasmania* (2017) 261 CLR 328, 368-369 [123]-[127] (Kiefel CJ, Bell and Keane JJ) 416-417 [278] (Nettle J); *Unions NSW v New South Wales* (2019) 264 CLR 595, 615 [42] (Kiefel CJ, Bell and Keane JJ), 638 [110] (Nettle J), 653–656 [161]–[167] (Edelman J); *Clubb v Edwards* (2019) 267 CLR 171, 208-209 [96]–[102] (Kiefel CJ, Keane and Bell JJ), 266-269 [270]-[275] (Nettle J), 341– 345 [491]–[501] (Edelman J); *Comcare v Banerji* (2019) 267 CLR 373, 402–405 [38]–[42] (Kiefel CJ, Bell, Keane and Nettle JJ), 455–458 [202]–[206] (Edelman J).

12 *Clubb v Edwards* (2019) 267 CLR 171, 331 [466] (Edelman J) (*'Clubb'*); Alec Stone Sweet and Jud Mathews, 'Proportionality Balancing and Global Constitutionalism' (2008) 47 *Columbia Journal of Transnational Law* 72, 74; Aharon Barak, *Proportionality: Constitutional Rights and their Limitations* (Cambridge University Press, 2012) 181-210.

13 *Palmer v Western Australia* (2021) 95 ALJR 229 (*'Palmer'*)

14 See, eg, *Tajjour v New South Wales* (2014) 254 CLR 508, 579-581 [148]-[152]; *Brown v Tasmania* (2017) 261 CLR 328, 389-391 [200]-[206]; *Clubb v Edwards* (2019) 267 CLR 171, 225 [161]-[162] (Gageler J); *Comcare v Banerji* (2019) 267 CLR 373, 408–409 [53]–[54] (Gageler J).

that may demonstrate that it was never justified.[15]

The law should be predictable, and we should easily be able to scrutinise 'the reasons for the rules which we follow'.[16] Constitutional freedoms and the rules that underpin them are grounded in the notion of democracy and the rule of law. Justice Dixon in *Australian Communist Party v The Commonwealth* said that the rule of law is an assumption which underlies the *Constitution*.[17] The majority of the Court in *McCloy* made the similarly obvious—but ultimately necessary—observation that:

> In a system operating according to a separation of powers, judicial restraint should be understood to require no more than that the courts undertake their role without intruding into that of the legislature.[18]

B   Approach to this analysis

Part II of this chapter explains the importance of analysing structured proportionality when considering constitutional freedoms. The concept of proportionality is said to have emerged in 18th century Prussian public law with the understanding that natural law mandated that a government's use of police powers should be proportionate.[19] *Structured* proportionality is said to have emanated from German public law (*"Verhältnismäßigkeit"*)[20] from where it has slowly crept

---

15 *LibertyWorks* (n 8) [298] (Steward J).

16 Oliver Wendell Holmes, 'Law in Science and Science in Law' (1899) 12 *Harvard Law Review* 443, 460 cited in *Palmer* (n 13) [145] (Gageler J).

17 (1951) 83 CLR 1. 'Moreover, it is government under the Constitution and that is an instrument framed in accordance with many traditional conceptions, to some of which it gives effect, as, for example, in separating the judicial power from other functions of government, others of which are simply assumed. Among these I think that it may fairly be said that the rule of law forms an assumption.', at 193.

18 *McCloy* (n 7) 216 [77] (French CJ, Kiefel, Bell and Keane JJ).

19 Shipra Chordia, *Proportionality in Australian Constitutional Law* (The Federation Press, 2020) 18.

20 Susan Kiefel, 'Proportionality: A Rule of reason' (2012) 23 *Public Law Review* 85. *Verhältnismäßigkeit* roughly translates to 'proportionality' or 'relativity', but it has been suggested it is closer in meaning to 'reasonableness', at 87.

to Canada,[21] the United Kingdom[22] and New Zealand,[23] before its entry into Australia.[24] Its Australian version requires three sequential inquiries into the 'suitability', 'necessity' and 'adequacy of balance' of an impugned law.[25]

Part III three examines the ascent of structured proportionality in Australia which culminated in its adoption in *McCloy*. This chapter also considers the concept of proportionality in the constitutional context of the High Court's legalist tradition. Then it highlights some of the key differences between the majority's acceptance of proportionality and the counterarguments given by Gageler and Gordon JJ and it analyses the recent decisions of *Palmer* and *LibertyWorks*.

Part IV considers what can be extrapolated from Gageler and Gordon JJ's rejection of structured proportionality and defines the themes which underly the rejection. It seeks to contextualise the opposition of Gageler and Gordon JJ within the history of Australian constitutional law - specifically, the conflict between the test and the High Court's legalist tradition. It concludes by explaining how structured proportionality in both its rigidity and origins, risks breaching the separation of powers and neglects the importance of judicial deference where a court is asked to invalidate the decisions of the legislature.

What is structured proportionality?

Chief Justice French said that proportionality is not a legal doctrine, but an analytical tool.[26] Chief Justice Kiefel said it is

---

21 See, eg, *R v Oakes* [1986] 1 SCR 103, 138-139 (Dickson CJ)

22 See, eg, *Bank Mellat v Her Majesty's Treasury (No 2)* [2014] 2 AC 700, 771 (Lord Sumption JSC), 790-791 (Lord Reed JSC).

23 *R v Hansen* [2007] NZSC 7 [103]-[104] (Tipping J).

24 *Palmer* (n 13) [143] (Gageler J).

25 Ibid.

26 *Attorney-General (SA) v Corporation the City of Adelaide* (2013) 249 CLR 1. 37 [53]-[55] (French CJ). Janina Boughey, 'Brett Cattle: New Limits on Delegated Law-making Powers?' (2020) 31 *Public Law Review* 347. Boughey says that proportionality is also a 'protean term referring to a range of legal tools that address different questions.' at 350.

'employed as a concept and an ideal; as a test and a conclusion. Its legal basis is reason.'[27] For Professor Stone proportionality is a 'highly substantive doctrine' for enforcing 'strong conceptions of constitutional rights' or a tool which enables assessment of the validity of a law that burdens a constitutional requirement.[28] The former describes foreign constitutional contexts; the latter, Australia.[29]

A The Constitutional Context

The majority in *McCloy* acknowledged that proportionality should be approached in light of a jurisdiction's constitutional, historical and institutional backgrounds.[30] For Australia, this is the principle of legalism. Australian legalism has been described as the application of legal rules and principles of interpretation; not reliance on the subjective values of individual justices.[31] Sir Owen Dixon believed there was no safer guide to the High Court's adjudication than through a 'strict and complete legalism'.[32] Professor Zines has remarked that this concept should be 'common knowledge' to Australian lawyers.[33]

---

27 Susan Kiefel, 'Proportionality: A Rule of reason' (2012) 23 *Public Law Review* 85.
28 Adrienne Stone, 'Proportionality and Its Alternatives' (2020) 48(1) Federal Law Review 123, 125.
29 Carlos Bernal, 'The Migration of Proportionality to Australia' (2020) 48(2) *Federal Law Review* 288, 289.
30 *McCloy* (n 7) 215 [72]. See, also, Barak (n 95).
31 Sir Anthony Mason, 'The Role of a Constitutional Court in a Federation: A Comparison of the Australian and the United States Experience' (1986) 16 *Federal Law Review* 1, 5; Sir Owen Dixon, *Jesting Pilate and Other Papers and Addresses* (Law Book, 1965). 'But it is a safe generalisation that courts proceed upon the basis that the conclusion of the judge should not be subjective or personal to him but should be the consequence of his best endeavour to apply an external standard' at 157.
32 *Swearing in of Sir Owen Dixon as Chief Justice* (1952) 85 CLR xi, xiv: 'Such a function has led us to all I think believe that close adherence to legal reasoning is the only way to maintain the confidence of all parties in federal conflicts. It may be that the Court is thought to be excessively legalistic. I should be sorry to think that it is anything else. There is no other safe guide to judicial decisions in great conflicts than a strict and complete legalism.'
33 Leslie Zines 'Legalism, Realism and Judicial Rhetoric in Constitutional Law' in Nye Perram and Rachel Pepper (eds), *The Byers Lectures: 2000-2012* (Federation Press, 2012) 50.

Gageler J analysed this idea, and legalism more broadly, in a 1987 article[34] that he still adhered to when later a justice of the High Court.[35] He wrote:

> What legalism has meant is the persistence of a practice of constitutional argument based on the belief that the Constitution sets definite substantive limits on government power and that it is possible for the judiciary to determine those substantive limits simply by a process of interpretative judgment based on the letter and spirit of the constitutional text. It has involved the belief that the Court can and must draw lines to contain government power and that adherence to the strict analytical and conceptual techniques of formal legal argument provides the only sure method of approaching what is necessarily a sensitive political function.[36]

His Honour further drew attention to Sir Isaac Isaacs in the *Engineers' Case*, who declaimed the judiciary's determination of 'political necessities'.[37] Gageler J noted that the substantive part of the *Engineers'* case begins with a statement on the High Court's role in constitutional adjudication: the *Constitution* is a legal and political document.[38] The Court in the *Engineers' Case* also acknowledged that:

> [A] judicial tribunal has nothing to do with the policy of an Act which it may be called upon to interpret...[t]he duty of the Court, and its only duty, is to expound the language of the Act in accordance with the settled rules of construction.[39]

---

34 Stephen Gageler, 'Foundations of Australian Federalism and the Role of Judicial Review' (1987) 17(3) *Federal Law Review* 162

35 Stephen Gageler 'Beyond the Text: A Vision of the Structure and Function of the Constitution' in Nye Perram and Rachel Pepper (eds), *The Byers Lectures: 2000-2012* (Federation Press, 2012) 202.

36 Gageler (n 34) 176.

37 Ibid citing *Engineers' Case* (n 3) 151.

38 Ibid 184.

39 *Engineers' Case* (n 3) 142 citing *Vacher & Sons Ltd v London Society of Compositors* [1913] AC 107, 118 (Lord Macnaghten).

Dixon J, writing in the context of the defence power, similarly remarked in *Stenhouse v Coleman*:

> But where the validity of a legislative instrument is affected by what is planned or is going forward in relation to the prosecution of the war, the presumption is, so to speak, reinforced by the respect which the court pays to the opinion or judgment of other organs of government with whom the responsibility for carrying on the war rests. When, for example, it appears that a challenged regulation is a means adopted to secure some end relating to the prosecution of the war, **the court does not substitute that of the Executive with its own opinion of the appropriateness or sufficiency of the means to promote the desired end.**[40]

These comments suggest an existing level of judicial deference in questions of constitutional invalidity determined by the High Court. Deference has been described as the process through which 'judges assign varying degrees of weight to the judgments of the elected branches.'[41] Sir Anthony Mason has said that the term has been viewed with disfavour in Australia and England and is better expressed as 'respect' for the authority of the legislature.[42] Additionally, Roux notes that the foundational approach in the *Engineers' Case* is already deferent.[43] But deference is also evident in implied freedom cases. An early example is Brennan J's caution that the High Court's role is supervisory: '[the Court] declares whether a balance struck by Parliament is within or without the range of legislative choice.'[44]

---

40 *Stenhouse v Coleman* (1944) 69 CLR 457, 470 (Dixon J) (emphasis added).
41 Aileen Kavanagh, 'Defending Deference in Public Law and Constitutional Theory' (2010) 126 *Law Quarterly Review* 222, 223.
42 Sir Anthony Mason, 'Proportionality and Calibrated Scrutiny: A Commentary' (2020) 48(2) *Federal Law Review* 286.
43 Theunis Roux, 'Reinterpreting "the Mason Court Revolution": An Historical Institutionalist Account of Judge-Driven Constitutional Transformation in Australia' (2015) 43 *Federal Law Review* 1, 17 in Murray Wesson, 'Crafting a Concept of Deference for the Implied Freedom of Political Communication' (2016) 27(2) *Public Law Review* 101, 108.
44 *Nationwide* (n 5) 50 (Brennan J).

In the s 92 context, Gordon J has agreed. Her Honour alluded to a need for deference as the Court is not 'well-placed' to make judgments on the complex issues which might affect trade, commerce or intercourse between states.[45] In 1987, Gageler J noted that the judiciary is more than just an 'external observer' of government function that 'merely declares uniform legal limits on legislative and executive power'.[46] His Honour has also acknowledged that there are times when 'judicial deference must give way to judicial vigilance.'[47]

There is a view that Australia has a 'more restrictive power of judicial review, and hence a different understanding of the separation of powers, to jurisdictions where the judiciary is expected to enforce constitutional rights.'[48] This necessitates hesitancy when considering the weight one should give to applications of structured proportionality from other jurisdictions. Nonetheless, a broader understanding of the concept of proportionality, informed by its origins in other jurisdictions, is still relevant to this analysis.[49]

B The origins of proportionality

One historical root of proportionality as a 'public law standard'[50]

---

45 *Palmer* (n 13) [199] citing *Betfair [No 1]* (2008) 234 CLR 418, 452-452 [12]-[20].

46 Gageler (n 35) 176.

47 Ibid 214.

48 Murray Wesson, 'The Reception of Structured Proportionality in Australian Constitutional aw' (2021) 20(10) Federal Law Review 1, 3 citing *Roach v Electoral Commission* (2007) 233 CLR 162, 178-9 [17] (Gleeson CJ).

49 It should also be acknowledged that the literature on proportionality's classical philosophical and legal origins is extensive. For an interesting discussion see Chordia (n 21) 12–18, which explores the concept's developments through Plato, Aristotle, Cicero and St Augustine and Hugo Grotius. See also, on the history of proportionality in a comparative law context: Aharon Barak, *Proportionality: Constitutional Rights and their Limitations* (Cambridge University Press, 2012); Mattias Kumm, 'Constitutional Rights as Principles: On the Structure and domain of constitutional justice' (2004) (2004) 2(3) *International Journal of Constitutional Law* 574; Moshe Cohen-Eliya and Iddo Porat, 'American balancing and German proportionality: The historical origins' (2010) 8 *International Journal of Constitutional Law* 263; Vicki C Jackson, 'Constitutional Law in an Age of Proportionality' (2015) 124(8) *Yale Law Journal* 3094, 3113; Anne Carter, *Proportionality and Facts in Constitutional Adjudication* (Hart Publishing, 2022) (forthcoming).

50 Barak (n 12), 177

can be found in Article 10 II 17 of the Prussian General Law
of 1793 (*Allgemeines Landrecht für die Preußishen*) which
circumscribed state powers by ensuring '[t]he office of the
police is to take the necessary measures for the maintenance of
public peace, security, and order'.[51] This clause is a foundation
on which the 'necessity' step of structured proportionality
is built.[52] It was in the context of previously unchecked,
authoritarian rule in Prussia, that the law's response was informed
by the rule of law ("*Rechtsstaat*") resulting in a codification of
proportionality to constrain executive action.[53] In 1928, Fleiner
euphemistically summarised the law of proportionality at the
time, saying: 'You should never use a cannon to kill a sparrow'.[54]
In the early 20th century, the Weimar era's reactionary 'war' of
rights adjudication by its *Reichsggericht* (Supreme Court) was
quickly extinguished by the Third Reich (where labelling a state
measure as 'political' was enough to shield it from the courts'
review).[55] West Germany thereafter ratified the *Grundgesetz
für die Bundesrepublik Deutschland* ('Basic Law for the Federal
Republic of Germany') 'under the watchful gaze of occupying
forces'.[56] It further entrenched the constitutional status of the
new German Federal Constitutional Court—which viewed itself
as playing a central role in the rebuilding of the German State.[57]

---

51 Alec Stone Sweet and Jud Mathews, Proportionality Balancing and Global Constitution-alism (2008) 47 *Columbia Journal of Transnational Law* 73, 101. Edelman J has also suggest-ed that while proportionality's origins are 'arguably' Germanic, it can also be seen to have an English origin traceable from Aristotle, to Aquinas, the 18th century Enlightenment, and the writings of Blackstone: *LibertyWorks* (n 8) [199] (Edelman J) citing *Bank Mellat v Her Majesty's Treasury [No 2]* [2014] AC 700, 788 [68] (Lord Reed).
52 Sweet and Matthews (n 51) 101.
53 Chordia (n 19) 19; Moshe Cohen-Eliya and Iddo Porat, 'American balancing and Ger-man proportionality: The historical origins' (2010) 8 *International Journal of Constitutional Law* 263. Friedrich the Great was a proponent of liberal social contractarianism and rationalism and believed his authority as Monarch was not unlimited but that he was 'the first servant of his state', at 271.
54 Barak (n 12) 179, citing Fritz Fleiner, *Institutionen des Deutschen Verwaltungsrechts* (Tübin-gen, 1928), 404.
55 Sweet and Matthews (n 38) 103-104.
56 Ibid 104.
57 Chordia (n 19) 29.

In this new environment West Germany committed to protecting fundamental rights where the 'prestige of...legislative authority was relatively low'.[58]

Interestingly, the Basic Law for the Federal Republic of Germany does not contain an explicit provision regarding proportionality.[59] Yet, since its establishment, the *Bundesverfassungsgericht* (German Constitutional Court) has strictly abided by the notion that all rights contained in the Basic Law are 'bound by the concept of proportionality and all its components'.[60] Throughout the development of proportionality testing, the German Constitutional Court would invoke its elements without citing authority or explication.[61] To Dieter Grimm, former Justice of the German Constitutional Court, 'the principle was introduced as if it could be taken for granted.'[62] Proportionality 'flows' from 'the rule of law or the essence of fundamental rights'.[63]

C Common law jurisdictions

Meanwhile, the common law world began to embrace proportionality in the Supreme Court of Canada decision of *R v Oakes ('Oakes')*.[64] Both Canada and the United Kingdom have since developed and applied their own forms of proportionality testing. The advent of structured proportionality in both jurisdictions followed the introduction of constitutional or statutory charters of rights. It is trite here to note the absence of a federal Bill of Rights in Australia.[65] As Edelman J (quoting

---

58 Sweet and Matthews (n 51) 109.
59 Ibid 179.
60 Ibid 180.
61 Sweet and Matthews (n 51) 108.
62 Ibid citing Dieter Grimm, *Proportionality in Canadian and German Constitutional Jurisprudence* (2007) 27 *University of Toronto Laws Journal* 383, 385.
63 Grimm (n 62) 386.
64 Chordia (n 19) 24.
65 Wesson (n 48) 8.

Dean of Harvard Law School Roscoe Pound) remarked, the history of a country's laws 'is largely a history of borrowings of legal materials from outside of the law…For except as an act of omnipotence, creation is not the making of something out of nothing.'[66] It is important to canvass the experience in the UK and Canada, to provide a common law comparison of a legal system's adoption of proportionality analysis.

1   Canada

The protections in the Canadian Charter of Rights and Freedoms ('Charter') are circumscribed by section one of the Charter, which states that the rights therein should be 'subject only to such reasonable limits prescribed by law as can be demonstrably justified in a free and democratic society'.[67] Four years after the Charter's enactment, Dickson CJ introduced a form of structured proportionality to determine whether a law could be so appropriately justified in *Oakes*. This structured test arose in Canada after the adumbration of some of its elements in earlier cases.[68] The Court employs a three-part inquiry, similar to what would be applied in *McCloy*, and asks whether: (1) the means chosen are rationally related to the legitimate object; (2) the means chosen 'minimally impair' protected rights; and (3) the benefits towards achieving the government's objective are sufficient to warrant the harm to interests protected by rights.[69] Though the Court made no direct reference to German jurisprudence,[70] Canadian scholarship up to the time of the decision had suggested that the jurisprudence of the

---

66 *Clubb* (n 12) 331 [464] (Edelman J).

67 *Canada Act 1982* (UK) ch 11, sch B pt I (*'Canadian Charter of Rights and Freedoms'*).

68 David Kenny, 'Proportionality and the Inevitability of the Local: A Comparative Local-ist Analysis of Canada and Ireland' (2018) 66(3) *American Journal of Comparative Law* 537, 542 citing *R v Big M Drug Mart Ltd* [1985] 1 SCR 295.

69 Vicki C Jackson, 'Constitutional Law in an Age of Proportionality' (2015) 124(8) *Yale Law Journal* 3094, 3113.

70 Chordia (n 19) 25.

European Court of Human Rights (which did look to German proportionality) would be helpful to decide Charter cases.[71] Dickson CJ stated that the justification of a measure involves a 'form of proportionality':

> First, the measures adopted must be carefully designed to achieve the objective in question.... Second, the means, even if rationally connected to the objective in this first sense, should impair 'as little as possible' the right or freedom in question. Third, there must be a proportionality between the effects of the measures which are responsible for limiting the *Charter* right or freedom, and the objective which has been identified as of 'sufficient importance'.[72]

Over time, the Canadian test has developed and changed. Mere months after *Oakes,* the Supreme Court in *R v Edwards Books & Art Ltd*[73] weakened the *Oakes* test considerably.[74] Further, the Supreme Court of Canada introduced varying categories whereby the test would apply more or less deferentially depending on, for example: policy areas; the nature of the competing laws; and the targeting of vulnerable groups.[75]

2   United Kingdom

The *Human Rights Act*[76] has been 'transformative' of the United Kingdom's House of Lords/Supreme Court.[77] Some suggest it has led to 'the emergence of de facto judicial supremacy in the

---

71 Ibid.

72 *R v Oakes* [1986] 1 SCR 103, 139.

73 *R v Edwards Books & Art Ltd* [1986] 2 SCR 713, 772.

74 Chordia (n 19) 25.

75 Ibid citing Sujit Choudhry, 'So What Is The Real Legacy of *Oakes*? Two Decades of Proportionality Analysis Under the Canadian *Charter's* Section 1' (2006) 24 *Supreme Court Law Review* 501, 511.

76 *Human Rights Act 1998* (UK).

77 Since 2009 the Supreme Court has been the United Kingdom's final court of appeal following the enactment of the *Constitutional Reform Act 2005* (UK) which moved final appeals from the houses of parliament to the new Supreme Court.

UK.'[78] Prior to the Act's enactment, Lord Phillips of Worth Matravers MR in *R (Mahmood) v Secretary of State for the Home Department* discussed the issue of proportionality in circumstances where a UK court is 'anxiously scrutinising an executive decision that interferes with human rights'. [79] Lord Steyn stated in *R (Daly) v Home Secretary* ('*R (Daly)* ')[80] that 'the court will ask the question, applying an objective test, whether the decision-maker could reasonably have concluded that the interference was necessary to achieve one or more of the legitimate aims recognised by the convention'[81] Following this statement Lord Steyn observed that the 'contours of proportionality are familiar'.[82] He used the three-stage test adopted by the Privy Council in *de Freitas v Permanent Secretary of Minister of Agriculture, Fisheries, Lands and Housing:*[83]

> Whether: (i) the legislative objective is sufficiently important to justify limiting a fundamental right; (ii) the measures designed to meet the legislative objective are rationally connected to it; and (iii) the means used to impair the right or freedom are no more than is necessary to accomplish the objective.[84]

His Honour differentiated between that test and the test proposed in *R (Mahmood) v Secretary of State for the Home Department*. He noted 'most cases would be decided in the same way whichever approach is taken' but the 'intensity of review is somewhat greater' under the *de Freitas* test.[85] This is because the structured approach requires consideration of weight and balance: the balance struck between the competing interest, and the weight accorded to those interests, to consider

---

78 Chordia (n 19) 27 citing Stephen Gardbaum, *The New Commonwealth Model of Constitutionalism: Theory and Practice* (Cambridge University Press, 2013) 180-181.
79 [2001] 1 WLR 840, 857 [40].
80 [2001] 2 AC 532, 546 [25] (Lord Steyn) ('*Daly*').
81 Ibid.
82 Ibid 547 [27] (Lord Steyn).
83 [1999] 1 AC 69, 80.
84 Ibid.
85 *Daly* (n 80) 547 [27] (Lord Bingham).

which should prevail.[86] Importantly, the facts in *R (Daly)* took place before the *Human Rights Act* came into effect and it was therefore decided on common law grounds.[87] Moreover, the notion of balancing was not explicitly raised until the case of *Huang v Secretary of State for the Home Department*,[88] where Lord Bingham said 'the need to balance the interests of society with those of individuals and groups' is an aspect of the law 'which should never be overlooked.'[89] Lord Reed approved the inclusion of the balancing stage in *Bank Mellat v Her Majesty's Treasury (No 2)* (*'Bank Mellat'*) qualifying, however, that it was nonetheless necessary to afford the legislature a 'margin of appreciation'.[90]

Two key similarities should here be noted. First, proportionality appears in jurisdictions after their entrenchment of express rights. Second, these common law jurisdictions have continued to adapt and refine what is inherently a German concept to suit their own legal environment. Like Canada, the structured test in England is—maybe oxymoronically—not fixed in its application and scope. As Edelman J has noted 'despite the presence of proportionality testing in many countries, there is no fixed approach within each stage.'[91] In *Bank Mellat* the Supreme Court considered a 'margin of appreciation' should be afforded to the decision maker.[92] One conclusion which can then be considered is that proportionality inescapably creeps into a jurisdiction when the judiciary engages with the validity of legislative limitations on the rights (whether express or otherwise) of people in their polity. As Professor Barak notes, proportionality is fundamental to the rule of law.[93] This

---

86 Ibid.
87 Ibid 454 [23] (Lord Bingham).
88 [2007] 2 AC 167.
89 Ibid 187 [19] (Lord Bingham).
90 *Bank Mellat v Her Majesty's Treasury (No 2)* [2014] AC 700 [75] (*'Bank Mellat'*) (Lord Hope)
91 *Clubb v Edwards* (2019) 267 CLR 171, 311 [408].
92 *Bank Mellat* (n 90) [75].
93 Barak (n 12) 3.

was apparent in the Prussian context hundreds of years ago as proportionality began to be considered in tandem with the growing concept of *Rechtsstaat*. It is therefore unsurprising that the High Court has had to confront this concept in relation to the implied freedom of political communication.

The long march of structured proportionality into Australian law

Having briefly traced the intra-jurisdictional origins of proportionality in an express rights context, it is necessary then to consider the Court's expansion of structured proportionality into both the express freedom established in s 92 and the implied freedom of political communication. Here, it should be remembered that the *Constitution* does not confer positive rights but rather imposes negative limitations on the exercise of legislative power.[94] Further, as Professor Barak stresses, every 'legal system that adopts proportionality must determine for itself...how the elements of proportionality are to be satisfied'.[95] The majority in *McCloy* agreed. Referring to Barak's influential writings they said, 'it is not to be expected that each jurisdiction will approach and apply proportionality in the same way' but instead it will do so 'by reference to its constitutional setting and its historical and institutional background.'[96]

Proportionality did not take clear shape in Australia until *McCloy*. But it is a concept that has been referenced in the High Court since Dixon J's 1933 judgment in *Williams v Melbourne Corporation*.[97] There, his Honour said the question

---

94 Sir Anthony Mason, 'The use of proportionality in Australian constitutional law' (2016) 27 *Public Law Review* 109, 115.

95 Aharon Barak, 'Proportionality (2)' in Michel Rosenfeld and András Sajó (eds), *The Oxford Handbook of Comparative Constitutional Law* (Oxford University Press, 2012) 739, 741.

96 *McCloy* (n 7) 215 [72] (French CJ, Kiefel, Bell and Keane JJ).

97 *Williams v Melbourne Corporation* (1933) 49 CLR 142,155-156.

was whether the impugned law went 'beyond any restraint which could reasonably be adopted' for the specific purpose it intended.[98] The precursor to structured proportionality was the requirement that a law be reasonably appropriate and adapted; a concept imported into Australia from the United States.[99] It is a phrase Kirby J regarded as 'ungainly': 'Just imagine what non-lawyers must make of it? It involves a ritual incantation, devoid of clear meaning.'[100] To Kiefel J the expression was 'rather cumbersome'.[101] Deane J's oft cited remark in the *Tasmanian Dam Case* goes even further:

> Implicit in the requirement that a law be capable of being reasonably considered to be appropriate and adapted to achieving what it is said to provide it with the character of a law with respect to external affairs is a need for there to be a reasonable proportionality between the designated purpose or object and the means which the law embodies for achieving or procuring it.[102]

As Sir Anthony Mason has written, structured proportionality can 'invite the court to make a decision which would ordinarily be a matter of legislative choice'.[103] Necessarily, it should not be done lightly. This is especially relevant when considering Australia in contrast to the jurisdictions discussed above. Further consistent in those examples is that none of the courts made explicit reference to the German jurisprudence. One key link between structured proportionality and a jurisdiction's application of it, is a foundation of express rights. It is a

98 Ibid 156.

99 It is generally considered to have been taken from the United States case of *McCulloch v Maryland* (1819) 17 US 316, 421: *Mulholland v Australian Electoral Commission* (2004) 220 CLR 181, 199 [399] (Gleeson CJ); see also *Clubb* (n 12) 331 [465] (Edelman J) citing *McCulloch v Maryland* (1819) 17 US 316, 421; *Rowe v Electoral Commissioner* (2010) 243 CLR 1, 131–133 [427]–[431] (Kiefel J); *Monis v The Queen* (2013) 249 CLR 92, 213 [345] (Crennan, Kiefel and Bell JJ) ('*Monis*').

100 *Coleman v Power* (2004) 220 CLR 1, 90 [234] (Kirby J) ('*Coleman*').

101 Kiefel (n 20) 88.

102 *Commonwealth v Tasmania* (1983) 158 CLR 1, 260.

103 Forward to Chordia (n 19) vi.

mechanism for courts to reign in legislative advances on their peoples' rights. While such *express* rights do not exist in Australia, High Court jurisprudence concerning the implied freedom of political communication and, more recently the freedom of trade, commerce and intercourse under s 92 of the *Constitution*, have seen the creation of a distinctly Australian form of proportionality.

A The Implied Freedom of Political Communication

The implied freedom of political communication was first recognised in two judgments in 1992.[104] The freedom is implied in the text and structure of the *Constitution* and requires a 'qualified, not an absolute, freedom of political communication.'[105] It limits legislative power so that the people of the Commonwealth can make a 'free and informed choice as electors.'[106] A law that restricts political communication must be, in Gageler J's words, 'consistent with the preservation of the integrity of the system of representative and responsible government established by chapters I and II of the *Constitution*, and of the method of constitutional alteration prescribed by s 128 of the *Constitution*.'[107] At the time of the freedom's inception, some considered it a 'radical departure from the status quo',[108] or based on a 'dubious' methodology.[109] But such critiques have been relatively isolated.[110]

---

104 *Nationwide* (n 5); *ACTV* (n 5).

105 *Unions NSW v New South Wales* (2019) 264 CLR 595, 56 [155] (Edelman J)

106 *Lange v Australian Broadcasting Corporation* (1997) 189 CLR 520, 560 (Brennan CJ, Dawson, Toohey, Gaudron, McHugh, Gummow and Kirby JJ) ('*Lange*').

107 *McCloy* 231 [128].

108 Chordia (n 19) 152 citing Jeffrey Goldsworthy, 'Implications in Language Law and the Constitution' in Geoffrey Lindell (ed), *Future Directions in Australian Constitutional Law* (Federation Press, 1994) 150.

109 Jeffrey Goldsworthy, 'Implications in Language Law and the Constitution' in Geoffrey Lindell (ed), *Future Directions in Australian Constitutional Law* (Federation Press, 1994) 150, 179.

110 Chordia (n 19) 152.

Initially, to determine if a law was inconsistent with the implied freedom the Court would assess whether 'the balance struck' was readily open to the legislature.[111] Mason CJ said the balance required was between 'the public interest in free communication against the competing public interests which the restriction is designed to serve.'[112] These comments reflect an understanding that to assess balancing requires consideration of the nature and degree of the burden imposed and thus the degree of justification required in a given case.[113] The inquiry was further refined by the High Court in *Lange v Australian Broadcasting Corporation* ('*Lange*')[114] and then in *Coleman v Power* ('*Coleman*').[115] The Court followed a two-step test, which asked:

1. Does the law effectively burden freedom of communication about government or political matters either in its terms, operation or effect?

2. Is the law reasonably appropriate and adapted to serve a legitimate end in a manner which is compatible with the maintenance of the constitutionally prescribed system of representative and responsible government?[116]

The Court noted there was 'little difference' between proportionality and this test.[117] Crennan, Kiefel and Bell JJ however were unsatisfied with the later reformulation in *Coleman*. This much is evident from their attempts at further refinement in *Monis v The Queen*[118] and *Tajjour v New South*

---

111 *Nationwide* (n 5) 52 (Brennan J).
112 *ACTV* (n 5) 143,145 (Mason CJ).
113 Chordia (n 19) 157.
114 *Lange* (n 106) 567.
115 *Coleman* (n 100) 51 [95]-[96] (McHugh J). His Honour said that Kirby J had correctly expounded the formulation in *Levy v Victoria* (1997) 189 CLR 579, 646. It should also be noted that subsequently the High Court saw the *Coleman* reformulation as inadequate: *Monis* (n 99) 192 [274] (Crennan, Kiefel and Bell JJ) and was further refined in *Tajjour v New South Wales* (2014) 254 CLR, 570-575 [110]-[133] (Crennan, Kiefel and Bell JJ).
116 *Coleman* (n 100) 51 [95]-[96] (McHugh J), 77-78 [196] (Gummow and Hayne JJ), 82 [211] (Kirby J); *Lange* (n 106) 567.
117 Ibid.
118 (2013) 249 CLR 92, 192 [274].

Wales.[119] The latter case saw their Honours set out the three inquiries of suitability, necessity and balance that would be adopted a year later in *McCloy*.[120]

The High Court's formulation of structured proportionality seeks to disaggregate the second part of the *Lange* test into three distinct steps.[121] This three-step approach was finalised by the plurality in *Brown v Tasmania*: [122]

1. Does the law effectively burden freedom of communication about government or political matters either in its terms, operation or effect?

2. If 'yes' to question 1, is the purpose of the law legitimate, in the sense that it is compatible with the maintenance of the constitutionally prescribed system of representative and responsible government?

3. If 'yes' to question 2, is the law reasonably appropriate and adapted to advance that legitimate objective in a manner that is compatible with the maintenance of the constitutionally prescribed system of representative and responsible government?

Structured proportionality testing is then applied to answer the third question. It inquires whether the law is:

(i)   **suitable** – as having a rational connection to its purpose;

(ii)   **necessary** – in the sense that there is no obvious and compelling alternative, reasonably practicable means of achieving the same purpose which has a less restrictive effect on the freedom; and

---

119 *Tajjour v New South Wales* (2014) 254 CLR 508 ('*Tajjour*').
120 Ibid 571 [112]-[116] (Crennan, Kiefel and Bell JJ).
121 Wesson (n 48) 5.
122 *Brown v Tasmania* (2017) 261 CLR 328, 363–4 [104] (Kiefel CJ, Bell and Keane JJ).

(iii)   **adequate in its balance** – requiring a value judgment, consistently with the limits of the judicial function, describing the balance between the importance of the purpose served by the restrictive measure and the extent of the restriction it imposes on the freedom.[123]

The majority's approval for this form of proportionality testing in *McCloy* did reference some international authorities discussed above. Those justices referred to Lord Reed in *Bank Mellat* and noted that proportionality testing's 'attraction as an heuristic tool' is that it breaks down the proportionality assessment into distinct aspects to explicitly reveal the judicial officer's value judgment.[124] For the majority, the development of structured proportionality was nothing more than a further explication of the principles established in *Lange*.[125] *Lange* 'pointed clearly in the direction of proportionality analysis;'[126] which is to say that the advent of structured proportionality was not a case of borrowing from other jurisdictions but the natural progression of the law.[127] Importantly, as later expounded by Edelman J in *Clubb*: structured proportionality should be precise and based on principle lest it 'become an unlicensed vehicle for a court to remodel public policy.[128]

1   Gageler and Gordon JJ's initial opposition

McCloy also saw the genesis of Gageler and Gordon JJ's opposition to structured proportionality. Gageler J's preference

---

123 *McCloy* (n 7) 194-195 [2]; 217 [79] (French CJ, Kiefel, Bell and Keane JJ) (emphasis added).

124 Ibid 217 [78] citing *Bank Mellat v HM Treasury [No 2]* [2014] AC 700, 790 [72]-[74]; *Pham v Secretary of State for the Home Department* [2015] 1 WLR 1591, 1722 [96].

125 Chordia (n 19) 164. Such a justification is also reflected in Kiefel CJ and Keane J's decision to apply structured proportionality in the context of s 92 of the *Constitution*: see below (n 178) and accompanying text.

126 *McCloy* (n 7) 214 [70].

127 *Palmer* (n 13) 243 [54] (Kiefel CJ and Keane J) citing Chordia (n 21) 164.

128 *Clubb v Edwards* (2019) 267 CLR 171, 310 [406]–[407].

was for a categorical approach through which the standard of
the court's review 'is calibrated to the degree of risk to the
system of representative and responsible government'.[129] His
Honour acknowledged that 'proportionality' is just a different
expression of the formulation 'reasonably appropriate and
adapted'.[130] The difference between them was unobjectionable
'provided such use does not bring with it considerations relevant
only to a different constitutional context'.[131] His Honour saw
'no magic in a label' in this context.[132] Ultimately, Gageler J
did not believe *McCloy* was the correct time for the exegesis
of his arguments, though he forewarned 'the content and
consequences of the approach now propounded by a majority
of this Court must await consideration in future cases.'[133] He
restricted himself to two brief reservations. They were concerns
of 'one size fits all'[134] and that 'adequate in its balance' is an
inappropriate criterion of validity:[135]

> No unitary standard of justification can or should be applied
> across all categories of cases. To date that has repeatedly
> been recognised when it has been accepted that a law
> which operates to impose a content-based restriction will
> demand closer scrutiny than a restriction based on the form
> or manner of communication, just as when it has been
> recognised that a law which operates to prohibit or regulate
> communications which are inherently political will demand
> closer scrutiny than a law which operates incidentally to
> restrict political communication.[136]

Gordon J approved of the previously established approach as it
had been used 'without apparent difficulty' since *Lange*.[137] For

---

129 *McCloy* (n 7) 238 [150] (Gageler J).
130 Ibid 234 [138] citing *Lange* (1997) 166 CLR 106, 562.
131 Ibid, citing *Mulholland v Australian Electoral Commission* (2004) 220 CLR 181, 200 [39] (Gleeson CJ) (*'Mulholland'*).
132 *McCloy* (n 7) 234 [138] (Gageler J).
133 Ibid 235 [141].
134 Ibid 235 [142]
135 Ibid 236 [145].
136 Ibid 238 [152] (citations omitted).
137 Ibid 282 [310].

her Honour, the questions posed in *McCloy* were answerable through the existing law—*McCloy* was not a controversy the Court was prevented from resolving through pre-existing 'methods of reasoning and analysis'.[138] Gordon J also raised an alternative, categorical approach, consistent with the common-law methodology that a law may be more or less justifiable dependent on category.[139]

Since *McCloy*, Gageler and Gordon JJ have 'maintained and elaborated' their objections to structured proportionality across a series of cases,[140] including *Brown v Tasmania*,[141] *Unions New South Wales v New South Wales*,[142] *Clubb v Edwards* ('*Clubb*'),[143] and *Comcare v Banerji* ('*Banerji*').[144] In *Brown v Tasmania*, Gageler J referred to his past attempts to explain that the test used to explore constitutional adjudication of the implied freedom:

> needs to be understood as a reflection of the underlying reason for the implication of freedom of political communication. The reason for the implication lies in the protection of political communication on which depends the efficacy of electoral accountability for the exercise of legislative and executive power within the constitutionally prescribed national system of representative and responsible government to which there is added a mechanism for constitutional change in which electors through referenda participate directly in the legislative process.
>
> The terms of the question do not deny that, as with all constitutional adjudication, patterns emerge as precedents accumulate. What they do deny is that the analysis appropriate to be brought to bear on the

---

138 Ibid 282 [311].
139 *Brown* (n 122) 477–8 [477]–[478].
140 Wesson (n 48) 6.
141 *Brown* (n 122) 376–9 [158]–[166] (Gageler J), 464–7 [426]–[438] (Gordon J).
142 (2019) 264 CLR 595, 633 [101] (Gageler J), 649–50 [150] (Gordon J).
143 (2019) 267 CLR 171, 224–5 [158]–[162] (Gageler J); 304–9 [389]–[404] (Gordon J).
144 (2019) 267 CLR 373 422 [97] (Gageler J); 440 [161] (Gordon J).

determination of rights in controversy in a particular
case can or should be constrained in the abstract. [145]

Gageler J's approach crystallised in *Clubb* into what he termed
'precedent-based calibrated scrutiny'.[146] This method varies the
level of scrutiny on an impugned law by the nature and intensity
of the risk which that law may pose to the implied freedom.[147]
Structurally, the analytical process for *Clubb* was formulated as
follows:

> [F]irst, to examine the nature and intensity of the
> burden which the protest prohibition places on political
> communication; **second**, to calibrate the appropriate
> level of scrutiny to the risk which a burden of that
> nature and intensity poses to maintenance of the
> constitutionally prescribed system of representative
> and responsible government; **third**, to isolate
> and assess the importance of the constitutionally
> permissible purpose of the prohibition; and **finally**,
> to apply the appropriate level of scrutiny so as
> to determine whether the protest prohibition is
> justified as **reasonably appropriate and adapted**
> to achieve that purpose in a manner compatible with
> maintenance of the constitutionally prescribed system
> of government.[148]

As to the construction of the test, Gageler J noted that to continue
using the language 'reasonably appropriate and adapted':

> not every law which effectively burdens freedom
> of political communication poses the same degree
> of risk to the efficacy of electoral accountability
> for the exercise of legislative and executive power.
> For that reason not every law which effectively
> burdens freedom of political communication in
> pursuit of a legitimate purpose demands the same
> degree of justification, and concomitantly not every

145 *Brown* (n 122) 377 [162]–[163](Gageler J).
146 *Clubb* (n 12) 225 [161] (Gageler J).
147 Ibid.
148 Ibid [162] (Gageler J) (emphasis added).

law which effectively burdens freedom of political communication needs to be subjected to the same intensity of judicial scrutiny.[149]

He presciently added:

> I doubt my capacity to spell out the approach with greater clarity, and I doubt that there is much more that I can usefully say in support of it at the level of constitutional and adjudicative principle. Like all of the numerous competing approaches to the judgment calls required of the High Court in matters arising under the Australian *Constitution* which have come and gone since 1903, it will be evaluated over time as case law accumulates by reference to its capacity to inform sound and consistent outcomes.[150]

Additionally, in *Banerji*, Gageler J confirmed that a law which conferred a discretion capable of imposing a direct and substantial burden on the freedom requires 'close scrutiny corresponding to a compelling justification' to infringe the implied freedom of political communication.[151]

1 *LibertyWorks*

With the departure of Bell and Nettle JJ from the High Court bench and their replacement with Steward and Gleeson JJ, the need to re-analyse the positions of the bench arises. *LibertyWorks* presents the perfect opportunity. It provides an opportunity to look to the two opinions of the two newest High Court justices, as well as to consider how the opposition of Gageler and Gordon JJ has further developed.

The plaintiff in *LibertyWorks* was a private think tank that organised political conferences. It lobbied for public policy change towards greater freedom of speech and political communication.[152] The

---

149 *Brown* (n 122) 378 [164] (Gageler J).
150 Ibid.
151 *Comcare v Banerji* (2019) 267 CLR 373, 422 [97] (Gageler J) ('*Banerji*').
152 *LibertyWorks* (n 8) [1] (Kiefel CJ and Keane J).

plaintiff challenged the 'registrable obligations' engaged by the plaintiff's activities under the *Foreign Influence Transparency Act 2018* (Cth).[153] The obligation to register with the relevant authority, before undertaking 'communication activities' in Australia, was argued to impermissibly burden the implied freedom.[154] By a 5:2 majority, the Court disagreed and held that the legislation did not constitute an impermissible burden on the implied freedom of political communication. The judgments of the plurality (Kiefel CJ, Keane and Gleeson JJ) and the separate reasons of Edelman and Steward JJ all followed the *McCloy* structured proportionality approach and upheld the law. Gageler and Gordon JJ both separately dissented. The plurality said the use of structured proportionality in an implied freedom context was 'well settled'.[155] They re-iterated that structured proportionality has been 'consistently maintained by a majority of this Court in each of the cases concerning the implied freedom since *McCloy*'.[156] Despite that view, the plaintiff made submissions that the laws were not 'reasonably appropriate and adapted' if a reasonable necessity test was applied.[157]

a) Justice Gageler

Gageler J noted he had 'adequately explained in the past' his analytical approach to the third stage of the three-part *McCloy* analysis.[158] He elaborated on his calibrated scrutiny approach saying that 'the level of scrutiny appropriate to be brought to bear on a law which imposes a burden on political communication [lies] within a spectrum.'[159] He concluded that the impugned law was incompatible with the constitutional freedom of political

---

153 Ibid [5].
154 Ibid.
155 *LibertyWorks* (n 8) [44] (Kiefel CJ, Keane and Gleeson JJ).
156 Ibid [48] (Kiefel CJ, Keane and Gleeson JJ).
157 Ibid [47] (Kiefel CJ, Keane and Gleeson JJ).
158 Ibid [93].
159 *Brown* (n 122) 389 [201] (Gageler J) citing *Tajjour* (n 119) 580-581 (Gageler J)

communication.[160]

Despite reaching this conclusion with his own method of analysis, Gageler J curiously also explained why the impugned law did not satisfy structured proportionality testing.[161] He stated that the legislation was not 'suitable' as there was no rational connection between improving transparency and the subjection of a registrant to register; not 'necessary' as there was an obviously compelling and reasonably practicable alternative; and lastly not 'adequate in its balance' as the requirement to register 'contributes nothing to the achievement of the benefit of improved transparency sought to be achieved.'[162] Nonetheless, the fact that his Honour reached an alternate conclusion to the majority (in applying both calibrated scrutiny and structured proportionality) does suggest that differing approaches are more than mere syntactical choices. As Gleeson CJ put it: 'there is no magic in a label.'[163] Furthermore, these differences in the chosen method of analysis are not inconsequential.[164] As Sir Anthony Mason once wrote 'the method of interpretation a court pursues has a close inter-relationship with the court's perception of its role.'[165]

b) Justice Gordon

Gordon J continued to follow the 'reasonably appropriate and adapted' analysis.[166] She returned to her reasons in *Clubb v Edwards* where a key theme underlying her opposition was structured proportionality's incongruity with the common law.[167]

---

160 *LibertyWorks* (n 8) [118] (Gageler J)
161 Ibid [119] (Gageler J).
162 Ibid.
163 *Mulholland* (n 131) 200 [39] (Gleeson CJ).
164 Evelyn Douek, 'All Out of Proportion: The Ongoing Disagreement about Structured Proportionality in Australia' (2019) 47(4) Federal Law Review 551, 566.
165 Ibid citing Sir Anthony Mason, 'The Role of a Constitutional Court in a Federation: A Comparison of the Australian and the United States Experience' (1986) 16 *Federal Law Review* 1, 2.
166 *LibertyWorks* (n 8) [134].
167 See, *Clubb* (n 12) 305 [391], 309 [401]-[403].

Her Honour was not shaken from her continued application of the reasonably appropriate and adapted standard. And, like Gageler J, she found that the law was invalid as it went further than was necessary to achieve its legitimate object.[168] But the contrary methods of analysis of both dissenting judges yielded the same result.

B Section 92

On 11 March 2020, the World Health Organisation declared COVID-19 a pandemic. Soon after, a state of emergency was declared across Western Australia. The constitutionality of the legislative regime[169] that sought to protect West Australians from the pandemic was then challenged in the High Court.[170] It was argued that the legislative regime infringed the guarantee in s 92 of the *Constitution* that interstate trade, commerce and intercourse should be 'absolutely free'. Prior to this case, the High Court had resolved how that s 92 freedom was to be interpreted in a trade and commerce case in *Cole v Whitfield*.[171] The interpretation of what 'intercourse' between the states in s 92 means was resolved in *Palmer* where the Court re-integrated these two limbs of s 92.[172] The standard of review used by the plurality was structured proportionality.[173] Gageler and Gordon JJ, unsurprisingly, did not.

---

168 *LibertyWorks* (n 8) [190]-[191].

169 *Emergency Management Act 2005* (WA), *Quarantine (Closing the Border) Directions* (WA).

170 *Palmer* (n 13).

171 Justice Gageler, writing extra-judicially, said the words of s 92 have caused 'more anxiety to lawyers than any other words of the Constitution.': Stephen Gaegler, 'The Section 92 Revolution' in James Stellios (ed) *Encounters with Constitutional Interpretation and Legal Education* (The Federation Press, 2018) 27. In *Palmer*, Gageler J said that *Cole v Whitfield* partially resolved the issue by cutting through 'the debris left by some 140 earlier failed judicial attempts to resolve that riddle': *Palmer* (n 13) 247 [84].

172 *Palmer* (n 13) 242 [48] (Kiefel CJ and Keane J): '[A] law which burdens interstate movement should be subject to a requirement of justification, in the same way as required where interstate trade and commerce is burdened.', 249 [92] (Gageler J), 267 [189] (Gordon J), 279 [241] (Edelman J).

173 Ibid 244 [62] (Kiefel CJ and Keane J), 284 [261] (Edelman J).

1 The Plurality

Though before *Palmer*, a law's validity under s 92 was assessed through the criterion of reasonable necessity,[174] the plurality argued that proportionality is not foreign to s 92 jurisprudence. Edelman J noted that in *Castlemaine Tooheys Ltd v South Australia* (*'Castlemaine'*) the majority said a legislative impact on interstate trade should 'not [be] disproportionate to the achievement of [its] objects.'[175] Kiefel CJ and Keane J suggested that 'it may be said that at least *Betfair [No 1]* recognised the connection between the test of reasonable necessity and the concept of proportionality.'[176] Their Honours reasoned that the content of that test 'clearly aligns it with the second test in structured proportionality'.[177] Structured proportionality 'simply explicates the [pre-existing] tests for justification'.[178] Their Honours also accentuated the important quality of transparency and predictability that structured proportionality brings:

> It cannot be suggested that structured proportionality is a perfect method. None is, but some method is necessary if lawyers and legislators are to know how the question of justification is to be approached in a given case.[179]

Similarly, Edelman J's argument foregrounds transparency: '[j]udicial reasoning concerning constitutional validity of legislation should not be a black box to be unlocked only when parties to a later case seek explanation for the earlier exercise of discretion.'[180] His Honour then quoted Professor Birks' discussion of 'unstructured discretion':

---

174 Ibid 240 [37] (Kiefel CJ and Keane J) citing *Betfair [No 1]* (2008) 234 CLR 418, 476-477 [201]-[103] (Gleeson CJ, Gummow, Kirby, Hayne, Crennan and Kiefel JJ).

175 Ibid 284 [262] citing *Castlemaine Tooheys Ltd v South Australia* (1990) 169 CLR 436, 473-474 (Mason CJ, Wilson, Dawson, Brennan and Toohey JJ).

176 Ibid 242 [52] (Kiefel CJ and Keane J).

177 Ibid.

178 Ibid [57] (Kiefel CJ and Keane J).

179 Ibid [56] (Kiefel CJ and Keane J).

180 Ibid 284 [263] Edelman J.

> The whole point of the rule of law is to ensure that power which cannot be put under the law should be accountable to the electorate and that, for the rest, we all live under the law, not under the wills and whims of a person or a group of people. The blessings of this commitment have been overlooked by the discretionary remedialists, who suddenly suppose that the judges should be the one group answerable only to God.[181]

The proponents' arguments can be distilled as follows. First, structured proportionality does not magically appear in the constitutional discourse—it is merely a deeper explanation of the method of reasoning previously applied. Second, this form of justification is necessary to bring greater transparency to the Court's reasons.

2   Nothing is broken; nothing should be fixed – Gageler J's opposition

Gageler J adopted Sir Anthony Mason's comment that 'the *Cole v Whitfield* interpretation has brought an element of certainty and stability to a question which was a source of confusion over a long period of time. So why abandon that interpretation?'[182] To this Gageler J simply added that '[n]othing is broken; nothing should be fixed.'[183] This argument takes a similar approach to Kiefel CJ and Keane J (structured proportionality simply 'explicates'

---

181 Ibid, citing Peter Birks, 'Three Kinds of Objections to Discretionary Remedialism' (2000) 29 *University of Western Australia Law Review* 1, 15. Cf *Dasreef Pty Ltd v Hawchar* (2011) 243 CLR 588. On predictability and transparency, albeit in the context of the principles of evidence, Heydon J said 'To make the criterion of admissibility turn not on the satisfaction of a rule but on the invocation of a discretion is to abandon the search for reasonable predictability... An expert witness's high qualifications and impeccable intellectual processes will produce only useless evidence unless there is a link between the opinion and a version of the primary facts made possible by the evidence. A proof of assumption rule is a significant safeguard against the dangerous consequences of experts giving opinions which fail to mesh with the concrete factual controversies before the court.' at 635–636 [119]–[120] (Heydon J).
182 Chordia (n 19) vi.
183 *Palmer* (n 13) [151] (Gageler J).

the previous test) and comes to a different conclusion. Kiefel CJ and Keane J do not disagree that 'nothing is broken', but believed structured proportionality brings greater transparency to the court's decisions. Gageler J understood the need 'to produce predictable outcomes through a transparent process of reasoning employing judicially manageable standards.'[184] Nonetheless, Gageler J cited the position of *Betfair [No 1]* as authority for the proposition that reasonable necessity 'should be accepted as the doctrine of the Court'.[185]

Though *Palmer* has re-joined the two limbs of s 92 as a holistic freedom, this does not mean the standard of justification has changed. The plurality's suggestion of a mere explication of the existing test seems contradictory to the reality of structured proportionality. Gageler J cited Gleeson CJ's warning in *Mulholland v Australian Electoral Commission* that proportionality could lead to 'elaborations that vary in content, and that may be imported sub silentio into a different context without explanation'.[186] To Gageler J the three-stage inquiry 'exhaustively defines, and in so doing confines, each of those standardised inquiries'.[187] Relevant considerations which may not be caught within the first two steps of 'suitability' or 'necessity' are merely 'pushed down to be swept up in the residual inquiry into 'adequacy of balance'.[188]

Gageler J is concerned with structured proportionality's 'rigidity'.[189] This objection forms the majority of his reasoning, though he also holds reservations about 'judicial importation' of a tool from completely different institutional, historical and

---

184 Ibid [141] (Gageler J).
185 Ibid [131] citing *Betfair [No 1]* (2008) 234 CLR 418, 477 [102]–[103] (Gleeson CJ, Gummow, Kirby, Hayne, Crennan and Kiefel JJ).
186 *Palmer* (n 13) 257 [135] citing *Mulholland* (n 131) 197-198 [34] (Gleeson CJ).
187 Ibid 258 [143] (Gageler J).
188 Ibid [143] (Gageler J).
189 Ibid [144]; see, also, Gordon J in *Murphy v Electoral Commissioner* (2016) 261 CLR 28, 123 [299] and *Brown* (n 122) 477 [477].

political settings, where it is used for different purposes.[190] Yet Gageler J did not eschew the invariable reality of evaluative judgments. He noted that in Australian constitutional history 'no good can come of attempting to avoid' or 'unduly canalise' them.[191] His Honour referred to Sir Kenneth Jacobs's comment that analysis through a standard of reasonableness or unreasonableness 'may often yield more certainty than many rules of law couched in terms of apparent precision and decisiveness'.[192] Parallels to Gageler J's earlier objections to structured proportionality in the implied freedom context can be seen here. So, while the context of the test's application may differ, the objections are still made within similar themes.

3   There can be no one-size fits all approach – Gordon J's opposition

Gordon J meanwhile, discussed her objection to structured proportionality in two precise paragraphs.[193] She first noted that 'it is unnecessary to repeat the concerns expressed elsewhere about the rigidity of structured proportionality' citing various reasons in *McCloy, Murphy v Electoral Commissioner*[194] ('*Murphy*'), *Brown* and *Clubb*.[195] Gordon J's significant objection, with regards to s 92, is with the 'necessity' stage of analysis, because '[t]o treat the existence of alternative means as conclusive that s 92 is infringed, in every case, would be an approach that is too rigid and prescriptive'.[196] Her Honour suggested that such an approach ignored the role of the Court in

---

190 *Palmer* (n 13) 259 [144] (Gageler J) citing Kenneth Jacobs, 'The Successor Books to 'The Province and Function of Law'—Lawyers' Reasonings: Some Extra-judicial Reflections' (1967) 5 *Sydney Law Review* 425, 428.
191 Ibid [146] (Gageler J)
192 Ibid [149] (Gageler J).
193 Ibid 269 [198] – [199].
194 *Murphy v Electoral Commissioner* (2016) 261 CLR 28 ('*Murphy*').
195 *Clubb* (n 12) 299.
196 Ibid [198].

questions concerning s 92. That role is to 'decide the matter, so far as may be, on the specific considerations or features which it presents'.[197] There may also be cases where alternative means are impossible:

> [F]or example, where the impugned provisions are part of a complex legislative scheme and there is no ready comparator, or as in this case, where an inquiry into the existence of alternative means would be futile. In the context of s 92, there can be no "one size fits all" approach.[198]

Then, she argued that the third balancing stage of structured proportionality introduces 'a new element that would be contrary to the foundations and current operation of s 92'.[199] As her Honour reminds us, s 92 is an absolute freedom subject to a reservation,[200] whereas the balancing stage of structured proportionality requires a value judgment that s 92 'neither permits nor requires'.[201] It is noted that 'the Court is often not well-placed to make such value judgments where the nature of trade, commerce and intercourse is complex, multi-faceted and evolving'.[202] To introduce values-based decision making is something 's 92 not only can avoid, but must'.[203]

The case against structured proportionality

Gageler and Gordon JJ's opposition to structured proportionality has been maintained for reasons of principle. As this chapter has shown, structured proportionality has a particular context and content; both in its application in Australia, and in other international jurisdictions. And their Honours suggest that

---

197 Ibid [198] citing *Gratwick v Johnson* (1945) 70 CLR 1,19.
198 Ibid.
199 Ibid [199]
200 Ibid.
201 Ibid.
202 Ibid citing *Betfair [No 1]* (2008) 234 CLR 418, 452-452 [12]-[20].
203 Ibid citing Chordia (n 19) 143,149,150-151.

this test—with a civil law origin and applications in express human rights jurisdictions— does not fit within the Australian constitutional context. Themes in their Honours' distaste for the method of analysis are apparent. In short: they both agree that it is an analysis too 'rigid' or 'prescriptive'; they are wary of 'importation' from legal cultures different to ours; and they form the opinion that it is unnecessary as the pre-existing tests are fit for purpose. Douek argues that structured proportionality is a *fait accompli* of the contemporary constitutional system.[204] Instead of skirmishes over methodological agreement and finding the 'right' approach, she suggests that 'greater attention should be paid to the questions that need to be addressed within that framework.'[205] However, what this chapter has sought to explain is that the disagreements are more than merely methodological or syntactical.

Further, there have been a number of recent requests by litigants to Australian federal courts to invalidate legislation whether it be the public service code of conduct,[206] foreign interference legislation,[207] or COVID-19 lockdown measures.[208] It is fair to

---

204 Evelyn Douek, 'All Out of Proportion: The Ongoing Disagreement about Structured Proportionality in Australia' (2019) 47(4) *Federal Law Review* 551, 571.
205 Ibid.
206 *Banerji* (n 151) (2019) 267 CLR 373.
207 *LibertyWorks* (n 8).
208 *Palmer* (n 13).

say that such actions will not abate in the near future.[209] It is therefore important for the legislature and executive branches to transparently understand the standard of review that they are being held to by the High Court.

This final section explains and categorises the objections under two themes. First, their Honours oppose it *structurally*: it is too rigid, and prescriptive, therefore encroaching onto the legislature and giving rise to value judgments. Second, they oppose it *institutionally*: it is contrary to the High Court's method of developing the law and its legalist tradition.

A The structural objection

One of Gageler J's objections is that the 'rigidity' of structured proportionality does not reflect the 'degrees of latitude' which might be afforded to government action.[210] He also suggests that the 'adequacy in balance' stage is not 'sufficiently' focused on the reasons which underlie the implication of the freedom itself and that it invites open-ended judicial balancing.[211] Gordon J espoused a similar objection in *Murphy*. She argued that the second stage (necessity) is too rigid as the judiciary is ill-

209 See, eg, *Farm Transparency International Ltd* v *New South Wales* [2021] HCATrans 151; Christopher Knaus, 'High court to hear bid to overturn New South Wales hidden camera laws', *Guardian* (online), (online at 4 October 21021) <https://www.theguardian.com/australia-news/2021/jun/29/high-court-to-hear-bid-to-overturn-new-south-wales-ag-gag-laws>. This case concerning the implied freedom of political communication which impugnes the *Surveillance Devices Act 2007* (NSW) to stop the use of recording devices on private premises; Jack Mahony, 'Queensland Premier wishes Flight Centre 'good luck' after CEO announces company is considering legal action', *Sky News* (online), (online at 4 October 2021) <https://www.skynews.com.au/australia-news/politics/queensland-premier-wishes-flight-centre-goodluck-after-ceo-announces-company-is-considering-legal-action/news story/b2d9b9227b6965ac2a09d10b7f4e8638>. The CEO of Flight Centre, an Australian tourism company, has also recently suggested that the company will pursue legal action if Australian states refuse to allow for interstate travel: 'We do have a constitution and the constitution clearly states in section 92 about the freedom of movement between states and we don't particularly want to have to take states to the high court but we will and it's not only us I can assure you.'
210 *McCloy* (n 7) 235 [143] (Gageler J).
211 Carter (n 223) 77 citing *McCloy* (n 7) 236 [145].

equipped to judge the existence of obvious, compelling, or practical alternatives to provisions of a legislative scheme. [212] To do so 'would create too great a risk of the judicial branch intruding on the legislative function conferred on the Parliament by the *Constitution*'.[213]

These arguments are rooted in the jurisprudence of the High Court. Gordon J's sentiments were shared by Brennan CJ, in *Levy v Victoria* and *Cunliffe v Commonwealth,* where he considered the question of alternative measures was primarily a matter for the Parliament, and opined that the Court should reserve its judgment solely to the question whether the law is appropriate and adapted to the fulfilment of its purpose.[214] In *Leask v Commonwealth,* Toohey J argued that to extend proportionality so that it became a general touchstone of constitutional power would bring the Court 'inexorably into areas of policy and of value judgments.'[215] Dawson J was similarly critical in *Leask v Commonwealth* saying proportionality relied on 'essentially political rather than judicial considerations'.[216] Gleeson CJ agreed with these criticisms in *Coleman,* emphasising the 'respective roles of the legislature and the judiciary in a representative democracy'.[217] In the s 92 context, the majority in *Castlemaine* warned that to substitute a judicial opinion for that of the legislature's 'without having access to all the political considerations that played a part in the making of that decision' would give rise to 'a new and unacceptable dimension to the relationship'.[218]

---

212 *Murphy* (n 194) 123 [303] (Gordon J).
213 Ibid.
214 *Levy v Victoria* (1997) 189 CLR 579, 598 (Brennan CJ); *Cunliffe v Commonwealth* (1994) 182 CLR 272, 325 (Brennan J).
215 *Leask v Commonwealth* (1996) 187 CLR 579, 616 (Toohey J) ('*Leask*').
216 Ibid 601 (Dawson J).
217 *Coleman* (n 100) 31 [31] (Gleeson CJ).
218 *Castlemaine Tooheys* (n 175) 473 (Mason CJ, Brennan, Deane, Dawson and Toohey JJ); Caroline Henckels, 'Proportionality and the Separation of Powers in Constitutional Review: Examining the Role of Judicial Deference' (2019) 45(2) *Federal Law Review* 181, 185.

There is a clear conclusion that can be drawn from the above: the rigidity of structured proportionality risks, in principle, infringing the separation of powers. This is especially apparent when considered in the context of the High Court's legalism and practice of judicial deference. Sir Anthony Mason said that structured proportionality 'does not overtly reflect the separation of powers considerations which are a fundamental element in Australian constitutional law.'[219] A constitutionally enshrined federal Bill of Rights might overcome this issue and would draw Australia into alignment with jurisdictions such as the United Kingdom and Canada where the emergence of structured proportionality makes sense contextually. However, as Mason CJ explained in *Australian Capital Television Pty Ltd v Commonwealth*, an active choice not to enshrine a bill of rights in our constitutional arrangements was made at federation.[220] On a similar note, Heydon J in *Momcilovic v The Queen* opined that '[t]he insertion of a bill of rights into the Commonwealth Constitution…could give the courts a role in interpreting statutes which departed from the separation of powers. But as the Constitution stands that is impermissible.'[221] These views also resonate with Brennan J's statement in *Re Limbo* that 'courts perform one function and the political branches of government perform another'.[222]

D The institutional objection

Gageler and Gordon JJ also outline an objection based on structured proportionality's conflict with the common law's

---

219 Sir Anthony Mason, 'Proportionality and Calibrated Scrutiny: A Commentary' (2020) 48(2) *Federal Law Review* 286.

220 *ACTV* (n 5). 'The framers of the Constitution accepted, in accordance with prevailing English thinking, that the citizen's rights were best left to the protection of the common law in association with the doctrine of parliamentary supremacy.' at 135–136.

221 *Momcilovic v The Queen* (2011) 245 CLR 1, 173 [433] (Heydon J).

222 Ibid citing *Re Limbo* (1989) 64 ALJR 241, 242 (Brennan J).

development in Australia. Anne Carter recently framed this as the 'common law objection'.[223] Notably Edelman J cited Carter in *LibertyWorks* to rebut the contention that proportionality is disliked 'because it is *foreign*'.[224] However, this is too reductive of the merits of Gageler and Gordon JJ's objection. Douek considers that the High Court has 'long hewn' closely to the common law tradition of case-by-case, fact-sensitive analysis and incremental development of the law over 'abstract adjudication'.[225] Gageler J has additionally suggested that lawyers brought up in the common law tradition would be less comfortable being constrained by the standardised pattern of structured proportionality.[226] His Honour's objection is not explicitly made in reference to an inconsistency with the common law.[227] But Sir Anthony Mason considered Gageler J's alternative of 'calibrated scrutiny' a 'traditional common law approach to the solution of legal problems'.[228] In *Clubb*, Gordon J said that structured proportionality would risk hampering the development of the *Lange* test under the common law method.[229] It can also hamper the incremental development of legal principles to crystallise the meaning of the standard of review.[230] This objection is not new. Dawson J went even further:

> To introduce the concept of proportionality, whether it be via the notion that a law must be reasonably appropriate and adapted to some end in view or by any other route, is to introduce a concept which is

---

223 Anne Carter, 'Moving Beyond the Common Law Objection to Structured Proportionality' (2021) 49(1) *Federal Law Review* 73.

224 *LibertyWorks* (n 8) [199] citing Carter (n 223) 94 (emphasis in original).

225 Evelyn Douek (n 205) 567 citing *In re Judiciary and Navigation Acts* (1921) 29 CLR 257, 267 (Knox CJ, Gavan Duffy, Powers, Rich and Starke JJ). Carter (n 223) similarly discusses the common law tradition of Australia Carter as being case specific, (there is careful consideration of the facts of each case); features analogical reasoning (from case to case); and is governed by precedent, at 81.

226 *Clubb* (n 12) 224 [159] (Gageler J).

227 Carter (n 223) 78.

228 Sir Anthony Mason (n 94) 121.

229 *Clubb* (n 12) 532 [404] (Gordon J).

230 Ibid.

alien to the principles which this Court has hitherto applied.[231]

This reflects a long-standing history of concern with proportionality's place in Australia. This is further seen in Gummow J's statement in *Roxborough v Rothmans of Pall Mall Australia Ltd* that 'general principle is derived from judicial decisions upon particular instances, not the other way around'.[232]

Carter makes an argument that the value judgments inherent in structured proportionality are not anathema to the common law tradition.[233] She cites Nettle J's decision in *Clubb*, where his Honour suggested that the task required at the balancing stage of structured proportionality is not different from other areas of law.[234] Nettle J provided the example that when identifying a duty of care or sentencing a criminal offender 'courts are not infrequently called upon to weigh competing values that could never plausibly be reduced to any single metric of evaluation.'[235] Yet in that same passage, Nettle J still acknowledged that understanding proportionality can be assisted by reference to 'principles of the common law'.[236] However, such an analogy may not be as convincing in the constitutional context of rights and freedoms. Sentencing evaluations and the identification of tortious duties of care may well involve value-laden judgment. But the real issue is that structured proportionality—in a constitutional law context—encroaches onto the legislature. It is a tool for determining the *validity* of a law; it is a means of the judiciary telling the legislature they went wrong. This is significantly different than other, non-constitutional, uses of proportionality. This difference is what gives more weight to the

---

231 *Leask* (n 215) 600–601 (Dawson J).
232 *Roxborough v Rothmans of Pall Mall Australia Ltd* (2001) 208 CLR 516, 544 [72] (Gummow J).
233 Carter (n 223) 91–93.
234 *Clubb* (n 12) 508 [271] (Nettle J).
235 Ibid.
236 Ibid.

objections from Gageler and Gordon JJ. It acknowledges that questions of balance and proportionality are extant in other areas of our law. However, those examples referred to by supporters of structured proportionality do not concern judicial decisions which declare legislative action constitutionally invalid.

E The trajectory of structured proportionality in Australia

Perhaps there is a way through this divide. Edelman J was right to say that judges' reasoning should not be a locked box, only unlocked through later cases' explication of their predecessors' decisions.[237] There could be potential for a unanimous breakthrough like in *Lange*, which the majority in *McCloy* considered a 'compromise' of the High Court.[238] Professor Zines was more cynical. For him the unanimity in *Lange* was 'a major miracle explicable only by divine interference with the forces of nature.'[239]

This chapter has argued that Gageler and Gordon JJ's opposition is not tenuous or superficial. Therefore, as the Court currently stands, unanimity would be more the product of miracle than compromise. Douek rightly notes that *Lange* quelled doubts about the survival of the implied freedom in the face of the

---

237 See *Palmer* (n 13) 284 [263] (Edelman J).

238 *McCloy* (n 7) 214 [71] (French CJ, Kiefel, Bell and Keane JJ). It is important to remember that prior to the Court's unanimous judgment in *Lange*, the implication of the freedom was not received well by some members of the bench. McHugh J denounced the majority's approach to implied freedom cases in *McGinty v Western Australia* (1996) 186 CLR 140, 229-235 as 'departing from legitimate judicial reasoning, and not following standards of interpretation' and resorted to external political theory: Leslie Zines 'Legalism, Realism and Judicial Rhetoric in Constitutional Law' in Nye Perram and Rachel Pepper (eds), *The Byers Lectures: 2000-2012* (Federation Press, 2012) 56.

239 Leslie Zines 'Legalism, Realism and Judicial Rhetoric in Constitutional Law' in Nye Perram and Rachel Pepper (eds), *The Byers Lectures: 2000-2012* (Federation Press, 2012) 56.

controversy over the 'activist nature of its discovery.'[240] But it may be premature even now, almost two decades after *Lange*, to suggest the doubts are 'quelled'. Steward J's questioning of the 'existence' of the implied freedom in *LibertyWorks* again leaves open a challenge to the freedom itself.[241] Critically, his Honour's brief exposition of these thoughts was triggered by the Court's divergence on the question of structured proportionality.[242] Therefore doubts similarly need to be quelled over the method that the High Court will use to invalidate laws that infringe upon the implied freedom and s 92.

The 'compromise' in *Lange* was viewed as more consistent with the Court's legalist heritage and a retreat from the 1990s activist climate.[243] It was an authoritative restatement of future limits so that judges in lower courts and the legislature knew where they stood. For greater predictability, similar clarity would be beneficial here. There is a compromise position which could be reached. For example, Professor Rosalind Dixon has suggested a hybrid form of 'calibrated proportionality' to address some of Gageler J's concerns.[244] Professor Stone has also discussed the need to incorporate a notion of deference into the test.[245]

Part two of this chapter looked to the history of structured proportionality. It outlined two important issues: (1) a court's turn to proportionality is fundamentally based on the rule of law; and (2) most common law jurisdictions that have adopted

---

240 Douek (n 205) 555. See also, generally, Jason L Pierce, *Inside the Mason Court Revolution: The High Court of Australia Transformed* (Carolina Academic Press, 2006);

241 *LibertyWorks* (n 8) [298]-[304]. A challenge that his Honour echoes from Callinan J in *Australian Broadcasting Corporation v Lenah Game Meats Pty Ltd* (2001) 208 CLR 199, 339–339 [336]-[348]; and Heydon J in *Monis v The Queen* (2013) 249 CLR 92, 181–184 [243]-[251].

242 Ibid [298].

243 Douek (n 205) 555 citing Shireen Morris and Adrienne Stone, 'Abortion Protests and the Limits of Freedom of Political Communication: *Clubb v Edwards; Preston v Avery*' (2018) 40(3) *Sydney Law Review* 395, 397-8.

244 See, Rosalind Dixon, 'Calibrated Proportionality' (2020) 48(1) *Federal Law Review* 92.

245 See, Adrienne Stone, 'Proportionality and Its Alternatives' (2020) 48(1) *Federal Law Review* 123.

structured proportionality did so after the entrenchment of express human rights instruments. A structured approach was an appropriate means to analyse the questions that then arose. Part three explained that since *Lange* the High Court has tangled with the best method of determining whether a law impermissibly burdens the implied freedom of political communication. For some at the bench, *McCloy* settled the debate, but Gageler and Gordon JJ have consistently articulated their own alternatives. A global pandemic has also seen the proportionality test newly applied in the realm of s 92 via *Palmer*. This demonstrates that the debate is still ongoing. Lastly, this part dove deeper into the reasons for Gageler and Gordon JJ's opposition. It is clear now that their opposition is more than syntactical—their Honours' objections go to the heart of our constitutional history and consider the importance, and relevance, of parliamentary sovereignty, legalism, and judicial deference.

It is thus clear that structured proportionality is far from a 'settled' part of the High Court's contemporary jurisprudence. This chapter has focused on the application of structured proportionality to questions of constitutional invalidity. However, it acknowledged that structured proportionality is a growing area of law and this tool may yet reach into other areas of public law, such as administrative law.

Attempts at incorporating structured proportionality in the administrative law domain have already begun. Justice Rares in *Brett Cattle Co Pty Ltd v Minister for Agriculture, Fisheries and Forestry* explained that it could be used as a 'tool of analysis for ascertaining the rationality and reasonableness of a legislative restriction'.[246] His Honour further added that structured proportionality was 'apposite' as a means of determining the

---

246 *Brett Cattle Co Pty Ltd v Minister for Agriculture, Fisheries and Forestry* (2020) 274 FCR 337, 410 [294].

validity of delegated legislation.[247] In *DBP16 v Minister for Home Affairs* Banks-Smith J reviewed the authorities which considered the application of structured proportionality.[248] However, her Honour declined to apply it in a case concerning a decision-maker's credibility assessment.[249] This judicial commentary is extensive and fertile ground for further analysis. Justice Davis of the Supreme Court of Queensland also recently spoke on proportionality's application to *Wednesbury* unreasonableness.[250] His Honour's closing remarks in that speech are elucidating:

> At present, there is not a huge appetite for [proportionality] at either trial or intermediate Court of Appeal level. That is hardly surprising though as any seismic shift in a test which has had so much attention from the High Court, must surely come from the High Court itself or the legislature.[251]

---

247 Ibid. His Honour's comments are reflective of the language of proportionality which has been used in similar cases, including the majority in *South Australia v Tanner* (1989) 166 CLR 161. Where it was held a law would be 'so oppressive and capricious if it lacks reasonable proportionality as not to be a real exercise of the [delegated law-making] power', at 168 (Wilson, Dawson, Toohey and Gaudron JJ).

248 *DBP16 v Minister for Home Affairs* [2020] FCA 781 (Banks-Smith J) referring to, *inter alia*, *Vanstone v Clark* [2005] FCAFC 189 (Weinberg J); *Brett Cattle Co Pty Ltd v Minister for Agriculture, Fisheries and Forestry* (2020) 274 FCR 337 (Rares J); *Minister for Immigration and Citizenship v Li* (2013) 18 249 CLR 332 (French CJ); *Minister for Immigration and Border Protection v Stretton* (2016) 237 FCR 1 [10] (Allsop CJ); *Lobban v Minister for Justice* [2015] FCA 1361 [96]–[97] (McKerracher J); *Renzullo v Assistant Minister for Immigration and Border Protection* [2016] FCA 412 [40] (McKerracher J); *Malek Fahd Islamic School Limited v Minister for Education and Training (No 2)* [2017] FCA 1377 [68] (Griffiths J); *DJS16 v Minister for Immigration and Border Protection* [2019] FCA 254 [14] (Mortimer J).

249 *DBP16 v Minister for Home Affairs* [2020] FCA 781 [97] (Banks-Smith J).

250 Peter Davis, 'Proportionality in Australian Public Law' (Speech, Australian Institute of Administrative Law, 8 June 2021). *Wednesbury* unreasonableness takes its name from the UK case of *Associated Provincial Picture Houses Ltd. v Wednesbury Corporation* [1948] 1 KB 223,230 (Lord Greene MR) In Australia, unreasonableness, as a ground for judicial review was expressed by French CJ in *Minister for Immigration and Citizenship v Li* (2013) 249 CLR 332 to contain considerations of proportionality 'a disproportionate exercise of an administrative discretion, taking a sledgehammer to crack a nut, may be characterised as irrational and also unreasonable simply on the basis that it exceeds what, on any view, is necessary for the purpose it serves' at 352, [30] (French CJ). See, also, Janina Boughey, 'The Reasonableness of Proportionality in the Australian Administrative Law Context' (2015) 43(1) *Federal Law Review* 59.

251 Ibid 24.

Proportionality analysis is now a pervasive aspect of Australian public law. It is more that an exotic jurisprudential pest[252] and will obviously endure in academic and judicial discourse. Yet when it comes to questions of constitutional invalidity, Gageler and Gordon JJ's objections and counterarguments are compelling. They are rooted in fundamental principles of our constitutional system.

Conclusion

Professor Andrew Lynch noted the High Court's composition was a critical factor in producing the majority decision of the *Engineers' Case*.[253] For Professor Lynch, Isaacs and Higgins JJ's continuing dissent across a number of cases prior to the *Engineers' Case* majority was a 'stunning demonstration of persistent dissent as a legitimate judicial method'.[254] It is a model of how a judge's 'stubborn expression of disagreement' may be rewarded by eventual victory.[255] The same could be argued for the persistent dissent of Gageler and Gordon JJ. Although they are now in the plurality, Kiefel CJ and Keane J have only a few years remaining before retirement from the bench. Alongside Steward J's scepticism, a High Court furnished with two new justices may move away from the *McCloy* formulation. Perhaps a *Lange*-like compromise may occur before then and bring unanimity to the bench and predictability to the Court's future decisions concerning proportionality. Or an administrative law challenge raising proportionality may enable analysis of whether the divide is replicable in a different legal context. In any event, proportionality will be a topic which attracts continued

252 *Murphy* (n 194) 52 [37] (French CJ and Bell J).
253 Andrew Lynch, 'Engineers and Persistent Constitutional Dissent' (2020) 31 *Public Law Review* 28, 31 citing John Goldring, 'The Path to Engineers' in Michael Coper and George Williams (eds), *How Many Cheers for Engineers?* (Federation Press, 1997) 1, 37.
254 Ibid 32.
255 Ibid.

consideration into the future.

When speaking on his vision for the structure and function of the *Constitution,* Gageler J said the following of the role of judges and lawyers in constitutional development:

> At any given time [constitutional law] exists within the collective imaginations of those who practice and administer it. They are relatively few, but they still cannot all be expected to see things the same way. They are the custodians for the present of a constitutional tradition which they must interpret each for themselves in terms that are meaningful to them and for their own time...The doctrine of precedent is a white-fella's version of respect for elders.[256]

The content and history of structured proportionality focuses our attention on some of the most fundamental aspects of the Australian constitutional system. Whether that is federalism and parliamentary sovereignty, constitutional freedoms, or the legalist tradition. This context also reminds us of the importance of understanding how our highest court makes its decisions and the methods it follows in so doing.

---

256 Gageler (n 35) 216.

6

The *Australian Constitution* and our First Peoples – a statutory solution seeded by *Mabo* (*No.2*)?

A. Keith Thompson

Abstract

In this chapter I disagree with the idea that aboriginal reconciliation in Australia requires constitutional amendment. Instead, following the example of New Zealand after the establishment of Waitangi Tribunal in 1975 and the enlargement of its jurisdiction in 1985, seven years before the *Mabo* (*No. 2*) *Case* was decided in 1992, I argue that Australia should have started its process of reconciliation in 1993 by statute with something much better than the *Native Title Act* (Cth) which followed. I observe that the High Court prepared the way for that process to begin when it overruled the *terra nullius* doctrine in the *Mabo* (*No. 2*) *Case* in a conscious exercise of its interpretive sovereignty despite two centuries of contrary executive policy decisions. I argue that the High Court's similar exercise of its interpretive sovereignty in the *Love Case* in 2020 shows that Australia would accept statutory changes which began a reconciliation process which New Zealand pioneered 40 years ago.

Keywords

Aboriginal reconciliation, interpretive sovereignty, Waitangi Tribunal, Makarrata Tribunal, *Mabo (No.2) Case, Love Case, Native Title Act 1993* (Cth)

Introduction

In *Roach v Electoral Commissioner*,[1] Justice Heydon obliquely criticised Justice Kirby's insistence that international legal materials were a legitimate influence in Australian jurisprudence.[2] In *Al-Kateb*, Justice McHugh had criticised this view by saying 'courts cannot read the Constitution by reference to the provisions of international law that have become accepted since the Constitution was enacted in 1900';[3] that 'this Court has never accepted that the Constitution contains an implication to the effect that it should be construed to conform with the rules of international law';[4] and that to do so would amount to '*amending* the Constitution in disregard of the direction in s 128 of the Constitution...that the Constitution is to be amended'[5] only by legislation approved in a referendum.

Justice Heydon said that

> [t]he proposition that the legislative power of the Commonwealth is affected or limited by developments in international law since 1900 is denied...by twenty-one of the Justices of this Court who have considered

---

1 *Roach v Electoral Commissioner* (2007) 233 CLR 162.
2 See for example, *Al-Kateb v Godwin* (2004) 219 CLR 562, 617-625 and his Philip A. Hart Memorial Lecture delivered at Georgetown University on April 16, 2019, "Constitutional Law and International Law: National Exceptionalism and the Democratic Deficit", *Georgetown Law Journal*, Volume 98, No. 2, January 2010 and (2010) 12 *UNDALR*, 95 <http://www.austlii.edu.au/au/journals/UNDAULawRw/2010/6.pdf>.
3 *Al-Kateb v Godwin* (2004) 219 CLR 562, 589 [62].
4 Ibid 591 [66].
5 Ibid 592 [68] (emphasis original).

the matter, and affirmed by only one.[6]

Yet Justice McHugh had earlier joined Chief Justice Mason in concurring with Justice Brennan in *Mabo* (*No.2*) in 1992[7] in overturning the *terra nullius* doctrine in Australia in reliance on international interpretations of the common law of the British Commonwealth.

While I am sure Justices McHugh and Heydon would protest that the international jurisprudence relied on in *Mabo* (*No.2*) was not the same international law they were talking about in *Al-Kateb* and *Roach*, the use and interpretation of international jurisprudential materials clearly has more nuance than those eminent rebukes to Justice Kirby allow. Justice Isaacs famously relied upon English common law to justify his sea change in the High Court's interpretation of the *Constitution* in the *Engineers'* *Case*, Justice Dixon affirmed many times that our *Constitution* is premised in common law materials (including common law materials from the United Kingdom), and the High Court relied upon common law materials to justify the shift away from the *terra nullius* doctrine that occurred in *Mabo* (*No. 2*). While contemporary public opinion in Australia seems to accept the view that our modern nation cannot atone for the past atrocities and lingering injustices that have been committed against our First Peoples without almost impossible constitutional change, in this chapter I assert that constitutional change is not necessary to effect that required atonement.

In particular, I assert that we do not need to amend the *Constitution* to achieve a just settlement with our First Peoples despite the praiseworthy efforts of the authors of the Uluru Statement from the Heart,[8] because New Zealand achieved

---

6 *Roach v Electoral Commissioner* (2007) 233 CLR 162, 224 [181].
7 *Mabo* (*No.2*) *v Queensland* (1992) (*Mabo* (*No. 2*)) 66 ALR 408.
8 "The Uluru Statement from the Heart", The Uluru Statement, 26 May 2017 <https://
  ulurustatement.org/the-statement>.

a change similar to that to which we aspire without such amendment. Indeed, there is no written constitution in New Zealand to amend, so those politicians had to find another way. Australia can do the same. This insight is particularly useful since constitutional amendment in Australia has proven so difficult.[9] To accomplish the just settlement process that was hinted at in *Mabo (No.2)*, we only need to start recognising the injustices that have been done to our First Peoples by passing ordinary legislation designed to accomplish that objective. The Keating government showed that could have been done immediately after *Mabo (No. 2)* when the *Native Title Act 1993* (Cth) was passed. Sadly however, that Act did not follow the ambitious path towards reconciliation which New Zealand had taken with 1985 amendments to the *Treaty of Waitangi Act 1975* just 8 years earlier. While the view of Justices Deane, Toohey and Gaudron that compensation should have been paid in the *Mabo (No. 2) Case*[10] was a bridge too far for the other members of the High Court in 1992, New Zealand's subsequent achievements using the Waitangi Tribunal show what could have been done without constitutional amendment, and thus what could still be done.[11] I also suggest that just as the decision in *Mabo (No. 2)* signalled that the time was right for reconciliation steps in relation to land to begin in Australia, so the majority decision in *Love* in 2020[12] raises the question as to whether the time may now be right for further steps in pursuit of more complete reconciliation.

My principal argument is that the High Court decision in *Mabo*

---

9 Note that there have been 8/44 successful constitutional amendments in Australia since federation (122 years as of this writing). 27/33 have been passed in the 232 years since US federation and 15 of those were passed in the first 90 years. Because of the difficulty of passing constitutional amendments in Australia, Australia has been dubbed the 'frozen continent' by many Australian constitutional law commentators though the phrase was first coined by Geoffrey Sawyer in his 1967 book *Australian Federalism in the Courts* (Melbourne University Press).

10 *Mabo (No.2)* 440, 444, 448 and 452 (per Deane and Gaudron JJ); and 483, 489, 491-492, and 498-499 (per Toohey J).

11 *Treaty of Waitangi Act 1975* (NZ).

12 *Love v Commonwealth (Love)* [2020] HCA 3.

(*No. 2*) was an exercise in what I define as its interpretive sovereignty. I further argue that just as that exercise of interpretive sovereignty precipitated the *Native Title Act 1993* (Cth) passed by the Commonwealth legislature, so the High Court decision in the *Love Case* could be used by the Commonwealth legislature to justify more comprehensive reconciliation legislation now. The High Court has exercised its interpretive power to promote sea change in the Australian legal environment sparingly, but it has used that power on a number of occasions. I refer to the decisions in the *Engineers'*,[13] *Tasmanian Dam*[14] and *Work Choices Cases*[15] as examples, but I explain that the decision in *Mabo* (*No.2*) is the best example in the First Peoples context.

In Part One, I define the High Court's interpretive sovereignty and trace it back to the majority decision in the *Engineers' Case* in 1920. I suggest that while Justice Isaacs said that he was returning Australian jurisprudence to its British common law roots, in fact he used the interpretive sovereignty of the High Court to assert the new nation's primacy over the states in the face of existing precedent. In Part Two, I explain that the *Engineers'* (1920), *Tasmanian Dam* (1983), *Mabo* (*No.2*) (1991) and *Work Choices* (2006) *Cases* are all examples of cases where the High Court exercised its interpretive sovereignty. But I also note the development of the implied freedom of political communication and more recent use of the European doctrine of structured proportionality as examples of the High Court using its interpretive sovereignty to change the social direction that Australia takes. The development of the implied freedom of political communication and the use of the European doctrine of structured proportionality both show that the High Court has moved on from the literalism that Chief Justice Dixon recommended in hard cases. Like the decisions in the

13 *Engineers v Adelaide Steamship Company* (*Engineers' Case*) (1920) 28 CLR 129.
14 *Commonwealth v Tasmania* (*Tasmanian Dam Case*) (1983) 158 CLR 1.
15 *New South Wales v Commonwealth* (*Work Choices Case*) (2006) 229 CLR 1.

Engineers', Tasmanian Dam, Mabo (No. 2) and *Work Choices Cases*, the implied freedom of political communication and the adoption of the doctrine of structured proportionality were controversial when they were first adopted, yet they have been accepted and that acceptance is a measure of our national trust that the High Court will do the right thing. That expectation of trust was set when our framers created a High Court modelled on the Supreme Court of the United States given its independence from the legislature.

In Part Three I lay out the rudiments of the Waitangi Tribunal justice mechanisms that New Zealand has created for its first peoples since 1975 in the *Treaty of Waitangi Act 1975* and its amendments. I note the passage of the original Act in 1975 and the most important amendment particularly that which was passed in 1985, seven years before the *Mabo (No. 2)* decision and eight years before the *Native Title Act 1993* (Cth) was passed in Australia. I explain that these New Zealand legislative provisions show that better legislation could have been passed in favour of our First Peoples when the *Native Title Act* was passed, but I observe that the *Native Title Act* could still be superceded by better legislation that closely follows the New Zealand Waitangi model.

In Part Four I suggest that the *Love* majority's use of Justice Brennan's criteria of Aboriginality and other reasoning in the *Mabo (No. 2) Case* confirm that our High Court judges remain alive to Australia's failure to protect the interests of our First Peoples. The *Love decision* also manifests the willingness of the High Court to protect our First Peoples without the need for amendment to the *Australian Constitution* when future occasion arises. I note that the Commonwealth legislature has not passed legislation to undo some of the effect of the majority judgment in *Love* as the Keating government did with the *Native Title Act* after *Mabo (No. 2)*. That is because they cannot. Just as the discovery of the implied freedom of political communication in the *Constitution* following the *Davis Case* in 1988, foreclosed legislation that would prevent reasonable political protest in the future, so the finding that Daniel Love and Brendan Thoms were not aliens within the meaning of the text of the *Constitution*, put further legislation in that matter beyond the reach of the Commonwealth legislature. I suggest that the High Court's discovery of modern implications in the word 'alien' as used in s 51 (xix) of the *Constitution* shows both that the High Court can use its interpretive sovereignty to foreclose injustice by the Commonwealth legislature and that it is willing to do so to prevent injustice to our First Peoples when litigation occasion arises.

I conclude with the recommendation that Australia should immediately take steps to implement an Australian version of the New Zealand Waitangi Tribunal regime, with our tribunal to perhaps be called the Makarrata Tribunal or Commission. Because of the salutary results that I say flow to our society when our High Court exercises its interpretive power, I also recommend that it should do so more regularly, particularly in First People's space. In particular, I suggest that because two influential majorities of the High Court have understood the spiritual connection of our First Peoples with their land and waters (in the *Mabo* (*No.2*) and *Love Cases*), they are the appropriate constitutional institution to press the case for change when appropriate cases are brought before them. I also suggest that the High Court's recent decision in the *Love Case* indicates that the time is right for the Commonwealth legislature to create a Makarrata Tribunal or Commission to repair past injustices towards Australia's First Peoples on the same basis as the Waitangi Tribunal has done in New Zealand. The legislative creation of a tribunal modelled on New Zealand's Waitangi Tribunal would remove the need for constitutional amendment which is practically foreclosed to the Commonwealth Parliament because we are the 'frozen continent' where formal constitutional change is concerned. While the Commonwealth legislature could give an Australian Makarrata Tribunal or Commission narrower terms of reference than the New Zealand legislature gave to the Waitangi Tribunal, I express the hope that they would not do so. Australia is a rich enough country to fully fund a scheme that would respond to all the injustices that a Makarrata Tribunal or Commission might identify.

Part One

Literal interpretation of the *Australian Constitution* and Interpretive Sovereignty

The interpretive sovereignty of the High Court is not as well understood as the judicial sovereignty of the Supreme Court of the United States (Supreme Court). That is because of some things that Justice Isaacs said in his judgment for the plurality in the *Engineers' Case* in 1920, and because Australia does not have a constitutional Bill of Rights which has made the judicial sovereignty of the Supreme Court more obvious. While it is true that Justice Isaacs sought to distance Australian jurisprudence from the American precedents which had guided some High Court decisions before 1920, Justice Isaacs still affirmed that the *Australian Constitution* was 'the political compact of the whole of the people of Australia'.[16]

Justice Isaacs' assertion of the *Australian Constitution's* supremacy has been reiterated by subsequent panels of the High Court, perhaps most definitively in the period of reconstruction that followed WWII. But while the states' attempt to unwind Commonwealth control of uniform taxation adopted during

16 *Engineers' Case*, 142.

the war[17] was rebuffed by the High Court in 1957 effectively because the states left their challenge too long,[18] the High Court still insisted that constitutional limitations on Commonwealth power be observed in all other matters. Thus, after a period of tolerance justified by post-war reconstruction needs, the High Court told the Commonwealth in *R v Foster* in 1949 that it could no longer exercise employment law powers as if it were a unitary state since those powers then belonged to the states.[19] Nor could the Commonwealth tell the states and local authorities where they should do their banking,[20] and despite its banking power,[21] the Commonwealth could not consolidate all of the nation's trading banks into one.[22] Nor could the Commonwealth Parliament tell the High Court how to interpret the *Constitution* by including a long preamble to justify its Act to dissolve the Communist Party.[23] The High Court's interpretive sovereignty was very clear in the early 1950s if it had been forgotten in the years since the *Engineers' Case* was decided and especially during WWII.

What did the *Engineers' Case* decide – interpretive sovereignty, Westminster deference or legalism?

There are many ironies in *Engineers'* decision, not least of them those referred to by RTE Latham in the chapter he wrote in WK Hancock's *Survey of British Commonwealth Affairs: Problems of Nationality 1918-1936* before his untimely death in the Battle

---

17 *South Australia v Commonwealth (First Uniform Tax Case)* (1942) 65 CLR 373.
18 *Victoria v Commonwealth (Second Uniform Tax Case)* (1957) 99 CLR 575.
19 *R v Foster* (1949) 79 CLR 43.
20 *Melbourne Corporation v Commonwealth (Melbourne Corporation Case)* (1947) 74 CLR 31.
21 *Australian Constitution* s 51 (xiii).
22 *Bank of New South Wales v Commonwealth (Bank Nationalisation Case)* (1948) 76 CLR 1.
23 *Australian Communist Party v Commonwealth (Communist Party Case)* (1951) 83 CLR 1.

of Britain.[24] Latham observed:

> The original bench of the High Court…treated the constitution as a federal compact…by applying the American doctrine of the immunity of federal and state instrumentalities, a sort of rule of mutual tolerance. A brilliant minority, appointed to the bench in 1906, broke British judicial tradition by persisting in consistent dissent…As the older judges left the bench…this solid minority became the majority. The revolutionary *Engineers' Case* marks the point at which their heterodoxy became the new orthodoxy. The reasoning is open to all sorts of criticism. The case was decided on high constitutional ground, when a much simpler argument would have sufficed. It cut off Australian constitutional law from American precedents…in favour of the crabbed English rules of statutory interpretation which are one of the sorriest features of English law, and…particularly unsuited to the interpretation of a rigid constitution. The majority judgment was, further, self-contradictory in two ways. It declared that the Constitution was to be interpreted by its words alone; yet the court, in reaching that very proposition, took notice of responsible government, a matter…extrinsic to strict law,…[but secondly] the real ground [of the decision] is nowhere stated…This real ground was…that the Constitution had been intended to create a nation, and that it had succeeded;…[so] that a merely contractual view of the Constitution was therefore out of date… and was stultifying the [vital] Commonwealth industrial power.[25]

As Blackshield and Williams' have noted, 'Latham's identification of "the real ground" of the *Engineers Case* was subsequently endorsed by Windeyer J in *Victoria v Commonwealth* (*Payroll*

---

24 RTE Latham, "The Law and the Commonwealth" in WK Hancock, *Survey of British Commonwealth Affairs: Problems of Nationality 1918-1936* (Oxford University Press, 1937), vol 1, 510.
25 Ibid 563-564.

Tax Case)'.[26]

These commentators might also have drawn attention to the irony of the *Engineers' Case* plurality recognition of 'the common sovereignty of all parts of the British Empire'[27] as another English doctrine that differentiated Australia's constitutional approach from the American precedents. But as RTE Latham also said, a statement in the judgment,

> That the words of the Constitution permitted the view of the federal relationship which the times demanded...would have made the Engineers' Case...a quasi-political decision, based on a far-sighted view of ultimate constitutional policy, of the type with which the Supreme Court of the United States in its greatest periods has made us familiar...[and] would have been no more political than several of Sir Isaac Isaacs most notable judgments.[28]

We may assume that the reason that Justice Isaacs framed the *Engineers'* decision in legal language rather than the quasi-political language that RTE Latham suggests, was because Justice Isaacs made his decision as a common law judge and there was as yet no established tradition of judicial interpretive sovereignty in the British Commonwealth to draw upon. The consequence, as Justice McHugh said in *Eastman v The Queen* in 2000 is that while

> [t]he majority justices in the *Engineers' Case* emphatically rejected the use of external political principles or policies to interpret the Constitution, and thereby committed the Court to the strict legalism of which Sir Owen Dixon became the leading exponent...[they] did not rule out the history or background of the Constitution as interpretative aids. [Indeed t]he majority justices in that case expressly

---

26 George Williams, Sean Brennan and Andrew Lynch, *Blackshield and Williams, Australian Constitutional Law and Theory, Commentary and Materials* (Federation Press, 2018), 291 [7.48].

27 *Engineers' Case*, 146, 148.

28 Latham (n 24) 564.

> said that the Constitution was to be read in the light
> of the circumstances in which it was made with
> knowledge of the combined fabric of the common law
> and the pre-Constitution statute law...[Thus] most of
> the concepts and purposes are stated at a sufficient
> level of abstraction or generality to enable it to be
> infused with *current* understanding of those concepts
> and purposes.[29]

While it is difficult to know exactly what Justice Isaacs meant when he recognised 'common sovereignty' as an (ironical) implication in the *Constitution* in the *Engineers' Case*,[30] he could not have been agreeing with Dicey's view that apex courts in a federation are the repositories of sovereign power.[31] The reason Justice Isaacs could not say that in 1920 was because it would have been one heterodox statement too far, and to settle the new orthodoxy he had been consistently expressing since 1906,[32] he had to hedge his judgment with as many traditional references to English orthodoxy as he could find. It is also possible that he intended no assertion of judicial supremacy and that my commentary misrepresents his words and his intent.[33]

The larger point however is that the decision in *Engineers'* was accepted. While Jeffrey Goldsworthy has 'questioned how it can be reconciled with the High Court's professed commitment to respecting the limits of "text and structure" in the interpretation

---

29 *Eastman v The Queen* (2000) (*Eastman Case*) 203 CLR 1, 47 and 50 (emphasis original).

30 Twice ironical, since a limited federal government could not be sovereign in the then established British sense, but also ironical if Justice Isaacs was referring to the legislative and executive sovereignty of the Imperial Parliament over Australia since federation began a process of independence. That process was further developed when Australia adopted the *Statute of Westminster 1931* (Imp) in 1942 and completed by the passage of the various versions of the *Australia Acts* in 1986.

31 A V Dicey, *Introduction to the Study of the Law of the Constitution* (Macmillan, 1st ed, 1885; 10th ed, 1959), 175.

32 See Latham (n 24) 563.

33 It is unlikely that he was not asserting any judicial supremacy at all, since both majority decisions expressly overruled what he called the doctrine of 'implied prohibition' and confirmed the 'supremacy...to every Commonwealth Act, over...all State Acts' (*Engineers' Case* 154-155 per Knox CJ, Isaacs, Rich and Starke JJ). See also Higgins J (ibid 164-167).

of the Constitution',[34] Justice Windeyer's view that it 'would…
be an error and the adoption of a heresy' to return to the theories
that it discarded, has prevailed.[35] Indeed, 'Sir Anthony Mason…
defended' the *Engineers' decision* later still as 'an instance
of evolutionary or progressive interpretation' and confirmed
'that Windeyer J was "ahead of his time in advocating this
approach"'.[36]

Interpretive sovereignty after WWII?

The limitations on Commonwealth power remain. Sometimes
the High Court finds that the Commonwealth legislature has
reached beyond the power that was provided in *Constitution*.
Particularly after the end of the Second World War, there were
strong statements from the High Court about Commonwealth
legislative overreach. For example, in the *Melbourne
Corporation Case*, Justice Dixon said

> The prima-facie rule is that the power to legislate with
> respect to a given subject enables the Parliament to
> make laws which…affect the operation of the States
> and their agencies…It is subject however, to certain
> reservations…The foundation of the Constitution is
> the conception of a central government and a number
> of State governments separately organized. The
> Constitution predicates their continued existence as
> independent entities…the considerations upon which
> the States' title to protection from Commonwealth
> control depends arise not from the character of the
> powers retained by the States but from their position
> as separate governments…the efficacy of the system
> logically demands that, unless a given legislative

---

34 Williams, Brennan and Lynch, *Blackshield and Williams* (n 26), 292 [7.49] referring to Jeffrey Goldsworthy, "Justice Windeyer on the *Engineers' Case*" (2009) 37 *Federal Law Review* 363.

35 *Victoria v Commonwealth (Payroll Tax Case)* (1971) 122 CLR 353, 396.

36 Williams, Brennan and Lynch, *Blackshield and Williams* (n 26), 292 [7.49] referring to Anthony Mason, "Justice Windeyer on the *Engineers' Case*" (2010) 12 *Constitutional Law and Policy Review* 41.

> power appears from its content, context or subject matter so to intend, it should not be understood as authorizing the Commonwealth to make a law aimed at the restriction or control of a State in the exercise of its executive authority.[37]

Two years later, the High Court found it necessary to go even further. In *R v Foster* in 1949,[38] a unanimous Court said

> When actual hostilities have ceased the scope of application of the defence power necessarily diminishes...The Constitution does not confer upon the Commonwealth Parliament any power in express terms to deal with the consequences of war...If it were held that the defence power would justify any legislation at any time which dealt with any matter the character of which had been changed by the war... then the result would be that the Commonwealth Parliament would have a general power of making laws...with respect to almost every subject. Nearly all the limitations imposed by the Commonwealth power by the carefully framed Constitution would disappear and a unitary system of government... would be brought into existence notwithstanding the deliberate acceptance by the people of a Federal system of government upon the basis of the division of powers set forth in the Constitution. We proceed to state reasons why the Court should not ascribe an operation so far-reaching and, indeed, revolutionary, to the defence power.[39]

After those post-war cases were decided against the Commonwealth, the attempted overreach subsided for a time, but the possibilities of sovereign-like power had not altogether departed from the mind of the Commonwealth executive and legislature. Hence in the *Communist Party Case*[40] another two years later, in a 6-1 majority decision with Chief Justice

---

37 *Melbourne Corporation Case*, 78, 82-83.
38 R *v Foster* (1949) 79 CLR 43.
39 Ibid 81-83.
40 *Communist Party Case* (1951) 83 CLR 1.

Latham, a former Leader of the Opposition and federal Attorney-General alone dissenting, the High Court made it clear that the Commonwealth legislature could not tell the High Court how to do its interpretive job. Justice McTiernan said that 'the question whether the Act is valid or invalid... is a judicial question which only the judicature has the power to decide finally and conclusively.'[41] Justice Dixon said the Commonwealth legislature had no power under the *Constitution* to dissolve the Communist Party and its affiliated bodies, forfeit their property or to declare that its officers or members were 'disqualified for certain classes of post'.[42] And Justice Fullagar famously explained this was all because 'a stream cannot rise higher than its source.'[43]

So once again, the High Court's interpretive sovereignty remained and to date, no High Court decision against the policy direction of the Commonwealth Executive or Parliament has occasioned protest like that which has occasionally followed controversial apex court decisions in Europe and the United States.[44] It is beyond the scope of this chapter to determine whether that lack of Australian protest is a consequence of Australian apathy, the high regard in which the High Court is held by the Australian people, or the circumspect manner in which the Court conducts itself. But there have been decisions

---

41 Ibid 205.

42 Ibid 183-184.

43 Ibid 258.

44 For example, the decision that crucifixes could not be displayed in public school class-rooms in Germany (*Classroom Crucifix II Case* in Germany (Federal Constitutional Court of Germany, 92 BVerfGEI (1995) 'triggered a storm of protest throughout Germany' with 'Chancellor Helmut Kohl call[ing] the decision "incomprehensible"' (WC Durham and BG Scharffs, *Law and Religion, National, International and Comparative Perspectives* (United States: Walters Kluwer, 2nd ed., 2019. 611). The similar 'Italian Crucifix Case' saw a unanimous (7-0) decision of a Chamber of the Second Section of the European Court of Human Rights in 2009 reversed by the Grand Chamber of that Court in 2011 15-2 following large scale protests in Italy which resulted in an Italian government appeal which was publicly supported by '[m]ore than twenty European nations' (ibid 613-617 referring to *Lautsi v Italy* ECHR (Grand Chamber), App. No. 30814/06 (18 March 2011). In the United States, many controversial United States Supreme Court judicial appointments and decisions have been followed by widespread protest.

that likely would have led to protests in other countries and did not in Australia even though they similarly broke new ground. I have chosen to discuss three below because they also broke new ground, but did not occasion protest or significant political dissent and thus represent successful examples of what Sir Anthony Mason called 'instance[s] of evolutionary or progressive interpretation'.[45]

Part Two

Tasmanian Dam, Work Choices and *Mabo* (*No. 2*) - cases that have interpreted the *Constitution* progressively despite Dixonian literalism

Despite RTE Latham's assertion that the 'real ground [of the *Engineers'* decision] was...that the Constitution had been intended to create a nation, and that it had succeeded',[46] Australian nationality was born in the trenches of the First World War,[47] which ended just two years before the decision in *Engineers'* was handed down. And there was no such thing as Australian citizenship until 1948, three years after the end of the Second World War.[48]

The framers intended that the colonies would become states, that their separate identity would continue and that the continuing state governments would be the primary governments of the federated nation. That is the reason the original panel of the High Court developed the reserved state powers and implied immunity of instrumentalities doctrines which were reversed by

---

45 Anthony Mason (n 36).

46 Latham (n 24), 564.

47 See for example Rob Lundie and Dr Joy McCann, "Australian as a Nation", 4 May 2015, *Parliament of Australia* <https://www.aph.gov.au/About_Parliament/Parliamentary_Departments/Parliamentary_Library/pubs/rp/rp1415/ComParl#_Toc418157267> referring to FK Crowley ed, *A New History of Australia* (Melbourne: Heinemann, 1974) 260-262.

48 The *Nationality and Citizenship Act 1948* came into force on 26 January 1949.

the decision in the *Engineers' Case*. Though as Justice McHugh said in the *Eastman Case*, the High Court majority

> emphatically rejected the use of external political principles or policies to interpret the Constitution... the concepts and purposes [we]re stated at a sufficient level of abstraction or generality to enable it to be infused with *current* understanding of those concepts and purposes.[49]

Arguably that is exactly what happened in the *Engineers' Case* itself. The generalised 'concepts and purposes' the framers had chosen before 1901 were infused with a post-WWI meaning in 1920 and then again with a post-WWII meaning after 1948 as the High Court reminded the Commonwealth that the War had ended and so had its defence power-justified practice of operating in the domain of the states.

However, though he is said to have regretted the statement,[50] when Sir Owen Dixon became Chief Justice in 1952, he said

> that a close adherence to legal reasoning is the only way to maintain the confidence of all parties in federal conflicts. It may be that the Court is thought to be excessively legalistic. I should be sorry to think that it is anything else. There is no other safe guide to judicial decisions in great conflicts than a strict and complete legalism.[51]

While William Gummow has surmised that Justice Dixon only regretted his reference to 'legalism' in this passage because of 'its impact upon the Menzies government' in the wake of 'the recent decision in the *Communist Party Case*',[52] it is clear that

---

49 *Eastman Case*, 1, 47 and 50 (emphasis original).

50 See for example William Gummow, "The 2017 Winterton Lecture: Sir Owen Dixon Today", *University of Western Australia Law Review* 43 (2016), 30, 51. See also William Gummow, "Sir Owen Dixon Today" in *Jesting Pilate and other papers and addresses*, Susan Crennan and William Gummow eds. (Sydney: Federation Press, 3rd ed., 2019), 67.

51 Owen Dixon, "Address on Taking Office as Chief Justice of the High Court" in *Jesting Pilate*, 289.

52 Gummow, "Sir Owen Dixon Today", Winterton Lecture, 51 and in *Jesting Pilate*, 67.

Justice Dixon did not resile from this statement intellectually. For as Merralls explained, he deplored judicial decisions where 'right judgment had yielded to expediency'[53] and was often unable 'to reject a conclusion of courts of the highest authority... [even] though shown to be founded on error'.[54] But as William Gummow also opined, not all of Justice Dixon's opinions have stood the test of time[55] though they have cast a long shadow over Australian jurisprudence.[56] Significantly, as Leslie Zines observed, 'there was lacking in Dixon's constitutional judgments recognition that legal reasoning could lead to more than one legally sustainable conclusion'.[57] And the cases considered in the following paragraphs identify High Court majority decisions which would not have accorded with Justice Dixon's 'strict and complete legalism'.

The *Tasmanian Dam Case*[58] - protecting state autonomy?

Arguably the High Court's decision in the *Tasmanian Dam Case* does not respect the continued existence and autonomy of Tasmania as a state which concerned Justice Dixon in the *Melbourne Corporation Case*. Nor did it prevent the Commonwealth from denying Tasmania the ability to develop its 'innominate and anomalous' property interests in the Franklin River system.[59] Yet Tasmania accepted the decision without the

---

53 James Merralls, "The Rt Hon Sir Owen Dixon, OM, GCMG, 1886-1972" in *Jesting Pilate*, 33.

54 Ibid 37.

55 Gummow (n 52), "Sir Owen Dixon Today", Winterton Lecture, 40 and in *Jesting Pilate*, 57. See also Williams, Brennan and Lynch, *Blackshield and Williams* (n 26), 175-178, [5.8] and [5.12-5.13].

56 Williams, Brennan and Lynch, *Blackshield and Williams* (n 26), 170-175, [5.1-5.7].

57 Gummow (n 52), "Sir Owen Dixon Today", Winterton Lecture, 51 and in *Jesting Pilate*, 66 referring to Zines' "2002 Sir Maurice Byers Lecture" (Perram and Pepper eds, *The Byers Lectures 2000-2012*, (Sydney: Federation Press, 2013) 48, 50-51).

58 *Tasmanian Dam Case* (1983) 158 CLR 1.

59 *Bank Nationalisation Case*, (1948) 76 CLR 1, 349 (per Dixon J).

issue of an injunction to enforce compliance[60] – even though it could not be said in 1983 that this use of the Commonwealth external affairs power was well settled.[61] In his dissent,[62]

---

60 Williams, Brennan and Lynch, *Blackshield and Williams* (n 26) note that when Commonwealth counsel asked the High Court for an injunction to formally prevent the Premier of Tasmania proceeding with its Hydro-Electric Dam project, Chief Justice Gibbs 'protested indignantly: "*Of course* the Tasmanian government will comply with the law as this Court has declared it to be!"' (Ibid 582 [13.136] (emphasis original).

61 The decision in *Koowarta v Bjelke-Petersen* (182) 153 CLR 168 in favour of the Commonwealth's external affairs power to implement the *International Convention on the Elimination of All Forms of Racial Discrimination* (opened for signature 21 December 1965, 660 UNTS 195, entered into force 4 January 1969) was a close 4:3 decision. When Australia had ratified the *International Covenant on Civil and Political Rights* on 13 August 1980, she did so with the following reservation:

Articles 2 and 50

Australia advises that, the people having united as one people in a Federal Commonwealth under the Crown, it has a federal constitutional system. It accepts that the provisions of the Covenant extend to all parts of Australia as a federal State without any limitations or exceptions. It enters a general reservation that Article 2, paragraphs 2 and 3 and Article 50 shall be given effect consistently with and subject to the provisions in Article 2, paragraph 2.

Under Article 2, paragraph 2, steps to adopt measures necessary to give effect to the rights recognised in the Covenant are to be taken in accordance with each State Party's Constitutional processes which, in the case of Australia, are the processes of a federation in which legislative, executive and judicial powers to give effect to the rights recognised in the Covenant are distributed among the federal (Commonwealth) authorities and the authorities of the constituent States.

In particular, in relation to the Australian States the implementation of those provisions of the Covenant over whose subject matter the federal authorities exercise legislative, executive and judicial jurisdiction will be a matter for those authorities; and the implementation of those provisions of the Covenant over whose subject matter the authorities of the constituent States exercise legislative, executive and judicial jurisdiction will be a matter for those authorities; and where a provision has both federal and State aspects, its implementation will accordingly be a matter for the respective constitutionally appropriate authorities (for the purpose of implementation, the Northern Territory will be regarded as a constituent State).

To this end, the Australian Government has been in consultation with the responsible State and Territory Ministers with the object of developing co-operative arrangements to co-ordinate and facilitate the implementation of the Covenant <http://www.austlii.edu.au/au/other/dfat/treaties/1980/23.html>.

62 In his *Tasmanian Dam* dissent, Dawson J observed that the reach of the external affairs power confirmed the year before in *Koowarta v Bjelke-Peterson* (1982) 153 CLR 168 did not arise at federation since the power to make treaties was then confined to the Imperial Crown. While that had changed with Australia's retrospective adoption of the *Statute of Westminster 1931* (Imp) in 1942, it was doubtful that Australia's executive treaty making power under s 61 enabled the executive to make treaties which would expand their legislative powers beyond the limitations imposed on those powers in s 51. He therefore opined that the Commonwealth could only make laws implementing international treaties that fell within its existing domestic law-making powers (*Tasmanian Dam Case*, 561-563).

subsequent extra-judicial comment,[63] and in later reluctant acceptance that the *Tasmanian Dam decision* had become the law of Australia,[64] Justice Dawson complained that the majority decision ignored the limits on Commonwealth legislative power intended by the framers.

He was not alone. There was a similar lament from Justice Callinan in dissent after the High Court extended the reach of the corporation's power in the *Work Choices Case* in 2006. But again, the majority decision in the *Tasmanian Dam Case* was accepted without citizen protest and judges like Justice Dawson who believed in Justice Dixon's 'strict and complete legalism', accepted its consequences because they believed they were bound by High Court precedent.

The *Work Choices Case* - the limitation of Commonwealth power?

While some commentators have opined that John Howard's success in the *Work Choices Case* in 2006 was the reason why he lost the 2007 federal election and his own seat in the

---

63 In this Southey Memorial Lecture at Melbourne University Law School in 1983, Justice Dawson lamented:

it must now be said that the potential scope of Commonwealth legislative power is coextensive with the potential scope of international agreement…[thus] the external affairs power, may, as a matter of constitutional theory, be regarded as open-ended…the Commonwealth presently has the capacity to cut a swathe through areas hitherto thought to be within the residual powers of the States ("The Constitution – Major Overhaul or Simple Tune-up?" (1984) *Melbourne University Law Review* 353, 358).

64 For example, in *Richardson v Forestry Commission* (1988) 164 CLR 261 he maintained that it was appropriate to restrict the Commonwealth to its s 51 subject matter legislative limits despite the result in *Tasmanian Dam* and said:

the fact that an agreement is made internationally will not determine whether its subject-matter is external or domestic in character. Since there is no practical limit to those matters which may form the subject of international agreement, the result of taking the opposite view is that there is no practical limit to the scope of the external affairs power. That is to say, the result is that par (xxix) has the potential to obliterate the division of legislative power otherwise effected by s 51. Simply as a matter of construction, I cannot believe that such as result was ever intended (ibid 320).

Parliament,[65] even the unpopularity of the industrial reforms at issue in that case did not lead to large scale protests when the High Court upheld his legislation.

The former Keating Labor government arguably laid the groundwork for Howard's *Work Choices* legislative reform by engaging the external affairs power in its promotion and defence of Commonwealth industrial reform a decade earlier.[66] But the Howard government's engagement of the corporation's power as its primary constitutional justification for the *Workplace Relations Amendment (WorkChoices) Act 2005* (Cth) broke new ground. It practically reversed the narrow approach to the interpretation of s 51(xx) which had endured since *Huddart Parker v Moorehead* in 1909[67] and adopted what had still been a dissenting approach to that interpretation five years earlier.[68] However, even though the legislation occasioned national controversy with extensive contrary advertising campaigns when proposed so that five states and numerous trade unions and peak bodies intervened in the litigation, there was again no protest after the High Court handed down its decision – despite Justice Callinan's anxious dissent. Also, in the spirit of Justice Dixon's 'strict and complete legalism', Justice Callinan said:

> There is nothing in the text or the structure of the
> Constitution to suggest that the Commonwealth's
> powers should be enlarged, by successive decisions

---

65 For example, "WorkChoices blamed for election loss", *ABC News*, 25 November 2007 < https://www.abc.net.au/news/2007-11-25/workchoices-blamed-for-election-loss/967664> and John Roskam "It's not because they weren't liberal enough that the Libs lost", *The Age*, 5 December 2007 <https://www.theage.com.au/national/its-not-because-they-werent-liberal-enough-that-the-libs-lost-20071205-ge6gcg.html>.

66 The validity of the *Industrial Relations Reform Act 1993* (Cth) was upheld by the High Court in *Victoria v Commonwealth (Industrial Relations Act Case)* (1996) 186 CLR 416.

67 *Huddart Parker & Co Pty Ltd v Moorehead* (1909) 8 CLR 330.

68 As Justice Kirby pointed out in his dissent in the *Work Choices Case*, the judgment of Gaudron J in *Re Pacific Coal Pty Ltd v Ex parte Construction, Forestry, Mining and Energy Union* (2000) 203 CLR 346 which the *Work Choices* majority relied on, was itself a dissenting judgment.

of the Court, so that the Parliament of each State is
progressively reduced until it becomes no more than
an impotent debating society…The Constitution
mandates a federal balance…That the federal balance
exists, and that it must continue to exist, and that
the States must continue to exist…until the people
otherwise decide in a referendum under s 128 of the
Constitution, are matters that necessarily inform and
influence the proper construction of the Constitution.
The Act here seeks to distort that federal balance by
intruding into industrial and commercial affairs of the
State.[69]

Australia's acceptance of the *Work Choices decision* may have
been vindicated by the Rudd government's reliance on the
same corporations power for its successor *Fair Work Act 2009*
(Cth) (which was never challenged in the High Court). But the
fact that there was no enduring protest or further High Court
challenge to the High Court's progressive interpretation[70] of the
corporations power in the *WorkChoices Case* are further witness
to the high regard in which the High Court and its judgments are
held by the nation.

The *Mabo* (*No.2*) *Case* – the High Court's use of common law doctrines that predate the *Constitution*

In their combined judgment in *Mabo* (*No.2*), Chief Justice Mason
and Justice McHugh used almost the same words that Justice Bell
was to use three decades later when she announced the majority
decision in *Love* (see below nn 105 and 123). For though the
overall 6-1 result in *Mabo (No.2)* was clear, the reasoning in
the four concurring majority judgments was different especially
when it came to the availability of compensation. The interests
of the Meriam people in their traditional lands in the Murray

---

69 *Work Choices Case*, 322, 333 (per Callinan J).
70 Mason (notes 36 and 45 above).

Islands survived both Queensland's annexation in 1879 and all that had happened afterwards, but even if they had sought compensation, they would not have been entitled to it (4-3). Mason CJ and McHugh J said:

> The main difference between those members of the Court who constitute the majority is that…neither of us nor Brennan J agrees with the conclusion to be drawn from the judgments of Deane, Toohey and Gaudron JJ that, at least in the absence of clear and unambiguous statutory provision to the contrary, extinguishment of native title by the Crown by inconsistent grant is wrongful and gives rise to a claim for compensatory damages…
>
> *We are authorised to say that the other members of the Court agree* with what is said in the preceding paragraph about the outcome of the case.[71]

As in his earlier dissent in the *Tasmanian Dam Case* and in subsequent extra-judicial commentary about that case,[72] Dawson J adhered to established precedential views without need to refer to the long accepted doctrine of *terra nullius*.[73] Brennan J's judgment (Mason CJ and McHugh J agreeing), which overruled the established precedential view despite Justice Dixon's 'strict and complete legalism', says a great deal more about the interpretive power and sovereignty of the High Court. He said:

> In discharging its duty to declare the common law of Australia, this Court is not free to adopt rules that

71 *Mabo (No.2)*, 410 (per Mason CJ and McHugh J) (emphasis added).
72 Notes 62-64 and supporting text.
73 The head note summary of his judgment (ibid 409) includes the following statements: The vesting of the radical title in the Crown on the assumption of Crown authority is incompatible with the continued existence in precisely the same form of any pre-existing rights, which rights are necessarily held of a former sovereign or no sovereign at all. There is no need to resort to notions of "terra nullius"in relation to the Murray Islands as the law that applied on annexation was the law of Queensland. The legislative and political policy of the 19th century, whether imperial or colonial, was demonstrably inconsistent with and regardless of any native interests in the land. However insensitive those policies may now seem, a change of view does not of itself mean a change in the law.

accord with contemporary notions of justice and human rights if their adoption would fracture the skeleton of principle which gives the body of our law its shape and internal consistency...Although our law is the prisoner of its history, it is not now bound by the decision of courts in the hierarchy of an Empire then concerned with the development of its colonies... Although this Court is free to depart from English precedent which was earlier followed as stating the common law of this country...it cannot do so where the departure would fracture what I have called the skeleton of principle...The peace of Australia is built on the legal system. *It can be modified to bring it into conformity with contemporary notions of justice and human rights, but it cannot be destroyed...but no case can command unquestioning adherence if the rule it expresses seriously offends the values of justice and human rights (especially equality before the law) which are aspirations of the contemporary Australian legal system. If a postulated rule of the common law expressed in earlier cases seriously offends those contemporary values, the question arises whether the rule should be maintained and applied. Whenever such a question arises, it is necessary to assess whether the particular rule is an essential doctrine of our legal system and whether, if the rule were to be overturned, the disturbance to be apprehended would be disproportionate to the benefit flowing from the overturning.*[74]

While the decision to award compensation was apparently judged as beyond 'contemporary notions of justice and human rights' in 1992 even though Justices Deane, Toohey and Gaudron considered that they had found common law precedent which would justify it,[75] Justice Brennan here confirmed that the High Court could upset common law precedent where that precedent 'seriously offends those contemporary values'. While

---

74 *Mabo* (*No.2*), 416-417 (per Brennan J) (emphasis added).
75 Ibid 440, 444, 448 and 452 (per Deane and Gaudron JJ); and 483, 489, 491-492, and 498-499 (per Toohey J).

Justice Brennan's reinterpretation of Australia's common law doctrines in relation to customary title did not reinterpret the *Constitution* as Justice Isaacs had done in *Engineers'* and was thus not counted in Justice Heydon's calculus against Justice Kirby in *Roach* noted in the introduction, Justice Brennan was using common law material in a similarly revolutionary way since with Chief Justice Mason and Justice McHugh in complete concurrence, he overruled the conventional view of customary land ownership which had obtained in Australia since settlement. It is thus an understatement to say that such use of common law materials to reinterpret the *Constitution* in *Engineers'* and to reinterpret the conventional understanding of customary land title in *Mabo (No.2)* in contradiction of White Australia policies is progressive which is the word Chief Justice Mason used to describe Justice Isaacs' judgment in *Engineers'*.[76] Both were revolutionary. But both revolutions could claim ironical support from the most orthodox High Court judge of them all. For Justice Dixon had repeatedly affirmed that the common law was transcendental enough to influence constitutional interpretation since the 'State...deriv[ed] from the law; not the law...from [the] State'.[77]

But what of the minority dissenting view of Justices Deane, Toohey and Gaudron that there was common law authority which supported the view that compensation should be paid? Did Justices Mason, Brennan and McHugh fail Australia on the cusp of an even greater decision that might have begun the process of Aboriginal reconciliation in earnest?

---

76 Mason (notes 36, 45 and 70 above).
77 Gummow (n 52), "Sir Owen Dixon Today", Winterton Lecture, 36-37 and in *Jesting Pilate*, 53-55. See also Sir Owen Dixon, "Concerning Judicial Method" [1956] 29 *ALJ* 468 and "The Common Law as the Ultimate Constitutional Foundation" in *Jesting Pilate*, 203 - 211.

The Australasian context for *Mabo* (*No. 2*)

While the 21st century political focus of progressive Australia is premised in the belief that Aboriginal reconciliation can only be achieved by constitutional amendment, New Zealand reforms in the decade which preceded the *Mabo* (*No. 2*) decision suggest otherwise. For while Justices Mason, Brennan and McHugh paused at the compensation juncture in 1992 because of their perception that compensation was then a bridge too far for the greater Australian community, Justices Deane, Toohey and Gaudron did not. Justices Mason, Brennan and McHugh believed they could 'bring [the Australian common law] into conformity with contemporary notions of justice and human rights' only if they believed 'the disturbance to be apprehended would [not] be disproportionate to the benefit flowing from the overturning'. While all six of the *Mabo* (*No. 2*) majority judges believed the Australian community would tolerate their decision to recognise the undisturbed occupation of the Murray Islands by the Meriam people as a form of native title, Justice Mason, Brennan and McHugh appear to have feared that the suggestion that any First Nations' Peoples should be compensated for the unjust acquisition of those or similar rights, would 'fracture the skeleton of principle which gives the body of our law its shape and internal consistency'.[78]

While those concerns are not elaborated in the *Mabo* (*No.2*) judgements, the New Zealand reforms following the Māori Land march[79] and occupation of Bastion Point on the Auckland

---

78 *Mabo* (*No. 2*) 416-417 (per Brennan J).

79 This march began at the top of New Zealand's North Island on September 14, 1975 and terminated on the steps of the New Zealand Parliament one month later on October 13, 1975 and was led by 79 year old Whina Cooper, later Dame Whina Cooper. On those steps, she presented then Prime Minister Bill Rowling with a petition for a change in New Zealand's underlying monocultural land law signed by 60,000 people. The march coincided with the passage through the New Zealand Parliament of the *Treaty of Waitangi Act 1975* which created the Waitangi Tribunal.

waterfront provide context[80] which included the creation of the Waitangi Tribunal. That Tribunal was created by the 1985 Amendment to the *Treaty of Waitangi Act 1975* (NZ) and was then authorised to hear for the first time, personal and tribal claims of breach of the underlying 1840 Treaty between the English and the Māori.[81] That tribunal returned Bastion Point to its Ngati Whatua owners on 1 July 1988, just four years before the *Mabo* (*No. 2*) decision was handed down.

It is submitted that if all six of the *Mabo* (*No.2*) majority judges had decided that compensation should be paid to First Nations' Peoples who had been deprived of their lands unjustly in 1992, then the Keating government's following *Native Title Act 1993* (Cth) might have gone a lot further. It might have included the creation of a Waitangi-like Tribunal with power to identify unjust takings of land since settlement and to compensate the descendants of those deprived within clearly defined statutory bounds just as had been done in New Zealand. Arguably, since the *Native Title Act 1993* (Cth) did not require constitutional amendment for its efficacy, an expanded version of that the *Native Title Act* could have kick started the process of reconciliation with Australia's first people as the Waitangi Tribunal legislation did in New Zealand. That kick start in New Zealand did not

---

80 Bill Rowling was replaced as Prime Minister by Robert Muldoon two months after the conclusion of the Māori Land march in October 1975 on 12 December 1975. Despite the legislation of the *Treaty of Waitangi Act 1975* by the previous government, Prime Minister Muldoon announced that Bastion Point was to be released for sale and executive subdivision. This land had been given to the Crown by the Ngati Whatua tribe for the defence of New Zealand during the 1885 Russian scare. Led by activist Joe Hawke, in response to that announcement and the fear that the new government would not honour the terms of the *Treaty of Waitangi Act 1975*, Bastion Point was occupied for 506 days from 5 January 1977 until 222 people were removed by police on 25 May 1978 ("Bastion Point", *New Zealand History* <https://nzhistory.govt.nz/keyword/bastion-point>.

81 "Treaty of Waitangi", *Ministry of Justice* < https://www.justice.govt.nz/about/learn-about-the-justice-system/how-the-justice-system-works/the-basis-for-all-law/treaty-of-waitangi/>. As Justice Brennan noted in his *Mabo (No.2)* judgment (ibid 432), in 1877, the New Zealand Supreme Court had previously held that the New Zealand Courts could not overrule a Crown grant issued in breach of Treaty rights except at the suit of the Crown itself (*Wi Parata v Bishop of Wellington* (1877) 3 NZ (Jur) NS 72, 77 (per Prendergast CJ).

require a constitutional amendment. New Zealand does not have a written constitution. But nearly all objective commentators agree that the real intent of the New Zealand legislature and people to reconcile with its First Peoples was advanced by those legislative changes. That real intent is considered to have been proven by the allocation of substantial taxpayers' money to fund tribal compensation in appropriate cases.

It is not clear whether the Australian High Court judges who decided *Mabo (No. 2)* contemplated those possibilities. The Keating government certainly used the material that the *Mabo (No. 2)* judgment provided when it passed the *Native Title Act 1993* (Cth) the following year. But it did not go as far as the New Zealand legislature went, arguably because the judgments of Justice Deane, Toohey and Gaudron were a minority view. But those minority expressions of common law doctrine need not have constrained the Commonwealth legislature in 1993 and they certainly do not constrain the Commonwealth legislature now. The only current constraint is the political question of whether Australia is ready to tackle these past injustices and prove its real intent by implementing mechanisms that enable the return of land in appropriate cases and the payment of compensation to tribal trusts in others.

Though I accept that this legislative recommendation is controversial, I note that each time the High Court has exercised its interpretive sovereignty, it has enabled the nation to move in a new direction. The *Engineers'*, *Tasmanian Dam*, *Mabo (No. 2)* and *Work Choice Cases* are all examples of the High Court enabling and even leading necessary change in Australia. In the *Mabo (No. 2) Case*, I am suggesting that the High Court could have gone even further and that might have forced the Commonwealth legislature to address Aboriginal reconciliation much more comprehensively and much earlier.

I suggest that the High Court's discovery and development of the implied freedom of political communication beginning in 1992 is another example of the High Court's power to advance long term justice and human rights in Australia. While the majority which decided the *Love Case* may have been lost due to retirements, the decision of those majority judges still confirms that the High Court can lead social change.

The implied freedom of political communication as a manifestation of High Court interpretive sovereignty

Arguably the question whether the High Court could overrule statutes that offend contemporary Australian values had already been answered four years before *Mabo* (*No. 2*) was decided in 1988 when the Mason Court found that ss 22 and 23 of the *Australian Bicentennial Authority Act 1980* (Cth) were invalid. Those sections had been used to prevent Lou Davis selling t-shirts bearing Aboriginal protest messages. In finding those sections of the Act invalid, Mason CJ, Deane and Gaudron JJ said:

> In arming the Authority with this extraordinary power the Act provides for a regime of protection which is *grossly disproportionate* to the need to protect the commemoration and the Authority…the framework of regulation…reaches far beyond the legitimate objects sought to be achieved and impinges on freedom of expression by enabling the Authority to regulate the use of common expressions and by making unauthorised use a criminal offence…This extraordinary intrusion into freedom of expression *is not reasonably and appropriately adapted* to achieve the ends that lie within the limits of constitutional power.[82]

Wilson, Dawson and Toohey JJ agreed but Justice Brennan came to the same conclusion by finding the legislation exceeded

---

82 *Davis v Commonwealth* (1988) 166 CLR 79, 100 (emphasis added).

the Commonwealth's incidental legislative power.[83] But there remained a concern that the Commonwealth could have redrafted these provisions making the Commonwealth's intent to limit freedom of expression in specified political matters unambiguous and clear in recognition of what is now called the principle of legality.[84] In that context, and given Justice Brennan's exposition of the High Court's duty to correct law that does not respect contemporary Australian values, it is not surprising that the Mason Court decided shortly after *Mabo* (*No.2*), that freedom of political communication was implied throughout the text and structure of the *Australian Constitution*. The result of the finding that freedom of political communication was implied in the *Constitution* was that the Commonwealth could no longer pass laws that interfered with the freedom of political communication unless they were 'proportionate', or 'reasonably and appropriately adapted' to ends otherwise within their constitutional power. The discovery of the implied freedom of political communication between the lines in the text of the *Australian Constitution* ensured that the Commonwealth legislature would no longer be able to pass laws that made Lou Davis' reasonable protests illegal.

The continuing evolution of the resulting implied constitutional freedom of political communication now includes a detailed test of structured proportionality, which has begun to be used by High Court majorities to determine the legitimacy of

---

83 Ibid 111-117.

84 Though the phrase, 'principle of legality' was arguably only coined by Lord Steyn in R *v Home Secretary: Ex parte Pierson* [1998] AC 539, the idea has ancient common law roots and was usefully defined by French CJ in *Momcilovic v The Queen* (2011) 245 CLR 1, 46 as follows:

> The principle of legality…is expressed as a presumption that Parliament does not intend to interfere with common law rights and freedoms except by clear and unequivocal language, for which Parliament can be held accountable to the electorate. It requires that statutes be construed, where constructional choices are open, to avoid or minimise their encroachment upon rights and freedoms at common law.

other freedoms under the *Constitution*.[85] The High Court's decisions in *Engineers'*, *Tasmanian Dam*, *WorkChoices*, and *Mabo* (*No. 2*) have led social change in Australia. The discovery and development of the implied freedom of political communication using the doctrine of structured proportionality has limited Commonwealth power in favour of common law rights recognised by the framers. The *Mabo* (*No.2*) case also precipitated follow-on Commonwealth legislation that provided more definition than a legal case can, but as I have suggested above, that legislation could have gone much further. In Part Three I discuss how much further the Commonwealth legislature could have gone without the need for constitutional change.

Part Three – The *Treaty of Waitangi Act 1975* (NZ) as an example of how Australia could advance the process of Aboriginal reconciliation without constitutional amendment

The Treaty of Waitangi was signed on 6 February 1840 and is named for the place in the Bay of Islands in New Zealand's far north where it was signed. It is short. Only three articles. The English decided to annex New Zealand to 'protect Māori, regulate British subjects and secure commercial interests.'[86] It

---

85 See for example, *Palmer v Western Australia* (2021) 95 ALJR 229 where it was used in relation to a case about the meaning of the freedom of interstate trade in s 92 of the *Constitution*. Note however, that Justices Gageler and Gordon have continued to express dissenting concern with the majority's ongoing use of structured proportionality to determine the legitimacy of Commonwealth laws that burden common law freedoms. In *LibertyWorks Inc v Commonwealth of Australia* [2021] HCA 18, Justice Gageler said a calibrated review of laws which burden freedom of political communication is more appropriate referring to *McCloy v New South Wales* (2015) 257 CLR 178, 238 [150]. While he did not exactly propose the use of the American 'strict scrutiny' and 'compelling interest' tests, it appears that he found these American common law ideas more helpful than structured proportionality in identifying when a law had gone too far in abridging constitutional freedom. Justice Gordon has preferred to work out when a statute offends a constitutional freedom using the 'reasonably appropriate and adapted' test (*LibertyWorks*, [134]) referred to in the *Davis Case* but which first appeared in Australia in *Williams v Melbourne Corporation* (1933) 49 CLR 142,155-156.

86 "The Treaty in Brief" New Zealand History <https://nzhistory.govt.nz/politics/treaty/the-treaty-in-brief>.

was prepared hastily, translated into Māori overnight, signed initially by about 40 chiefs and then by another 500 by the end of September.[87] In defining its affect in *Mabo* (*No. 2*), Justice Deane, Toohey and Gaudron quoted Chapman J from an 1847 case where he said that 'it does not assert either in doctrine or in practice any thing new and unsettled'.[88] To assist that understanding it is convenient to set out the three articles in full:

> Article the first
> The Chiefs of the Confederation of the United Tribes
> of New Zealand and the separate and independent
> Chiefs who have not become members of the
> Confederation cede to her Majesty the Queen of
> England absolutely and without reservation all the
> rights and powers of Sovereignty which the said
> Confederation or Individual Chiefs respectively
> exercise or possess, or may be supposed to exercise
> or to possess over their respective Territories as the
> sole sovereigns thereof.
>
> Article the second
> Her Majesty the Queen of England confirms and
> guarantees to the Chiefs and Tribes of New Zealand
> and to the respective families and individuals
> thereof the full exclusive and undisturbed possession
> of their Lands and Estates Forests Fisheries and
> other properties which they may collectively or
> individually possess so long as it is their wish and
> desire to retain the same in their possession; but
> the Chiefs of the United Tribes and the individual
> Chiefs yield to Her Majesty the exclusive right
> of Preemption over such lands as the proprietors
> thereof may be disposed to alienate at such prices
> as may be agreed upon between the respective
> Proprietors and persons appointed by Her Majesty to
> treat with them in that behalf.

---

87 Ibid.
88 *Mabo* (*No. 2*) 444 (per Deane and Gaudron JJ) and 488 (per Toohey J) referring to *R v Symonds* [1847] NZPCC 387, 390 (per Chapman J).

Article the third
In consideration thereof Her Majesty the Queen of
England extends to the Natives of New Zealand Her
royal protection and imparts to them all the Rights
and Privileges of British Subjects.[89]

While the Māori version of the treaty is not as complete,[90] neither represents the law of New Zealand. However, since the Waitangi Tribunal was established under the *Treaty of Waitangi Act 1975* (NZ) that tribunal has had 'exclusive authority to determine the meaning of the Treaty in the two texts' and 'it is the spirit of the Treaty that matters most' with its broad-brush principles recognised as 'embody[ing] a partnership in which the Crown, chiefs and tribes would all have a place.'[91] Since the 1985 amendments were passed to the *Treaty of Waitangi Act 1975* (NZ), 'any Māori can take a claim to the Tribunal that they have been disadvantaged by any legislation, policy or practice of the Crown since 1840.'[92] While '[t]he Tribunal does not enforce the law, [it] has the power to make recommendations to government',[93] and since the Tribunal's inception, most '[h]istorical Treaty breaches...[have been] settled by negotiations with the Crown through the Office of Treaty Settlements'.[94]

There have been many questions to resolve in that recommendation and negotiation practice. Those questions have included how to compensate people long since departed and

---

89 John Wilson, "Nation and Government – The Origins of Nationhood", *Te Ara - The Encyclopedia of New Zealand*, 1 September 2016 <https://teara.govt.nz/en/document/4216/the-three-articles-of-the-treaty-of-waitangi>.

90 Ibid.

91 Ministry for Culture and Heritages, "Differences between the texts", 5 October 2021 <https://nzhistory.govt.nz/politics/treaty/read-the-Treaty/differences-between-the-texts>.

92 New Zealand Ministry of Justice, "Treaty of Waitangi", 11 March 2020 < https://www.justice.govt.nz/about/learn-about-the-justice-system/how-the-justice-system-works/the-basis-for-all-law/treaty-of-waitangi/>.

93 Ibid.

94 Ibid.

what those reparation packages should look like since 'a simple damages approach to reparations...would be beyond the capacity of the country to pay.'[95] As then Chief Judge J.V. Williams[96] explained to an Australian Human Rights Conference in 2001, the answers to those questions have largely been resolved by recommending 'reparations...at the Tribal level rather than the personal.'[97] While

> [t]he Treaty of Waitangi Act gives no specific criteria for reparations...[t]he approach of the Waitangi Tribunal is to support packages which restore a lost economic base bearing in mind the extent and nature of the loss and the current needs of the grieving community. This tends to make settlements more future looking and should help get communities out of grievance mode and into development sooner. Equally important emphasis in a reparations package must be given to what, in the Treaty is called – tino rangatiratanga. This is tribal autonomy. In many ways the greatest Treaty breach throughout New Zealand's colonial history was the theft of the ability of the tribes to rule themselves in accordance with tikanga Maori or Maori custom. The refusal to allow tribes to make their own collective decisions about how they would deal with both threats and opportunities which colonialisation presented. Once that was lost, it was not long before the land, the fisheries and the resources of the tribe were lost as well. Undermining the autonomy of an indigenous community has always been the most effective way of getting at its resources. It follows that restoration of that autonomy is the most important aspect of any settlement package.[98]

---

95 Chief Judge J. V. Williams, "Reparations and the Waitangi Tribunal", a paper presented to the "Moving Forward" national conference hosted by the Australian Human Rights Commission, the Aboriginal and Torres Strait Islander Commission and the Public Interest Advocacy Centre in Sydney on 15 & 16 August, 2001 < https://humanrights.gov.au/our-work/aboriginal-and-torres-strait-islander-social-justice/reparations-and-waitangi-tribunal>.

96 Chief Judge Williams of the Māori Land Court became a member of the New Zealand Supreme Court on May 2, 2019.

97 Chief Judge Williams, "Reparations and the Waitangi Tribunal".

98 Ibid.

It is also noteworthy that New Zealand did not implement its current Waitangi reparations structure and system overnight. The 1985 amendments were part of New Zealand's Fourth Labour Government's policy of giving greater acknowledgement to the treaty. The amendments required the original Tribunal to have a Māori majority and replaced the initial 1975 jurisdictional bar which had limited Tribunal investigation to Treaty breaches occurring after 1975. The 1985 amendments enabled the Tribunal to investigate claims dating back to 1840 when the Treaty was signed.

This settlement regime stands in significant contrast to the regime that was established by the Keating government's *Native Title Act 1993* (Cth) which was diluted further by the Howard government's *Native Title Amendment Act 1998* (Cth). Neither Act recognises 'the full exclusive and undisturbed possession of [Aboriginal] Lands and Estates Forests Fisheries and other properties which they may collectively or individually possess so long as it is their wish and desire to retain the same in their possession' which were 'confirm[ed] and guarantee[d]' to the Māori people of New Zealand under the second article of the Treaty of Waitangi. Justices Deane, Toohey and Gaudron acknowledged that those Treaty of Waitangi articles in New Zealand were a simple restatement of the common law of England extant at the time throughout the British Empire. The truth is that the *Native Title Act 1993* (Cth) was passed to prevent the possibility that Australia's First Peoples might be able to assert those further English common law rights. While the New Zealand Treaty recognised that after 1840 the Queen would have a right of pre-emption over Māori lands in the future, it was only to be at agreed prices and otherwise generally in accord with established British common law. There was to be no duress or taking advantage of the uneducated and illiterate. Indeed, the principle of just terms compensation is now more

familiar because of the *Australian Constitution's* restatement
of the *Magna Carta* principle that proper Crown compensation
is required for any property acquired from subjects.[99] Bottles
of whisky, blankets and the occasional musket traded at gross
undervalues in return for permanent land resources have all
been unpicked in accordance with the underlying principles of
British common law even though those principles were ignored
even in New Zealand until 1975...and even longer in Australia.

The *Native Title Act 1993* (Cth) was passed with alacrity as
ostensible protection of First Peoples' common law rights. But
in fact that legislation simply continued the Australian practice
of abridging First Peoples' common law rights. While the
Howard government's 1998 amendment has been criticised for
its further dilution of even those rights which were allowed by
the original Keating government version of the *Native Title Act*,
when the candour and real intent of the New Zealand regime is
compared with the cynical design of this Australian legislation,
neither Australian government has earned any bouquets. The
truth is, even the Keating Labor government's legislation simply
perpetuated traditional injustice. To overcome that justice deficit,
the *Native Title* regime needs to be completely repealed and a
new regime which follows the spirit of the New Zealand scheme
needs to be implemented in its place. But that new Australian
regime does not require constitutional amendment. Ordinary
legislation will be sufficient because the *Native Title Act 1993*
(Cth) was itself ordinary simple majority legislation. However,
in the spirit of sincere and honest reconciliation, perhaps the
Australian equivalent of the Waitangi Tribunal should be called

---

99 Section 51(xxxi) of the Australian Constitution provides power to the Commonwealth
to acquire property from states or individuals for any purpose for which it has power to
make laws provided just terms are provided. Clause 28, 30 and 31 of the original 1215
version of the *Magna Carta* provided that no movable goods could be taken by a royal
official without immediate payment or consent, and clauses 19 and 21 of the reissued
1225 version of *Magna Carta* specified what were then recognised as fair market prices
for various of those goods.

the Makarrata Tribunal or Commission. Whatever it is called, it needs to open the windows of justice and be empowered to recommend just terms settlements to the Commonwealth government as the Waitangi Tribunal does in New Zealand. The Australian version of the Waitangi Tribunal must be empowered to recommend the same just terms that the *Constitution* says should be provided whenever the Commonwealth acquired property from its constituent states or human persons. But if such a Tribunal or Commission is to contribute to a genuine reconciliation and rehabilitation of our First Peoples, its terms of reference need to be as broad and generous as those with which the New Zealand government empowered the Waitangi Tribunal.

Is Australia ready for such change? Justice Brennan, with Chief Justice Mason and Justice McHugh concurring did not think so when they handed down their majority judgments in *Mabo (No. 2)* in 1992. They did not think Australia was ready for a finding that compensation should be paid to our First Peoples when land had been taken from them unjustly as Justices Deane, Toohey and Gaudron recommended. Justices Brennan and McHugh and Chief Justice Mason inferred that such a decision 'would fracture the skeleton of principle which gives the body of our law its shape and internal consistency'.[100] Those deciding judges thought Australia was not ready for that recommendation, that it was a bridge too far – in their additional words, 'the disturbance to be apprehended would be disproportionate to the benefit flowing from the overturning'.[101] Does the *Love decision* suggest that Australia is now more ready for this change?

---

100 *Mabo (No.2)*, 416 (per Brennan J).
101 Ibid 417 (per Brennan J).

Part Four

The *Love case* – is the High Court limited by the words of the *Constitution*?

Again, in the *Eastman case*, Justice McHugh said that the majority justices in the *Engineers' Case* had

> committed the Court to the strict legalism of which Sir Owen Dixon became the leading exponent. However...[they] did not rule out the history or background of the Constitution as interpretative aids. [Indeed t]he majority justices in that case expressly said that the Constitution was to be read in the light of the circumstances in which it was made with knowledge of the combined fabric of the common law and the pre-Constitution statute law...Nevertheless, even when we see meaning in a constitutional provision which our predecessors did not see, the search is always for the objective intention of the makers of the Constitution....[but that search] does not equate with a Constitution suspended in time. Our Constitution is constructed in such a way that most of the concepts and purposes are stated at a sufficient level of abstraction or generality to enable it to be infused with *current* understanding of those concepts and purposes. This is consistent with the notion that our Constitution was intended to be an enduring document able to apply to emerging circumstances while retaining its essential integrity....Those who framed [it] knew that the meaning...would have to be deduced by later generations...The Court has not accepted that the makers' actual intentions are decisive. [102]

While it is easy to point to the well-known racist views of

---

102 *Eastman,* 47 and 50 (emphasis original).

Justices Isaacs and Higgins[103] to debunk an equalitarian interpretation of the *Constitution* as Justice Gaudron did in the *Stolen Generations Case,*[104] the four separate majority decisions in *Love* used the 'history or background' of the *Constitution* in a novel way which infused them with a different and new '*current* understanding of th[e constitutional] concepts and purposes.'

Justice Bell wrote the leading judgment and said:

> It is not offensive, in the context of contemporary international understanding, to recognise the cultural and spiritual dimensions of the distinctive connection between indigenous peoples and their traditional lands, and in light of that recognition to hold that the exercise of sovereign power of this nation does not extend to the exclusion of the indigenous inhabitants of the Australian community...Notwithstanding the amplitude of the power conferred by s 51 (xix) it does not extend to treating an Aboriginal Australian as an alien...*I am authorised by the other members of the majority* to say that although we express our reasoning differently, we agree that Aboriginal Australians (understood according to the tripartite test in *Mabo [No 2]*) are not within the reach of the "aliens" power conferred by s 51(xix) of the *Constitution.*[105]

Though the majority all agreed on the *Mabo (No.2)* definition of an Aboriginal Australian, Justice Bell also acknowledged Justice Deane's broader definition in the *Tasmanian Dam Case*[106] and affirmed that the 'context of contemporary international understanding' influenced her judgment, despite the aversion

---

103 George Williams, "Race and the Australian Constitution: From Federation to Reconciliation", *Osgoode Hall Law Journal* 38.4 (2000) 643, 651 citing Australia, House of Representatives, *Hansard* (24 April 1902), 11977 and 11979. Justice Michael Kirby has noted the racist views of Sir Isaac Isaacs and said they may be excused because they were accepted at the time ("Sir Isaac Isaacs – A Sesquicentenary Reflection", (2005) 29 (3) *Melbourne University Law Review*, 880).

104 *Kruger v Commonwealth (Stolen Generations Case)* (1997) 190 CLR 1, 113. Though note Justice Brennan's contrary comments in *Mabo* (n 72) and supporting text.

105 *Love v Commonwealth (Love)* [2020] HCA 3 [73]-[75], [81] per Bell J (emphasis added to words used similarly by Mason CJ and McHugh J in *Mabo (No.2)* referenced above (n 71).

106 Ibid [75].

of Justices McHugh and Heydon to such influences referenced above contra Justice Kirby.[107]

Justice Nettle intuitively resisted the previous High Court view that anyone born abroad was an alien and said that justice in this case required a re-examination of 'the essentials of alienage'.[108] He also said it was inconsistent with 'the common law's acknowledgement of traditional laws' to classify anyone as an alien who was recognised by Aboriginal elders as a member of Aboriginal society.[109] And he said that treating Aboriginal Australians as aliens in law or in practice was inconsistent with the Crown's 'unique [common law] obligation' to protect them which the Commonwealth had effectively conceded.[110]

Justice Gordon said that Aboriginal Australian were not 'others, outsiders or foreigners' within the meaning of the word 'alien' in s 51(xix).[111] Further, Aboriginal Australians were 'owned by the land' and thus by the nation so that they could not be alien to it.[112] The two-way 'spiritual' connection between the land and waters of Australia and its Aboriginal people was not and could not be severed by federation. Nor had such severance been proposed in the Convention Debates.[113] Indeed at federation, Australia's non-alien Indigenous population was 'not limited to persons' born here or who 'could trace...their ancestry through Indigenous ancestors'.[114] The English assertion of sovereignty over Australia 'brought with it the common law' which recognised that 'Indigenous peoples can and do possess certain rights and duties that are not possessed by, and *cannot*

---

107 See notes 1-6 above and supporting text.
108 *Love* [236] and [263].
109 Ibid [272].
110 Ibid [273] and [282] – [283].
111 Ibid [296], [343]-[344].
112 Ibid [341].
113 Ibid [342].
114 Ibid [345].

be possessed by, the non-Indigenous peoples of Australia'.[115] Neither the *Constitution* nor legislation passed since federation had changed any of that.[116]

Justice Edelman added that the fact that Mr Love and Mr Thoms were Aboriginal people made it unnecessary to inquire whether they had been absorbed into the Australian community or not.[117] While it was possible that Aboriginal people might renounce their aboriginality and become aliens, that had not happened in this case.[118]

While all four majority judges agreed that as Aboriginal Australians, Mr Love and Mr Thoms were not within the reach of the aliens power, that was the lowest common denominator of the ratio decidendi in this case. There was much more to their status than the tripartite test in *Mabo (No.2)* expressed, and the extent of the protection to which they were entitled under the common law which pre-dated federation and the *Constitution*, did not have to be worked out in this case. But it was made clear that pre-existing English common law in Australia and the international human rights context would have a part to play in that future story, despite some previous aversion of the High Court to the use of such international materials.[119]

The majority of the High Court in *Love* thus confirmed that the story of Aboriginal recognition under the *Australian Constitution* is not complete, and the majority judges signalled new directional possibilities. While the High Court has never possessed legislative power, after *Mabo (No.2)* was decided, the Keating government legislated to further define the land title

---

115 Ibid [357] (emphasis original).
116 Ibid [358]-[359].
117 Ibid [464].
118 Ibid [465].
119 Note again that there was no aversion to the use of international materials in *Mabo (No. 2)*. Indeed, those materials informed the High Court's understanding of the pre-existing common law.

rights the High Court had identified.[120] And while the Howard government amended that legislation to validate some pastoral and mining leases which had been illegally issued subsequent to the *Mabo (No. 2)* and *Wik decisions*,[121] the *Love decision* provides a foundation for a future settlement which is infused with current understanding of the need for resolution of past grievances and reconciliation. That is, a future federal government with a more complete vision of Aboriginal reconciliation could follow the lead of the Keating government and legislate to flesh out the ideas expressed in one or more of the four separate majority judgments in *Love*. Of course such a government could also propose formal constitutional change with the same goal. But since formal constitutional change has proven very difficult in Australia, the purpose of this chapter has been to show that the Aboriginal reconciliation process does not depend on formal constitutional change. Indeed, simple legislative change implementing a Waitangi-like tribunal could prepare the way for a future constitutional change if it later appeared that constitutional change might still be beneficial. While Australia has not yet made a settlement with its First Peoples that comes close to that which New Zealand has implemented, and while the High Court is unlikely to be presented with a case which would enable judicial commentary on a Makarrata Commission which would provide a 'First Nation's Voice' in the *Australian Constitution* as was proposed in the Uluru Statement from the

---

120 *Native Title Act 1993* (Cth). Arguably, the same process followed the High Court's decision that the ACT's same-sex marriage legislation was invalid in 2013 (*Commonwealth v ACT* (2013) 250 CLR 441). Following a referendum, the Turnbull government passed the *Marriage Amendment (Definition and Religious Freedoms) Act 2017*. That legislative solution to the legalisation of same-sex marriage created a more certain and nuanced same-sex marriage law in Australia than resulted from the United States Supreme Court decision in *Obergefell v Hodges* (2015) 576 US 644. However, note that I do not consider that the *Native Title Act 1993* (Cth) properly respects the customs and land title of Australia's First Peoples.

121 *Native Title Amendment Act 1998* (Cth). For a summary of John Howard's 'Ten Point Plan' see SK Wirk Online Education, *n.d.* "A brief summary of the *Native Title Amendment Act 1998 (Cth)*" <https://www.skwirk.com.au/skwirk/uploadFiles/content/database/files/chapter.1138.body.html>.

heart in 2017,[122] this review of the High Court's jurisprudence in *Mabo* (*No.2*) and *Love* identifies a way forward without the immediate need for formal constitutional change.

Both cases featured multiple majority judgements. In *Love*, Justice Bell echoed what Chief Justice Mason and Justice McHugh had said in *Mabo* (*No.2*) to explain what those majorities agreed on. In Justice Bell's words –

> I am authorised by the other members of the majority to say that although we express our reasoning differently, we agree that Aboriginal Australians (understood according to the tripartite test in *Mabo [No 2]*) are not within the reach of the "aliens" power conferred by s 51(xix) of the *Constitution.*[123]

When Chief Justice Mason and Justice McHugh used those same words, they were drawing attention to the divergence within the overall majority over the issue of compensation which the plaintiffs had not requested.[124] Justices Deane, Toohey and Gaudron found ample common law authority to justify the *Mabo* (*No.2*) Court in finding that some of Australia's First Peoples who had been deprived of their native land interests unjustly should be compensated.[125] Justice Brennan's majority judgment, with which Chief Justice Mason and Justice McHugh concurred, explained why they did not agree with Justices Deane, Toohey and Gaudron over compensation in 1992. Justice Brennan once again had said:

> In discharging its duty to declare the common law of Australia, this Court is not free to adopt rules that accord with contemporary notions of justice and human rights if their adoption would fracture the skeleton of principle which gives the body of our law

---

122 "The Uluru Statement from the Heart", The Uluru Statement, 26 May 2017 <https://ulurustatement.org/the-statement>.

123 *Love* [81] per Bell J.

124 *Mabo (No.2)*, 410 (per Mason CJ and McHugh J).

125 Ibid 440, 444, 448 and 452 (per Deane and Gaudron JJ); and 483, 489, 491-492, and 498-499 (per Toohey J).

its shape and internal consistency...Although our law
is the prisoner of its history, it is not now bound by the
decision of courts in the hierarchy of an Empire then
concerned with the development of its colonies...
Although this Court is free to depart from English
precedent which was earlier followed as stating the
common law of this country...*it cannot do so where
the departure would fracture what I have called the
skeleton of principle*...The peace of Australia is built
on the legal system. It can be modified to bring it into
conformity with contemporary notions of justice and
human rights, but it cannot be destroyed...but no case
can command unquestioning adherence if the rule it
expresses seriously offends the values of justice and
human rights (especially equality before the law)
which are aspirations of the contemporary Australian
legal system. If a postulated rule of the common law
expressed in earlier cases seriously offends those
contemporary values, the question arises whether the
rule should be maintained and applied. Whenever
such a question arises, *it is necessary to assess
whether the particular rule is an essential doctrine
of our legal system and whether, if the rule were to be
overturned, the disturbance to be apprehended would
be disproportionate to the benefit flowing from the
overturning.*[126]

The simple reason for pause at the compensation juncture in
1992 was the perception that compensation was a bridge too
far for the greater Australian community in 1992. Those judges
could 'bring [the Australian common law] into conformity with
contemporary notions of justice and human rights' only if they
believed 'the disturbance to be apprehended would [not] be
disproportionate to the benefit flowing from the overturning'.
While six of the *Mabo* (*No.2*) judges believed the Australian
community would tolerate their decision to recognise the
undisturbed occupation of the Murray Islands by the Meriam
people as a form of native title, they feared that any suggestion

---

126 *Mabo (No.2)*, 416-417 (per Brennan J) (emphasis added).

that other First Peoples should be compensated for the unjust acquisition of those or similar rights in 1992, would 'fracture the skeleton of principle which gives the body of our law its shape and internal consistency'. While those concerns are not elaborated further in the *Mabo* (*No. 2*) judgements, New Zealand reforms following the Māori Land march[127] and occupation of Bastion Point on the Auckland waterfront provide context[128] which included the creation of the Waitangi Tribunal. Following the recommendation of that Tribunal, Bastion Point was returned to its Ngati Whatua owners on 1 July 1988. It appears that a majority of Australia's High Court judges did not think Australia was ready in 1992 for New Zealand's more complete approach to reconciliation with her First Peoples. Perhaps Australia is ready now. I hope that the High Court will continue to express itself in favour of a more just reconciliation with Australia's First Peoples when appropriate cases allow that expression. They were endowed by the framers with the interpretive sovereignty that enables them to do so.

Conclusion

In this chapter, I have suggested the existence of a doctrine of High Court interpretive sovereignty in Australia that is almost as powerful as the doctrine of judicial sovereignty in the United States. Though lay Australians may believe the Commonwealth government has sovereign power to do whatever it considers is in the interests of the nation as a whole, that belief is mistaken. Unlike courts functioning in countries with unitary governments like those in the United Kingdom and New Zealand, the High Court has the power to review and invalidate any Commonwealth legislation challenged in a case as well as decisions based on

---

127 See details in n 79 above.
128 See details in n 80 above.

that legislation by government ministers and administrative departments.

Despite the strict literalism to which Chief Justice Dixon referred when he became Chief Justice in 1952, the High Court has a history of making choices which have advanced the social interests of the nation in hard cases. In the words of RTE Latham, in the *Engineers' Case*, the Court followed the 'brilliant minority...[that] broke British tradition by persisting in consistent dissent' and took a decision motivated by the view 'that the Constitution had been intended to create a nation' so that the old 'contractual view of the Constitution was...out of date'.[129] That High Court initiative has been repeated a number of times, perhaps most notably in the *Tasmanian Dam* and *Work Choices Cases* despite articulate dissenting defences of the literalistic common law tradition articulated by Justice Dixon.

The High Court's interpretive sovereignty that was used by majorities in *Engineers'*, *Tasmanian Dam* and *Work Choices Cases*, was also used in *Mabo* (*No.2*). As in the *Engineers' Case*, the majority judges in *Mabo* (*No.2*) mined common law materials to craft their decision, but Justice Dawson was correct in both *Tasmanian Dam* and *Mabo* (*No.2*) to observe that those decisions also flew in the face of a great deal of Australian policy and practice, which had been entrenched by generations of earlier and contrary Australian common law decisions. However, it is also clear that the majority judges in those cases knew exactly what they were doing, though Justice Brennan was the most transparent in *Mabo* (*No. 2*) when he said that we are doing as much as we can do to achieve a just result for these people who have been oppressed in the past.

Justices Bell, Nettle, Gordon and Edelman expressed similar sentiments in *Love*. Federal government policy and legislation

---

129 RTE Latham (n 24), 563-564.

that flew in the face of the meaning of the *Constitution* could not justify the deportation of Aboriginal Australians as aliens. I suggest that the time has come for the Australian federal government to create a tribunal which like the Waitangi Tribunal in New Zealand since 1985, has power to identify all the injustices that our First Peoples have suffered since settlement and to recommend the payment of compensation in appropriate cases by the federal government. As in New Zealand, the identification of what constitute appropriate cases will have to be worked out by the new tribunal.[130] While it should have the power to disregard trivial, frivolous and vexatious claims as in New Zealand,[131] any grievance that flows from a law or executive action or the policy or practice of a colonial or subsequent Australian government since settlement should fall within the new tribunal's remit.[132]

In deference to the framers of the Uluru Statement from the Heart, I recommend the Australian version of the New Zealand Waitangi Tribunal should be named the Makarrata Tribunal or Commission.

If the federal government will not legislate to create such a tribunal or commission, then I challenge the High Court to return to the judgments of Justices Deane, Toohey and Gaudron in *Mabo* (*No. 2*) and restate the common law authority for the payment of just terms compensation they identified in that case. I also challenge the High Court to take every opportunity that presents to restate the case for reconciliation with Australia's First Peoples. As I have suggested elsewhere,[133] the legal authority justifying government compensation for land taken

---

130 See for example the comments from Chief Judge Williams above in notes 95 to 98 and in the supporting text.

131 *Treaty of Waitangi Act 1975* (NZ) s 7.

132 Ibid s 6 as inserted by s 3 of the *Treaty of Waitangi Amendment Act 1985* (NZ).

133 A. Keith Thompson, "The spiritual foundations of s 51(xxxi)' in *Liber Amicorum for Gabriel Moens*, Augusto Zimmermann ed, (Redcliffe Queensland: Connor Court, 2018).

unjustly has a very long tail. It was certainly well established in the customary materials which motivated the compensation provisions of *Magna Carta* in 1215 and 1225 and referred to briefly in note 99 above.

Index

Aboriginal reconciliation – 5, 7, 11, 16, 19-20, 211-258

Act of Settlement 1701 (Eng) – 67

Agreement between Australia and the Republic of Indonesia on the Framework for Security Cooperation 2006 - 114

alien, meaning of – 217, 250

Al-Kateb v Godwin (2004) – 212, 213

Allan, James - 160

Andrews v Howell (1941) – 59, 116-117

Anti-Discrimination Act 1977 (NSW) – 139

Anti-Discrimination Act 1991 (Qld) - 139

Anti-Discrimination Act 1998 (Tas) – 138, 142

Anti-Discrimination (Racial Vilification) Amendment Act 1989 (NSW) - 139

anti-discrimination laws – 18, 135-143, 157

Aquinas, Thomas - 174

arbitral awards – 8, 17, 64, 65, 84, 85

Aristotle – 173, 174

Aroney, Nicholas – 33, 45, 52

Associated Provincial Picture Houses Ltd v Wednesbury Corporation (1948) - 207

Attorney-General (NT) v Emmerson (2014) – 80

Attorney-General (Qld) v Lawrence (2013) - 69

Attorney-General (SA) v Corporation of the City of Adelaide (2013) – 145

Augustine of Hippo - 173

Austin v Commonwealth (2003) – 27-29, 38-39, 49-52, 57

Australian Bicentennial Authority Act 1980 (Cth) - 239

Australian Bill of Rights, absence of – 15, 16, 20, 165, 176, 201, 218

Australian Building Construction Employees' and Builders' Labourers' Federation v Commonwealth (1986) - 70

Australian Capital Television Pty Ltd v Commonwealth (1992) – 145, 147, 165, 182, 183, 201

Australian Disaster Preparedness Framework - 116

Australian Government Crisis Management Framework – 101-102

Australian Government Disaster Response 2020 – 102

Australian Government Overseas Disaster Assistance Plan 2018 – 102

Australian Human Rights Commission – 24, 157-161, 244

Australian Railways Union v Victorian Railways Commissioners (1930) - 33

Banking Act 1948 (Cth) – 34-36, 38-41, 46

Bank of New South Wales v Commonwealth (Bank Nationalisation Case) (1948) – 50, 219

Bank Mellat v Her Majesty's Treasury (No 2) (2014) – 169, 174, 179, 185

Banks-Smith, Justice Katrina - 207

Barak, Aharon – 167, 170, 174, 179, 180

Bartolini, Giulio – 114, 116

Barton, Justice Sir Edmund – 31, 68

Barwick, Chief Justice Sir Garfield – 35, 40-41

Bastion Point – 236, 237, 255

Beck, Luke – 122-123

Bell, Justice Virginia – 28, 108, 183, 189, 232, 249, 253, 256

Benson, Iain T – 113

Berg, Chris – 131, 136, 142, 150

Bergin, Anthony – 97

Berkovic, Nicola – 141

Bernal, Carlos - 170

Betfair Pty Ltd v Western Australia (2008) – 173, 193, 195, 197

Bill of Rights 1689 (Eng) – 132

Bingham, Lord Chief Justice Thomas – 179

Birks, Peter - 194

Black Summer bushfires – 93-95, 99, 123, 125

Blackstone, Sir William - 66

Blicharz, Grzegorz – 136

Bodey, Michael - 154

Bolt, Andrew – 131, 136, 153-155

Boughey, Janina – 169, 207

Breheny, Simon - 152

Brennan, Chief Justice Sir Gerard – 19, 39, 72, 73, 78, 172, 200-201, 213, 232-237, 239, 247, 253, 256

Brett Cattle Co Pty Ltd v Minister for Agriculture, Fisheries and Forestry (2020) – 169, 206, 207

Bromberg, Justice Mordecai – 153-154

Brown v Tasmania (2017) – 167, 184, 187-189, 191, 196

Bruce, Tammy – 136, 137

Brutus v Cozens (1972) - 150

Boyle, Thomas - 5, 11, 18, 20, 23, 163-209

Brett Cattle Co Pty Ltd v Minister for Agriculture, Fisheries and Forestry (2020) – 169, 206, 207

Builders' Labourers' Federation of New South Wales v Minister for Industrial Relations (1986) – 69, 71

Burke, Edmund - 117

Burmah Oil Co (Burma Trading) Ltd v Lord Advocate (1964) – 106

Burns, Garry – 141

Byers, Sir Maurice – 170, 171, 204, 228

calibrated scrutiny – 172, 186, 188, 190, 191, 201, 202, 205, 241

Callinan, Justice Ian – 61, 205, 230, 231

Canadian Charter of Rights and Freedoms (1982) – 176-177

Carter, Anne – 173, 199, 202, 203

Castlemaine Tooheys Ltd v South Australia (1990) - 193, 200

Ceylon, *Constitution* of (1947) – 67

chameleon doctrine – 86

Chapman, Anna – 139, 151

Chapman, Justice Henry - 242

checks and balances – 63

Chordia, Shipra – 168, 173-175, 177, 178, 181, 182, 183, 185, 195, 197

Choudhry, Sujit - 177

Chu Kheng Lim v Minister for Immigration, Local Government and Ethnic Affairs (1992) – 70, 78, 87

Cicero - 173

Cigamatic Case (1962) – 17, 30, 37, 42, 44-46, 53

Clark, Andrew Inglis - 36

Clarke v Federal Commissioner of Taxation (2009) – 28, 29, 51-52

Classroom Crucifix II Case (1995) - 225

Clubb v Edwards (2019) – 167, 176, 179, 181, 185, 187, 188, 191, 192, 196, 202, 203, 205

Cohen-Eliya, Moshe – 173, 174

Coke, Sir Edward – 132

Coleman v Power (2004) – 146, 152

Cole v Whitfield (1988) – 58, 192, 194

Comcare v Banerji (2019) – 167, 187, 189, 198

common sovereignty – 222

Commonwealth Electoral Act 1918 (Cth) – 52

Commonwealth v ACT (Same Sex Marriage Case) (2013) - 252

Communist Party Case (1951) – 83, 111, 168, 219, 224-225, 227

Companies Acts 1936 (NSW) – 45-46

compensation for unjust land acquisition – 214, 232-234, 236-238, 245-247, 253-254, 257, 258

Convention on Assistance in the Case of a Nuclear Accident or Radiological Emergency 1986 - 114

Cook, Walter Wheeler – 47

Cooper, Dame Whina - 236

Coper, Michael - 208

Covid-19 - 7, 9, 10, 16-18, 25, 26, 93, 94, 96, 102, 123, 125, 192

Crennan, Justice Susan – 108, 183

Crowe, Jonathan – 70

Crowley, FK - 226

Cunliffe v Commonwealth (1994) – 200

D'Emden v Pedder (1904) - 32

D'Souza, Dinesh – 137

Dasreef Pty Ltd v Hawchar (2011) - 194

Dawson, Justice Sir Daryl – 78, 200, 202, 229, 230, 233, 239, 256,

Davis, Justice Peter – 207

Davis, Lou – 239-240

Davis v Commonwealth (1988) – 106, 107, 110, 216, 217, 239-241

DBP 16 v Minister for Home Affairs (2020) - 207

Deakin, Alfred – 32, 122-123

Deakin v Webb (1904) - 32

Deane, Justice Sir William – 19, 39, 70, 78, 181, 214, 233-236, 238, 239, 242, 245, 247, 253, 257

defence power, refer section 51 (vi) (*Australian Constitution*)

deference to the legislature – 20, 164, 165, 169, 172-173, 200, 205, 206, 219-223

de Freitas v Permanent Secretary of Minister of Agriculture, Fisheries, Land and Housing (1999) - 178

Demosthenes - 146

Dicey, AV – 19, 222

Dickson, Chief Justice Brian – 176-177

Dimarco, Michael - 5, 7, 16, 20, 23, 27-61

Dinnison v Leak (2016) – 159-161

Dinnison, Melissa – 159-161

Disaster Management Act 2003 (Qld) - 97

Discrimination Act 1991 (ACT) - 139

Dixon, Chief Justice Sir Owen - 8, 32-38, 40, 43-46, 48, 49, 56, 59-61, 68, 83, 85, 87, 90, 111, 116, 122, 166, 168, 170, 172, 180, 213, 215, 221, 223, 225, 227, 228, 235, 248, 256

DJS16 v Minister for Immigration and Border Protection (2019) - 207

Dixon, Rosalind - 205

Donaghue, Stephen – 33, 37, 39, 52

Douek, Evelyn – 170, 191, 198, 202, 204-205

Duncan v Independent Commission Against Corruption (2015) – 73, 75-77

Durham, W Cole - 225

Eastman v The Queen (2000) – 221, 222, 226, 227, 248

Eatock v Bolt (2011) – 153-155

Eburn, Michael – 97-100, 104, 109

Edelman, Justice James – 28, 29, 45, 47, 53, 55, 59, 61, 88-91, 167, 176, 179, 181, 185, 190, 193, 202, 204, 251, 256

Emergencies Act 2004 (ACT) – 97

Emergency Management Act 2013 (NT) – 97

Emergency Management Act 2004 (SA) – 97

Emergency Management Act 2006 (Tas) – 97

Emergency Management Act 1986 (Vic) – 97

Emergency Management Act 2013 (Vic) - 97

Emergency Management Act 2005 (WA) – 9, 97, 192

Emergency Management Australia – 101, 103

emergency powers - 5, 9, 10, 17, 18, 25, 26, 93-127, 192

Engineers' Case (1920) – 17, 30, 32, 33, 49, 56, 165, 171, 172, 208, 213, 215, 218-223, 226, 227, 234, 235, 238, 241, 248, 256

Ernst, Christine – 33, 37, 39, 52

Evans, Michelle - 32

evolutionary interpretation – 223, 226

executive power, refer section 61 (*Australian Constitution*)

external affairs power, refer section 51 (xxix) (*Australian Constitution*)

Fairfax v Federal Commissioner of Taxation (1965) - 40

Fair Work Act 2009 (Cth) – 232

Fardon v Attorney-General (Qld) (2004) – 79

Federal Commissioner of Taxation v Munro (1926) - 164

federalism – 27, 28, 30-33, 36, 60, 120, 123, 209

Fierravanti-Wells, Senator Concetta - 11

Finlay, Lorraine - 5, 10, 20, 24, 93-127, 152, 155-158

Forrester, Joshua – 10, 152, 155, 158

First Nation's Voice - 252

First Uniform Tax Case (1942) – 218

Fisher, Asaf - 146

Fleiner, Fritz – 174

Flint, David - 150

Foreign Influence Transparency Act 2018 (Cth) - 190

Forge v Australian Securities and Investment Commission (2000) – 69, 79-80

Fox, Charles James – 133-134

Franklin, Roger - 160

freedom of association – 148-149

freedom of speech – 10, 18, 129-162, 190

French, Chief Justice Robert – 51, 106, 111, 120, 145, 169

Friedrich the Great - 173

frozen continent – 214, 217

Gageler, Justice Stephen – 5, 11, 19, 163-209, 241

Garran, Sir Robert - 117

Gaudron, Justice Mary – 19, 73, 77, 214, 233-236, 238, 239, 242, 245, 247, 249, 253, 257

Gaynor, Bernard – 141

General Law 1793 (Prussia) - 174

Gerangelos, Peter – 82-83

German Basic Law (1949) – 174-175

Gibbs, Chief Justice Sir Harry – 58, 228

Gleeson, Chief Justice Murray – 50, 195, 200

Gleeson, Justice Jacqueline – 166, 189, 190

Global Financial Crisis – 107-108, 110

Goldring, John - 208

Goldsworthy, Jeffrey – 182, 222

Gordon, Justice Michelle – 5, 11, 19, 53, 163-209, 241, 250, 256

Graham v Paterson (1950) – 121

Gratwick v Johnson (1945) - 197

Gray, Anthony - 5, 8-10, 17, 20, 24, 63-92, 131, 132, 134, 144, 162

Griffiths, Chief Justice Sir Samuel – 31, 68

Grimm, Justice Dieter – 175

Grollo v Palmer (1995) – 79

Grotius, Hugo - 173

Gummow, Justice William – 45, 73, 77, 108, 146, 203, 227, 228

HA Bachrach Pty Ltd v Queensland (1998) – 72, 75, 76, 85-86, 88, 91

Hallowell, Billy - 140

Hancock, WK – 219

Hare, Ivan – 145

Hart, Philip A - 212

Harvey, Matt - 106

hate speech – 130, 146

Hawke, Joe - 236

Hayes, Sharon - 157

Hayne, Justice Kenneth – 73, 75, 77, 109, 146

Henckels, Caroline - 201

Heydon, Justice Dyson – 109, 201, 212, 213, 250

Higgins, Justice Henry – 208, 249

Hohfeld, Wesley - 47

Holmes, Jonathan – 154-155

Holmes, Justice Oliver Wendell Jr - 168

Hope, RM - 117

House of Commons – 10, 132-134

Howard, Prime Minister John – 230, 231, 245, 246, 252

Huang v Secretary of State for the Home Department (2007) – 179

Huddart Parker v Moorehead (1909) – 68, 231

Human Rights Act 1998 (UK) – 177-179

Hume, David - 33

hurt feelings test - 150

Hyogo Framework for Action (2005-2015) - 115

implied freedom of political communication - 5, 7, 16, 18, 129-167, 172, 180, 182-185, 187-190, 196, 199, 204-206, 215, 216, 238-241

immunity or restriction (*Melbourne Corporation Principle*) – 17, 38-39, 46-50, 52, 56, 61

inconsistency under the *Australian Constitution*, refer section 109

Industrial Relations Reform Act 1993 (Cth) - 230

In re Judiciary and Navigation Acts (1921) – 43, 202

intergovernmental immunity – 17, 30, 32, 33, 42, 47

International Convention on the Elimination of All Forms of Racial Discrimination 1965 - 229

International Covenant on Civil and Political Rights 1966 - 229

International Finance Trust Co Ltd v New South Wales Crime Commission (2000) – 79-80

interpretive sovereignty – 211, 212, 214-215, 217-226, 233, 238-241, 255, 256

interstate intercourse – see section 92 (*Australian Constitution*)

Iron Ore Processing (Mineralogy) Pty Ltd Agreement Amendment Act 2020 (WA) – 64-66, 74-92

Isaacs, Justice Sir Isaac – 32, 122, 164, 171, 213, 215, 218, 221-222, 234-235, 249

Italian Crucifix Case (2009) – 225

Italian Crucifix Case (2011) - 225

Jackson, Vicki C – 173, 176

Jacobs, Justice Sir Kenneth - 196

Jarret, Judge Michael - 158

Kable v Director of Public Prosecutions (1996) – 64, 69, 71, 75, 78, 81, 86, 87

Karst, Kenneth L - 165

Kartinyeri v Commonwealth (1998) – 83

Kavanagh, Aileen - 172

Keating, Prime Minister Paul – 20, 214, 216, 231, 237, 238, 245, 246, 251, 252

Kehoe, John - 123

Kelly, Mary – 157

Kenny, David - 176

Kiefel, Chief Justice Susan – 82, 109, 168-170, 181, 183, 190, 193, 195, 208

Kirby, Justice Michael – 39, 50, 73, 75-77, 118-119, 145-146, 181, 213, 231, 249, 250

Kirk, Justice Jeremy – 35, 41

Kirmani v Captain Cook Cruises Pty Ltd (No. 1) (1985) - 113

Kitto, Justice Sir Frank – 81

Knaus, Christopher - 199

Knox, Chief Justice Sir Adrian – 32

Kohl, Chancellor Helmut - 225

Koowarta v Bjelke-Peterson (1982) – 113, 229

Kumm, Mattias - 173

Kurti, Peter - 140

La Nauze, JA - 122

Lange v Australian Broadcasting Corporation
  (1997) – 182-187, 202, 204-206, 208

Latham, Chief Justice Sir John - 8, 34, 35,
  40, 224, 226

Latham, RTE - 32, 219, 221, 222, 224, 226,
  256

Lautsi v Italy (2011) - 225

Leak, Bill – 159-161

Leask v Commonwealth (1996) – 200, 203

Lee, HP – 106, 107, 125

Leeth v Commonwealth (1992) - 70

legalism – 164, 170-171, 201, 204, 206, 219-
  223, 227, 228, 230, 231, 233, 248

legal positivism – 134

Levy v Victoria (1997) – 183, 200

Libel Act 1792 (Eng) – 133

LibertyWorks v Commonwealth (2021) – 166-
  169, 174, 189-192, 198, 202, 205, 241

Lindell, Geoffrey – 182

Lipsett, EH – 130, 163

Liyanage v The Queen (1967) – 67-68, 75

Lobban v Minister for Justice (2015) - 207

*Local Government Association of Queensland
  (Incorporated) v State of Queensland* (2001)
  – 37

Locke, John - 132

Love Case (2020) – 20, 211, 212, 214-217,
  232, 238, 247-256

Love, Daniel – 217, 251

Lundie, Rob - 226

Lynch, Andrew – 33, 120-121, 208

Mabo (No. 2) Case (1992) - 5, 19, 211-258

MacArthur, Brian - 134

Magna Carta – 17, 246, 258

Mahony, Jack - 199

Makarrata Commission – 212, 217, 218,
  247, 252, 257

*Malek Fahd Islamic School Limited v Minister for
  Education and Training (No 2)* (2017) - 207

Māori Land March – 236, 255

margin of appreciation - 179

marketplace of ideas – 21

Marquis of Queensbury Rules – 130

*Marriage Amendment (Definition and Religious
  Freedoms) Act 2017* (Cth) - 252

Marshall, Chief Justice John – 31-32

Martinkovits, Jai - 150

Mason, Chief Justice Sir Anthony – 19, 29,
  39, 50, 51, 55, 59, 82-83, 111, 170, 172,
  180, 181, 183, 191, 201, 202, 205, 213,
  222, 226, 232, 233, 235, 236, 239, 240,
  247, 253

Mason, Mas – 8

Matthews, Jud – 167, 174, 175

McCann, Joy - 226

McCloy v New South Wales (2015) – 147, 166-
  170, 176, 180, 182, 184-187, 190, 196, 199,
  204, 206, 208, 241

McCulloch v Maryland (1819) - 181

McCormick, Ange – 159

McGinty v Western Australia (1996) - 204

McGowan, Premier Mark - 8, 123

McHugh, Justice Michael – 19, 50-51, 146,
  204, 212-213, 221, 226, 232, 233, 235, 236,
  247, 248, 250, 253

McTiernan, Justice Sir Edward – 34, 224

Meagher, Dean - 150

Meagher, RP - 45

Melbourne Corporation Case (1947) *and principle*
  - 5, 7-8, 16, 17, 23, 27-61, 219, 223, 228

Mellifont v Attorney-General (Queensland)
  (1991) - 44

Menzies, Justice Sir Douglas – 81

Meriam people – 232, 236, 254

Merralls, James – 227, 228

Mineralogy Case (2021) - See *Palmer v Western
  Australia* (2021)

Minister for Emergency Management and
  National Recovery and Resilience – 102

*Minister for Immigration and Border Control v
  Stretton* 2016) - 207

Minister for Immigration and Citizenship v Li
  (2013) - 207

Mistretta v United States (1989) – 80-81

Moens, Gabriël A - 5, 7-13, 24, 136, 137,
  139, 257

Momcilovic v Commonwealth (2011) – 201, 240

Monis v The Queen (2013) – 144, 181, 183,
  184, 205

Montesquieu - 66

Morris, Anthony – 158

Morris, Shireen - 205

Morrison, Prime Minister Scott – 11, 16,
  18, 94-95, 99, 102

Muehlenberg, Bill – 143

Muldoon, Prime Minister Robert - 236
Mulholland v Australian Electoral Commission (2004) – 181, 186, 191, 195
Murphy v Electoral Commissioner (2016) – 196, 199, 200, 208
Murray Islands – 232, 233, 236, 254
National Cabinet – 16, 18, 96
National Coordination Mechanism -102
National Disaster Risk Reduction Framework – 102, 116
National Emergency Declaration Act 2020 (Cth) – 10, 18, 93, 95-99, 101-104, 125-126
National Strategy for Disaster and Resilience - 102
nationhood power – 18, 94, 105-112, 126, 243
Nationwide News Pty Ltd v Wills (1992) – 147, 165, 172, 182, 183
Native Title Act 1993 (Cth) – 20, 211, 212, 214-216, 237, 238, 245, 246, 252
Native Title Amendment Act 1998 (Cth) – 245, 252
Near v Minnesota (1931) - 165
Nettle, Justice Geoffrey – 53, 189, 203, 250, 256
New South Wales, *Constitution* of – 70
Ngati Whatua people - 253
Nicholas v The Queen (1998) – 72, 75, 77, 78
Northern Australia Aboriginal Justice Agency v Northern Territory (2015) – 79
Obergefell v Hodges (2015) - 252
O'Connor, Justice Richard – 31,
Palmer, Clive - 8-9, 63-92
Palmer v Western Australia (2021) - 5, 8-9, 17, 20, 63-92, 167-169, 173, 185, 192-193, 195, 196, 198, 204, 206, 241
Pape v Commissioner of Taxation (2009) – 106-107, 109-111
parliamentary sovereignty – 19, 20, 123, 134, 143, 201, 206, 209
Payroll Tax Case (1970) – 30, 32, 34, 40, 50, 220, 222
Pepper, Justice Rachel - 170, 171, 204, 228
Permanent Trustee Australia Ltd v Commissioner of State Revenue (Vic) (2004) – 59
Perram, Justice Nye – 170, 171, 204, 228
Pham v Secretary of State for the Home Department (2015) - 185
Phillips, Lord Chief Justice Nicholas – 178

Pirrie v McFarlane (1925) – 33, 36
Plaintiff S157/2002 v Commonwealth (2003) – 71
Plato – 131, 173
Polyukhovich v Commonwealth (1991) – 70, 113
popular sovereignty – 143-149
Porat, Iddo – 173, 174
Porteous, Archbishop Julian – 141-142
Pound, Roscoe - 176
Powell, Jackson – 156, 158
Prior, Cindy – 155-159
Prior v QUT (2016) – 155-159
progressive interpretation – 223, 226
Protocol on Preparedness, Response and Cooperation to Pollution Incidents by Hazardous and Noxious Substances 2000 - 114
Quarantine (Closing the Border) Directions (WA) – 9, 192
Queensland Electricity Commission v Commonwealth (1985) – 29, 38, 39, 50-52
Quick, Sir John - 117
Quinlan, Michael - 113
R v Barger (1908) – 32
R v Burgess; Ex parte Henry (1936) - 113
R v Coldham; Ex parte Australian Social Welfare Union (1983) – 35, 46
R v Edward Books & Art Ltd (1986) – 177
R v Foster (1949) – 219, 224
R v Hansen (2007) – 169
R v Home Secretary; Ex parte Pierson (1998) - 240
R v Kirby; Ex parte Boilermakers' Society of Australia (1956) – 68, 72, 85, 87, 91
R v Oakes (1986) – 175-177
R v Public Vehicles Licensing Appeal Tribunal (Tas); Ex parte Australian National Airways Pty Ltd (1964) – 122
R v Sharkey (1949) – 113
R v Symonds (1847) - 242
R v Trade Practices Tribunal; Ex parte Tasmanian Breweries Ltd (1970) – 69, 81
R (Daly) v Home Secretary (2001) – 178, 179
R (Mahmood) v Secretary of State for the Home Department (2001) - 178
Racial Discrimination Act 1975 (Cth) – 135, 146, 150-161, 229
Radcliffe, Viscount Cyril John – 106
Rares, Justice Steven – 206, 207
Ratnapala, Suri – 70

Raz, Joseph - 55

Re Australian Education Union; Ex parte Victoria (1995) – 35, 49, 50, 57

reasonably appropriate and adapted – 181, 183, 184, 186, 188, 190-191, 202, 241

referral of state powers (s 51(xxxvii) – 94, 97, 119-124, 126

Reed, Lord Justice Robert – 179, 185

Reid, Lord Justice James - 150

Re Lee; Ex parte Harper (1986) – 39

Re Limbo (1989) – 201

Re Pacific Coal Pty Ltd v Ex parte Construction, Forestry, Mining and Energy Union (2000) - 231

Re Residential Tenancies Tribunal (NSW); Ex parte Defence Housing Authority (1997) – 37

Renzullo v Assistant Minister for Immigration and Border Protection (2016) - 207

reserved state powers – 32, 33, 52, 226

reverse *Melbourne Corporation principle* – 17, 42, 45, 46, 53

Rich, Justice Sir George – 34, 35, 49

Richardson v Forestry Commission (1988) - 230

Roach v Electoral Commissioner (2007) – 173, 212, 213, 234

Roberts v Bass (2002) – 145, 146

Rosenfeld, Michel – 181

Roskam, John - 230

Roux, Theunis – 172

Rowe v Electoral Commissioner (2010) – 181

Rowling, Prime Minister Bill - 236

Roxborough v Rothmans of Pall Mall Australia Ltd (2001) - 203

Royal Commission into National Natural Disaster Arrangements – 94-95, 97-98, 101, 104-105, 121, 123

Rudd, Prime Minister Kevin – 232

Ruddock v Vardarlis (2001) – 58, 107

rule of law – 17, 20, 25, 26, 63, 83, 162, 165, 168, 174, 175, 180, 194, 205

Sadurski, Wojciech – 135

Sajó, András - 181

Sakr, Johnny – 138

Scharffs, Brett G - 225

Schauer, Frederick - 165

Second Uniform Tax Case (1957) – 218-219

section 51 (vi) (*Australian Constitution*, defence power) – 18, 59, 94, 105, 116-119, 126, 165, 172, 224, 227, 231

section 51(xix) (*Australian Constitution*, aliens power) – 217, 230, 249, 250, 251, 253

section 51 (xxix) (*Australian Constitution*, external affairs power) – 18, 43, 94, 105, 112-116, 152, 181, 229-231

section 61 (*Australian Constitution*, executive power) – 4, 8, 18, 52, 54, 66, 67, 73, 105-112, 126, 172-174, 178, 187, 189, 199, 211, 222-225, 229, 257

section 92 (*Australian Constitution*, freedom of interstate trade) - 9-11, 44, 58, 163, 164, 167, 173, 180, 182, 185, 192-193, 195, 197, 199-200, 205, 206, 241

section 107 (*Australian Constitution*, continuation of state powers) – 31-33

section 109 (*Australian Constitution*, inconsistency) – 31, 121, 123, 183, 202

section 128 (*Australian Constitution*, alteration by referendum) – 18, 97, 124-125, 182, 212, 231

Sendai Declaration – 115

Sendai Framework for Disaster Reduction (2015-2030) – 115-116

separation of judicial power – 17, 64, 68-70, 72, 74, 76, 81, 82, 85-88, 90, 91, 168,

separation of powers - 5, 8, 24, 63-92, 164, 168, 169, 173, 200, 201

Sex Discrimination Act 1984 (Cth) – 135

Shanahan, Angela - 140

Shell Company of Australia Ltd v Federal Commissioner of Taxation (1930) - 164

Ship Money Case (R v Hampden) (1637) – 67

Smith, Hugh – 117, 118

Socrates – 131, 162

South Australia v Tanner (1989) - 207

South Australia v Totani (2010) – 69, 79, 81, 82, 86

Southey, Allen Hope - 229

Soutphommasane, Tim – 159-160

Spence v Queensland (2019) – 17, 27-29, 33, 36, 38, 45-47, 49, 52-53, 55, 57, 59, 61

Starke, Justice Sir Hayden – 34, 35, 49

State Emergency and Rescue Management Act 1989 (NSW) – 97

Statute of Westminster 1931 (Imp) – 222, 229

Stellios, James – 29, 40, 41, 44, 48, 50, 52, 57, 192

Stenhouse v Coleman (1944) – 165, 172

Steward, Justice Simon – 166, 167, 189,

190, 205, 208
Steyn, Lord Justice Johan – 178
Stolen Generations Case (1997) – 36, 249
Stone, Adrienne – 153, 166, 170, 205
Stone, Geoffrey R - 165
Strickland v Rocla Concrete Pipes Ltd (1971) - 33
strict and complete legalism – 170, 171, 220, 227, 228, 230, 231, 233, 248, 256
structural implication – 39-41
structured proportionality - 5, 7, 11, 20, 163-209, 215, 216, 240, 241
Sweet, Alec Stone – 167, 174, 175
Switzer, Tom - 143
Tajjour v New South Wales (2014) – 167, 184
Tasmanian Dam Case (1983) – 29, 38, 39, 110, 181, 215, 226, 228-230, 233, 238, 241, 249, 256
Tax Bonus for Working Australians Act (No 2) 2009 (Cth) – 107
terra nullius doctrine – 211, 213, 233
Thomas, Hedley – 156, 157, 159
Thomas v Mowbray (2007) – 86-87, 117-119
Thompson, A. Keith - 1, 4, 5, 7, 11, 13, 15-21, 25, 113, 211-258
Thoms, Brendan - 217, 251
Thwaites, Callum – 156, 158
Toohey, Justice John – 19, 73, 77, 200, 214, 233-236, 238, 239, 242, 245, 247, 253, 257
Treason and Sedition Act 1795 (Eng) – 133
Treaty of Waitangi (1840) – 237, 241-245
Treaty of Waitangi Act 1975 (NZ) – 214, 216, 236, 237, 241-247, 257
Trone, John - 8, 9, 11
Tsesis, Alexander - 163
Twomey, Anne – 29, 37, 40, 45, 108
Uluru Statement from the Heart (2017) – 213, 252-253, 257
Unions New South Wales v New South Wales (2019) – 145, 147, 167, 182, 187
United States v Klein (1871) - 67
University of Notre Dame Australia - 4, 7, 15, 20, 23, 25
Uther v Federal Commissioner of Taxation (1947) – 43-45
Vacher & Sons Ltd v London Society of Compositors (1913) - 171
van Gend, David – 140-141
Vanstone v Clark (2005) - 207
Victoria v Commonwealth (Industrial Relations

Act Case) (1996) – 113, 231
Victoria v Commonwealth and Hayden (AAP Case) (1975) – 107, 111
Volokh, Eugene - 140
Wainohu v New South Wales (2011) – 69, 79, 86
Waitangi Tribunal – 211, 212, 214, 216, 217, 218, 236, 237, 243, 244, 246, 247, 252, 255, 257
Ward, Elizabeth – 117, 119
Weinstein, James – 144-145
Wesson, Murray – 172, 173, 176, 184, 187
West v Commissioner of Taxation (NSW) (1937) – 33, 37
Western Australia v Commonwealth (Native Title Act Case) (1995) – 50
Wildheart, Yari – 147-149
Williams, Brennan and Lynch (Blackshield and Williams, *Australian Constitutional Law and Theory*) – 31, 32, 34, 40, 43, 220, 222, 223
Williams, Daryl - 120
Williams, George – 33, 208, 249
Williams, Justice Sir Dudley – 35
Williams, Justice JV – 244, 257
Williams v Commonwealth (2012) – 36, 106
Williams v Melbourne Corporation (1933) – 166, 181, 241
Windeyer, Justice Sir Victor – 30, 41, 81, 220, 223
Windschuttle, Keith – 160
Winterton, George – 227, 228, 235
Wik Peoples v Queensland (1996) – 252
Wilson, John - 243
Wi Parata v Bishop of Wellington (1877) - 237
Woinarksi, Judge SHZ, - 32
Wood, Alex – 155-156, 158
Work Choices Case (2006) – 215, 226, 230-232, 256
Workplace Relations Amendment (WorkChoices) Act 2005 (Cth) - 231
World Health Organisation – 192

XYZ v Commonwealth (2006) - 113

X7 v Australian Crime Commission (2013) - 69

Zimmermann, Augusto - 5, 9, 10, 18, 20, 25, 129-162, 257
Zines, Leslie – 18, 41, 57, 170, 204, 228

www.ingramcontent.com/pod-product-compliance
Lightning Source LLC
Chambersburg PA
CBHW060241220326
41598CB00027B/4007